A Plea for Embodied Spirituality

A Plea for Embodied Spirituality

The Role of the Body in Religion

Fraser Watts

scm press

© Fraser Watts 2021
Published in 2021 by SCM Press
Editorial office
3rd Floor, Invicta House,
108–114 Golden Lane,
London EC1Y OTG, UK
www.scmpress.co.uk

SCM Press is an imprint of Hymns Ancient & Modern Ltd
(a registered charity)

Hymns Ancient & Modern® is a registered trademark of
Hymns Ancient & Modern Ltd
13A Hellesdon Park Road, Norwich,
Norfolk NR6 5DR, UK

British Library Cataloguing in Publication data

A catalogue record for this book is available
from the British Library

978-0-33406-007-9

Typeset by Regent Typesetting

Contents

Acknowledgements   ix

1 Introduction   1
2 Minds, Bodies and Persons   11
3 The Embodied Origins of Religion   27
4 The Ascetic Life   39
5 Extreme Spirituality as 'Flow' Experience   55
6 Attending to Our Bodies   68
7 Embodiment: Postures and Meanings   81
8 Enacting Liturgy   95
9 Emotions and their Expression   108
10 Healing   124
11 Spiritual Bodies, Apparitions and Visions   143
12 Concluding Reflections   157

Appendix: The Body in World Faith Traditions by Sara Savage   162
References and Further Reading   195
Index of Names and Subjects   215

For
Roger Bretherton
and
James W. Jones

and to the memory of
Owen Barfield

Acknowledgements

I am much indebted to the John Templeton Foundation for the grant that funded my Embodied Cognition Project, and to all the colleagues who worked with me on the project, especially my friend and colleague Léon Turner, and also James W. Jones, whose book *Living Religion* (2019) was a great help in preparing this one. Léon Turner and I also worked with Robin Dunbar, Miguel Farias and others on a project entitled Religion and the Social Brain, funded by the Templeton Religion Trust, which underpins Chapter 3.

There are other friends and colleagues whose work has been very helpful at particular points. I am grateful to Rupert Sheldrake, a fellow 'Epiphany Philosopher', for his recent books on spiritual practices (*Science and Spiritual Practices* (2017) and *Ways to Go Beyond and Why They Work: Seven Spiritual Practices in a Scientific Age* (2019)), which have fed into Chapters 4, 5 and 6; to Mark Williams for help with mindfulness in Chapter 6, and to Thomas Dixon, whose work on emotion helped me with Chapter 9.

Chapter 10 on spiritual healing arises from a Humble Approach Initiative on spiritual healing, funded by the John Templeton Foundation, that met in Cambridge in 2004, and which I had the pleasure of co-chairing with Sarah Coakley. Two edited books came from that consultation, *Spiritual Healing: Scientific and Religious Perspectives* (Watts, 2011a), and *Spiritual Healing: Science, Meaning, and Discernment* (Coakley, 2020).

I am also very grateful to Sara Savage for allowing me to publish her excellent essay on the body in world religions as an Appendix in this book, and a big thank you goes to Geoff Dumbreck and Bonnie Poon Zahl, who helped her in its preparation. It is a very valuable resource and I am delighted that it has been possible to publish it here.

I

Introduction

The body is strangely neglected in religious practice. We humans are embodied creatures, so the body is inevitably involved in religion in some way or other. However, there seems to be a strange lack of interest in many circles in how people are using their bodies in religious and spiritual practice, with the result that many religious people don't use them as well or as skilfully as they might. When it comes to religion and spirituality, we just don't, for the most part, operate as though mind and body were integrated facets of a single, whole human person.

There are exceptions, of course, and it is striking that those forms of religious and spiritual practice that take the body seriously are those that are growing most conspicuously at the present time. Pentecostal religion makes good use of the body, and Pentecostalism is currently the fastest growing form of Christianity. Meditation in general, and mindfulness in particular, often make very deliberate and carefully considered use of the body, and mindfulness is also growing rapidly at present.

I think it would be reasonable to say that forms of religion and spirituality that make full use of the body are growing, and other forms that neglect it are in decline. The conclusion I draw is that if those involved in religion and spirituality want them to grow, they should take the body more seriously. Apart from the exceptions I have mentioned, the implicit assumption seems to be that religion and spirituality are not primarily about the body.

This book was written during the coronavirus pandemic in which large numbers of people became physically ill, and many died. However, there has been a conspicuous silence from most religious leaders about the body. Many churches regularly offer prayer for healing, but in this medical crisis almost nothing was said about the possibility of the healing of the body. Also, though many died, almost nothing was said by religious leaders about the death of the body, or what might lie beyond physical death. The implicit assumption seems to be that religion is religion, and what happens to the body is something else.

The widespread lack of interest in the body in religion is puzzling. It seems to reflect a kind of dualism. The implicit assumption seems to be that religion is about mind, soul and spirit, but not really about the body. Philosophers who consider the relationship between mind and body have, in the period since the Second World War, largely moved on from dualism. Intellectually, we seem to have become entirely persuaded that people are integrated wholes, with embodied minds or ensouled bodies.

However, this official philosophical rejection of dualism seems to be accompanied by a good deal of residual, implicit dualism among the general public. It is bizarre that people even consider it to be a line of defence in a court of law that their neurones (or genes) made them do what they did, as though their neurones were not really them, but something separate or alien (Wiseman, 2019). As Mary Midgley has argued in her trenchant way, when we do things, it is *we* who do what we do, not some bit of us (Midgley, 2010).

The central theme of this book is that the body can play an important role in the religious life. Indeed, it is hard to be religious in a purely mental or spiritual way, without drawing on the resources of the body. However, for various reasons, including philosophical dualism and moral panic about carnal pleasures, the crucial role of the body in religion is often not fully acknowledged.

I hope this book will help to overcome this curious avoidance of the important role of the body in religion. The body does actually play a very important role in religion, in all sorts of ways, even though religious instruction tends to focus more on the mental aspects of religion, especially on what to believe. Participants in mainline Christianity are given relatively little help in how to use their bodies wisely and skilfully in practising their faith. This book will consider the contribution of the body to religious life more explicitly, and I hope that it will help people to use the body more effectively in their spiritual practices.

I believe that wise use of the body in the religious life can lead to the spiritual transformation of the person. The whole person can be transformed, not just mind and heart, but also the body. The body in itself can begin to participate in what St John's Gospel calls 'eternal life'. Contemporary religion has largely neglected the call to offer our bodies for redemption and transformation. This book tries to set out what is possible, and how it can come about.

There are thus religious reasons for focusing on the role of the body in religion. Forms of religion that neglect the role of the body are truncated, and are likely to have limited appeal. If religion is to fulfil its potential to transform people, it is important to understand the potential role of the body and to use the body wisely. I believe that the lack of understanding of the role of the body in religion is contributing to the drift away from organized religion in our time.

Embodied Cognition

The body is also neglected in our present *understanding* of religion. It would be an exaggeration to say that no one in religious studies is considering the body, and I have discovered a surprisingly rich and extensive literature in the course of writing this book. However, the body is not a coherent subfield of research in the study of religion. One striking feature of that is that the authors of most of the books to which I refer here seem unaware of other books on religion and the body. In that sense, it is a very scattered literature.

My approach here will be multidisciplinary, drawing on theology, religious studies, psychology, history, biology and social science. Understanding the potential of the body in religion is a complex and multi-faceted task. Though there is some directly relevant literature to draw on, it is in many ways quite path-breaking work. It is surprising and disappointing, perhaps even slightly shocking, that so little work has been done on the potential of the body in the religious and spiritual life. As in all my work, I approach the understanding of the role of the body and religion in dialogue with my primary discipline of psychology.

Fortunately, there has been considerable recent interest in psychology in the role of the body in shaping how we think. What is called 'embodied cognition' has become a hot topic, and it makes the exploration of the role of the body and religion that I have undertaken here a timely one. Religion involves a way of understanding things, a framework of meaning, that enables us to make sense of particular events. There has been growing recognition recently among psychologists that cognition does not develop in isolated disembodied individuals. It depends on the context and is shaped by the context.

The path-breaking book that opened the eyes of many psychologists to this, including my own, was *The Embodied Mind: Cognitive Science and Human Experience* by Francisco J. Varela, Eleanor Rosch and Evan Thompson, first published in 1991, with a revised edition in 2017 (Varela et al., 2017). It has proved one of the most influential books in psychology in recent decades. Interestingly, it is a book that takes religious ideas much more seriously than most contemporary psychology. The focus is on the Buddhist tradition, whereas my main focus here is on Christianity (though there is an Appendix by my friend and colleague Sara Savage that looks systematically at the role of the body in a range of world faith traditions).

Though there are significant differences between Christianity and Buddhism in what people *believe*, there is a lot of common ground between them about how to *practise* religion, and how belief and practice are intertwined. So, much of what Varela et al. have to say about the role of the body in shaping cognition, drawing on Buddhism, is relevant to Christianity as well. This new focus on the role of the body in shaping cognition is only one aspect of a broad understanding of the importance of context in shaping how we understand things. People have come to talk about '4E' cognition, i.e. cognition that is embodied, embedded, enacted and extended (Newen et al., 2018).

How we understand things is *embodied* in the sense that it is shaped by what we do with our bodies. The state of our bodies affects our judgements; hills look steeper and distances look longer if we are tired. We can improve our attention by sitting up straight. We can influence the emotions we feel by expressing our emotions physically. Holding something warm, like a cup, makes us feel that other people are warm. Sitting on an unstable chair leads us to feel that relationships are unstable. Making gestures influences how we think and feel. I could give many more examples. The evidence that our thoughts, feelings and judgements are shaped by physical experience is overwhelming (see Jones, 2019; Teske, 2013).

Our human experience of the world is very much shaped by the words we use to describe our experiences. All our language is figurative or metaphorical (Arbib and Hesse, 1986; Lakoff and Johnson, 1980). There is a hidden trace of embodied experience in every word we use, even when we think we are describing something abstract or subjective. It seems that all language is metaphorical, in the sense that words began by referring both to something physical and embodied as well as to something subjective (Barfield, 1984). When we hear words about actions, there is activity in the parts of our brain that would be involved in actually making those actions.

Our thinking is also shaped by the social context in which we are *embedded*. Our ways of understanding things are not always consciously articulated in our minds; they are sometimes *enacted* rather than put into words and arise from our actions. Finally, though this is the most controversial of the 4Es, cognition is *extended* in the sense that it is not confined within the skin; our understandings often arise in the context of our interaction with what is around us.

4

Despite the explicitly religious context in which embodied cognition was first advocated by Varela et al., psychology has largely dropped the religious focus in its discussion of embodied cognition. For example, the *Oxford Handbook of 4E Cognition* (Newen et al., 2018) has nothing to say about religion, and that is true of most of the recent books on embodied cognition. It has also taken time for those interested in religion to appreciate the significance of this new work on embodied cognition.

I started work on this through a research project I led at the University of Cambridge from 2011 to 2013 on embodied cognition, funded by the John Templeton Foundation. That led to a series of journal articles, including an introductory one (Watts, 2013a), a review of the scientific evidence (Teske, 2013), an exploration of the significance of embodied cognition for a theological understanding of the human person (Turner, 2013), and for the moral life (Brown and Reimer, 2013). Other colleagues explored the relevance of embodied cognition for Judaism (Weiss, 2013) and Buddhist and Hindu traditions (Gosling, 2013).

Books exploring the significance of embodied cognition for religion are now appearing. First was *The Physical Nature of Christian Life: Neuroscience, Psychology, and the Church* by Warren Brown and Brad Strawn (2012), and later continued by them with *Enhancing Christian Life: How Extended Cognition Augments Christian Community* (2020). I have been particularly influenced by *Living Religion: Embodiment, Theology, and the Possibility of a Spiritual Sense* by James W. Jones (2019; see also Jones 2020), who spent a sabbatical year with my research group at Cambridge during our project on embodied cognition. Léon Turner has continued his exploration of the relevance of embodied cognition to theological anthropology, and has a book in preparation, *I Am Who I Am*. Tobias Tanton has looked at the relevance of embodied cognition to religious hermeneutics and has a book in preparation, *Corporeal Theology: The Nature of Theological Understanding in Light of Embodied Cognition*.

The most accessible theological introduction to the importance of embodied intelligence is in a chapter on bodies in Rowan Williams' *Being Human: Bodies, Minds and Persons* (2018). He emphasizes the different mood and character of embodied intelligence. Embodied thinking is less narrowly focused and controlling than humans can sometimes be. On the contrary it is more imaginative, cooperative and practical. Others, coming from a more secular perspective, such as Philip Shepherd (2010), are also emphasizing the practical importance of recovering a more embodied mode of thinking. The body has also been a recurrent theme in the theological explorations of Sarah Coakley (2010, 2015, 2020).

Outline of the Book

In this book, I have tried to gather together what we know about the role of the body in religious practices, especially in the Christian tradition. I have been pleasantly surprised by the richness of what I have found, but it is only recently that people have started to bring it together. I have tried to focus on what religious people actually do with their bodies, but also to keep embodied cognition in play as a unifying theoretical perspective.

Chapter 2 explores Christian attitudes to the body which, it must be admitted, are rather mixed. On the one hand the core doctrines of Christianity are strikingly pro-body (creation, incarnation, Eucharist, resurrection). However, this is in tension with other strands, such as moral panic about the body, and a philosophical dualism that is inclined to seek escape from the body. I argue that the Greek distinction between *sarx* (flesh) and *soma* (body) goes a long way to resolving this. We need a view of the human person that recognizes the many facets of person-hood, but does not try to set up divisions between them. I challenge the materialistic view that sees the physical realm as the source of everything else, and argue for a more systemic view that sees body, mind and spirit as intertwined and inter-dependent.

Chapter 3 focuses on the evolutionary origins of religion. It is signifi-cant that religion started with bodily practices, specifically with trance dancing. That is the soil out of which fully fledged religion grows. I draw on the approach to religion of Robin Dunbar (in press) in emphasizing the contribution of embodied religious practices to social cohesiveness, often mediated by endorphin release. Religion began by being embodied and social; it was only later in human evolution that it becomes doctrinal and individualistic. Religion was about praxis before it was about belief. Religious beliefs are often, erroneously, taken to be the core of religion. That is reflected in the assumptions about religion made in the New Atheism, and in the currently fashionable Cognitive Science of Religion.

Shamanic practices came first; doctrinal religion came later. Trance dancing served various functions in early hunter-gatherer societies, includ-ing healing and social bonding. It also gave rise to spiritual experiences, and to the sense of participating in a transcendent spiritual world. Given that religion evolved from trance dancing, it is not surprising that, for many people, religion works best when it gets back to something close to its evolutionary roots. So, it is only to be expected that the fastest grow-ing form of Christianity today, Pentecostalism, is the one that is closest to the evolutionary origins of religion.

Chapter 4 turns to the ascetic life. Over the centuries, Christians have gone to remarkable extremes in their physical practices, including fasting and sleep deprivation, restraints on movement, and self-injurious practices such as flagellation that lead to blood-letting. Opus Dei continues to use the cilice and the discipline, and has dedicated followers. Such practices may seem puzzling, though the reasons why people engage in them are intelligible. For example, it may well be true that severe ascetic practices improve self-discipline and can lead to heightened religious experiences. Many who have engaged in them believe they are denying the body and rising above it but I suggest that is a misunderstanding. In fact, I suggest, they are using the body in a particular way to energize and develop their religious life.

The motivation for undertaking ascetic practices will be explored, as well as their potential benefits and dangers. Asceticism sits well with the recent psychological work on the strength model of self-control that has recently been developed by Roy Baumeister. The concept of 'spiritual fitness' is also coming into vogue, and connects in interesting ways with physical fitness. Many see only an analogy between physical and spiritual fitness, but I propose that there is potentially a spirituality of the gym in which physical training can be integrated with spiritual practice, and contribute to spiritual development.

There is a wide range of rather extreme and energetic religious and spiritual practices on the contemporary scene, and Chapter 5 focuses on some of them. One currently popular practice is pilgrimage; it has migrated out of conventional religious circles and is now being under-taken by a wide range of people, some of whom would see themselves as more spiritual than religious. Going on a pilgrimage is in a broad sense an inherently religious activity, and that doesn't depend on being accompanied at every step by explicitly religious thoughts and devotions. I also look at snake-handling and fire-walking, trying to understand why people do such things, and what the effects are.

There are also extreme physical practices that are somewhat analogous to religious ascetic practices but are approached in a completely secular way, and I look at extreme sport as a spiritual practice. There are various reasons why these extreme practices are appealing, but I suggest that a key factor is that they provide people with a 'flow' experience in which they are completely absorbed in what they are doing, and thought and action are completely integrated.

Chapter 6 looks at another way of using the body in spiritual practices, one that is illustrated by body-focused forms of meditation such as mindfulness. A focus on the breath is one of the most common ways of meditating, and there is often cultivation of a 'mindful' relation to the whole body. Meditation produces significant changes in people – physical, emotional and cognitive. Though meditation comes from a religious stable, the fact that it is an embodied practice, and can be detached from doctrinal claims, makes it more acceptable in secular contexts than explicitly religious practices.

People are often unhappy with their bodies, ranging from the preoccupation with body ideals often found in young people, to older people who are having to cope with failing bodies. Both raise important issues about spirituality, and suggest a range of different spiritualities of the body, which I also consider in Chapter 6. There is a case for a 'befriending' of the body in the spiritual life, in which people are neither dominated by their bodies nor hostile to them, but work with the body in their spiritual life, and draw on its wisdom. The experience of pain is a good example, and I draw on the scientific evidence that underlines the importance of processes of interpretation in pain, and the benefits of meditation in pain management

Chapters 7 looks at how the body is used in prayer and liturgy. The recent scientific and philosophical work on 'embodied cognition' to which I have already referred offers a fresh approach to the role of the body in religion, and shows how thoughts and judgements can be shaped by physical postures and activities, such as genuflexion, blessing etc. Much embodied practice in religion, such as kneeling, seems designed to express feelings, and to encourage an attitude of devotion.

Body language in religion can help to induce particular moods and attitudes. The positions adopted for prayer are somewhat different in different faith traditions, but it is interesting that they mainly use the vertical axis rather than the horizontal one. Religious language is also often highly embodied and I explore the history of embodiment in the language we use about religion and other things.

Chapter 8 explores how recent work on cognition as enacted, embedded and extended provides us with a framework for understanding what is going on in the enactment of liturgy. Liturgical cognition is shaped by the physical practices that accompany it. In religion, more than in most areas of contemporary life, cognition is often implicit and enacted rather than being fully articulated. Religious rituals provide a prime example of enacted cognition in practice, and are rich in body language. When a religious community performs rituals in a coordinated way it can deliver a strong sense of social bonding and of becoming a spiritual community.

Chapter 9 turns to emotions, which have played an important role in religion and provide a way of integrating mind and body. There seems to have been a historical development from a primary focus on emotional expression in earlier periods to seeing emotion increasingly as a matter of subjective experience. Despite this subjective emphasis, work on the sociology of religious emotions has emphasized how much emotions are affected by the society and culture in which they occur. In this chapter I look at a selection of emotions in which religion has taken a particular interest for óne reason or another, including anger and aggression, tears and grief, shame and guilt, and awe and wonder.

From the late nineteenth century there has been growing interest in the role of healing, which is the focus of Chapter 10. Theology and psychology provide complementary perspectives on healing. Spiritual practices such as prayer are generally good for health, so it is no surprise if prayer for healing has health benefits. There is more controversy about whether spiritual healing should be theologized in terms of divine action, and I argue that spiritual healing need not be seen as 'miraculous' in the sense that there is no conceivable natural explanation for it. The scientific exploration of possible mediating processes in healing is neutral about the role of divine action. Some of the likely psychosomatic mechanisms for spiritual healing are becoming increasingly clear.

Chapter 11 turns to issues about the body that arise in connection with the resurrection and afterlife. Intriguingly, belief in the afterlife is increasing, even though belief in God is declining; the two things are becoming decoupled. There is also much interest in eternal life in science fiction. The predominant view among those who believe in an afterlife is dualistic, i.e. that the soul or personality survives the death of the body. Is there a way of conceptualizing afterlife that is credible but more embodied? It is helpful in this connection to re-explore the resurrection body of Jesus, following the lead of St Paul, who asserts the resurrection of a body of some kind, but is equally clear that it is not a body of flesh and blood. As he sees it, resurrection does not involve revival of the life of the flesh, but transformation of the flesh into something radically different. This opens up the possibility and promise of an eschatological transformation of the human body.

Properly understood, the religious life offers a transformation of all aspects of the human person, including body, mind and spirit; and an integration of the different aspects, so that they work fruitfully together in a systemically inter-connected way. In Chapter 12 I make a threefold plea: first, for a more integrated view of the human person that takes seriously the roles of the body in religious life; for a better understanding of the contribution that embodied practices can make to religion; and for a wiser and more deliberate use of the body to enrich spiritual practices and increase their impact.

I take both an insider's and an outsider's view of religion in this book. The psychology of religion looks at religion from the outside, and tries to understand what is going on there. Those involved in psychology of religion are often, like myself, also active participants in religious communities. That means that they can draw on their intuitions about what is going on, but they also try to check out their intuitions, as far as possible, with the objectivity of a detached observer.

I am mostly concerned here with religious practices, though in some parts of the book I engage with religious beliefs. That is especially true of the next chapter, which looks at beliefs about the human person, and two chapters towards the end of the book on healing and the afterlife. Though I hold Christian beliefs myself I don't assume that my readers do. It is also not my purpose here to try to persuade people to change what they believe. My task here is to examine these religious beliefs in relation to relevant scientific evidence.

2

Minds, Bodies and Persons

In the first part of this chapter I reflect on the marked ambivalence about the body to be found in the Christian tradition. I then consider the way the human person is conceptualized in the New Testament, and suggest that the distinction between body and flesh is crucial for resolving that ambivalence. Finally, I consider two important issues in contemporary Christian thinking about the human person – how to understand the relationship between mind and brain, and the shift in recent decades to a more relational understanding of the human person.

There is an obvious and rather glaring paradox about the body in Christianity. On the one hand, several core Christian doctrines emphasize the importance of the body in the unfolding purposes of God, and many Christian practices involve the body. On the other hand, the role of the body is often downplayed or even the ignored in Christian thinking. At worst, there is a moral panic about the body that assumes that we have to rise above our bodies if there is to be any hope of salvation.

Modern science, in contrast, has often espoused 'physicalism', the claim that everything arises from matter, or even that it is the only reality and that everything else is just an epiphenomenon. Applied to the human person, that translates into the view that the physical body is the fundamental or foundational thing in each human being, and that everything else spins off from that. On the face of things, we have a clash between science and religion, with religion at best ignoring the body and at worst disapproving of it, and science regarding the body as the fundamental reality in each person.

These are fiendishly complicated issues and it would be beyond the scope of one short chapter in this book to sort them out. However, I hope at least I can point us in the right direction. I want to encourage a balanced attitude to the body that takes it seriously, and sees the benefits of the body as well as the dangers.

I also want to find a path between a physicalist view of the human person that sees the body as the all-important foundation for everything else, and a dualist view that sees mind and body (or mind and soul) as separate and comparable realities. To anticipate, I suggest that body, mind and spirit are facets of the human person that are so intertwined that it makes no sense to get into debates about what causes what. Recent psychological work on embodied cognition points towards seeing the different facets of the human person as so highly interconnected that we can move on from tired debates about causal processes. I suggest that the view of the human person in embodied cognition and in Hebrew thought sit very comfortably together.

I also want to consider the role of embodiment in developing a sense of both individuality and personhood. A sense of individuality seems to have developed more strongly from the seventeenth century onwards, and to have been intertwined with a stronger sense of people having different and separate bodies. In more recent decades, there seems to have been a developing sense of personhood, with a strong sense of each person being formed by relationships with those around them. Embodiment seems to have been involved, in different ways, in both these developments

Christian Ambivalence About the Body

Religious Affirmation of the Body

Let us first look at attitudes to the body in the Judeo-Christian tradition. The doctrine of creation implies a positive view of the body. I assume that the Genesis creation narratives are not intended to be scientific accounts of how creation happened. However, it is significant that the Genesis account of creation starts with heaven and earth, land and sea, light and darkness before there are living creatures and humans. I take that, not as claiming a temporal sequence, but as a statement about what is primary. Only at the end of this narrative does God breathe life into humans (Genesis 2.7). Primacy is given to the creation of matter.

In Christianity, there is also the belief that God becomes incarnate in the person of Jesus. In Jesus, God lives as a human being, with flesh and blood, and all that goes with that. Far from trying to escape the body, God embraces the human body and lives an embodied existence. The gospel narratives about Jesus include the resurrection of his body. The Christian proclamation is that Jesus rose from the dead, and that there was a physical resurrection. The Christian creeds assert belief in the resurrection of the body for all who are in Christ.

The Gospels tell of how Jesus, on the night before his crucifixion, took bread and wine, gave thanks over it, and shared it with his disciples, saying 'this is my body' and 'this is my blood'. Ever since, it has been an almost universal practice of Christians to take bread and wine, and give thanks over it in Jesus' name. Christians unite themselves with Jesus by eating bread that is held to be the body of Christ.

Christians begin their life of discipleship with a ritual baptism in which the body is submerged under water and brought up again, or the body is sprinkled with water. There is believed to be a spiritual reality to baptism, but baptism is marked by immersing the body in water, or pouring water over the person. There is no baptism without bringing the body into contact with water.

Many religious people adopt particular positions or postures in the course of their religious practices, assuming that it makes a difference whether they are kneeling, sitting, standing or whatever. Manual gestures are widely used, whether that is people in the Catholic tradition crossing themselves, or people in the Charismatic tradition raising a hand as they sing Charismatic songs.

We thus have a sweeping and comprehensive set of doctrinal reasons and mainstream practices for regarding the body as having a central place in the purposes of God and the life of Christians. And yet, despite all this, there is a tendency to take a negative view of the body, sometimes to ignore it and try to rise above it, or to focus in a rather obsessional way on the regulation of the body.

We should note just how body-oriented the Jewish religion is. The book of Leviticus is almost entirely about bodily practices, which form a very important part of Jewish life. Howard Eilberg-Schwartz talks about the Jews, with some justification, not as a 'people of the book', but as a 'people of the body' and draws attention to how much the Hebrew Bible has to say about 'bodily emissions, skin diseases, circumcision, proper positions for sexual intercourse, how to urinate, how to empty one's bowels' (1992, p. 3). Judaism is a religion of the kitchen, bedroom and bathroom, and much of this has carried over into Christianity as well, as is reflected in the first Christian debates about sexuality.

Moral Panic About the Body

Though the body plays an important role in the Judeo-Christian tradition, it also often raises moral concerns. The background assumption is often that the body drags people down spiritually and corrupts them. There has been much wariness about the body in the Christian era. A good deal of this seems to arise from wariness about human sexuality. In the early centuries, in the period of the Roman Empire, there was particular caution about sexual pleasure, and a strong feeling that sex was for procreation, not for physical pleasure (Brown, 2008).

On this view, our present state is a kind of anomaly, caught between God's original creation (marred by the 'Fall') and our final destination. Differentiation into male and female is itself a kind of anomaly and a consequence of the Fall. Sexual desires enabled humans to have continuity through reproduction, but it was a perilous solution. Peter Brown says it was 'like trying to run an engine on an explosive *Ersatz* fuel' (2008, p. 296). The sexual act was tolerated reluctantly and the only way to make it safe was to do it solely for the purpose of reproduction and within marriage.

Many patristic writers are clearly shocked by sexuality, including Augustine, who seems puzzled by how God could have given humans anything as dangerous as sexual appetites. Procreation is acceptable in itself, but 'concupiscence', i.e. sexual appetite, entered into it and made it sinful. For Augustine, a clear indication of the sinfulness of concupiscence is that 'man by his very nature is ashamed of sexual lust'. Jerome in his *Commentary on the Epistle to the Galatians* expresses this view particularly strongly when he says that sexual relations, even in marriage, are filth and lust unless they take place under the eyes of God and with the sole purpose of procreation (Brown, 2008).

There was a strong attraction to the idea of virginity which was seen as a marker of a more general virtue of the soul. Gregory in *de Virginitate* says that 'release from marriage is the peculiar characteristic of the angelic nature' (Brown, 2008, p. 14). A puzzling paradox in the exhortation of virginity as the ideal state is that it was a doctrine developed by men who seemed to be mainly concerned about male sexual desire. However, the idealization of virginity focuses particularly on women. Men need to be sexually restrained so that women can be pure and virginal.

It is a view of sexual desire that seems inherently dualistic. A disapproval of carnal pleasure leads to a wariness about the physical body and a desire to transcend it to achieve a more spiritual state. It has its origins in St Paul's contrast between spirit and flesh, but takes it much further. It leads on to the view that the flesh needs to be 'mortified' through ascetic practices, something that we will consider in Chapter 4.

With hindsight it seems that in Late Antiquity there was a widespread failure to hold a proper balance between the dangers of the flesh and the positive potential of the body. In the early centuries the former overrides the latter. Maybe in contemporary religion things have gone too far in the opposite direction. As I see it, the New Testament holds a balance between the dangers and the potential in our corporeal nature, but it is a difficult balance to hold.

During the early centuries there was gradual imposition of a theological approach to sex that replaced an earlier and more social pattern of sexual regulation in terms of concepts such as shame and property. There was a transition from a framework of 'shame' to one of 'sin', leading to an unprecedented level of state interference in sexual matters (Harper, 2013). That focused especially on the campaign to eradicate prostitution.

Recent Centuries

It would be outside the scope of this chapter to attempt a complete historical survey of the role of religion in repressive attitudes to carnal pleasure. However, it is worth noting that there seems to have been an oscillation between relatively permissive and relatively repressive periods. Gordon Rattray Taylor in *The Angel Makers* has mounted an interesting and convincing argument that this is connected with the gendered nature of society in particular periods (1973). He argues that repressive periods are more patriarchal, and permissive periods are more matriarchal. Repressive attitudes towards carnal pleasure are often being intertwined with religion, but not necessarily so.

There is also an important distinction between an individual and a social focus. Some individuals have used extreme and self-injurious practices to 'mortify' their own flesh, and as a result have probably intensified their own personal religious experience. Such extreme religious practices are considered in more detail later in Chapter 4. There seems to have been an increase in such practices in the late medieval period (Kroll and Bachrach, 2006).

Religion has often become intertwined with the social regulation of sexual behaviour. The eighteenth century was in many ways a highly regulated and restricted period, and religion played a significant role in that (Gibson and Begiato, 2017). The teachings of the Church forbade fornication, masturbation etc, and tried to restrict sexual activity to marriage. It also had a significant role in public regulation, through the courts of the established Church. This faded away as industrialization led to large sections of society becoming unchurched, and religion became more a matter of individual piety than of social regulation.

The move away from restrictions on sexual activity that took place in the 1960s seems to have been intertwined with secularization. The libertarianism of the 1960s appeared to be secular rather than religious.

However, since then, secular thinking has moved back in a restrictive direction, of which a conspicuous feature is the considerable effort now being invested in the prevention of sexual abuse. Many soap opera and reality television shows are concerned with the regulation of personal and sexual relationships. For example, in *The Only Way is Essex,* the vast majority of conversations focus on the regulation of relational behaviour. However, perhaps for the first time, this move back to a repressive culture is not intertwined with religious authority. On the contrary, there has been much criticism of churches for permitting abusive behaviour.

Though sexual ethics in early Christian centuries tended to be dualistic, there is no need for it to be. An example is the twentieth century Catholic theologian, André Guindon (1976, 1986). He accepts that sex is for 'fecundity', but wants to interpret that more broadly than just procreation. He distinguishes different kinds of sexual fecundity:

- Integrated: Sexuality makes possible the integration of sensuality and tenderness.
- Relational: The integration of personal sexuality is achieved in the context of a relationship with another person.
- Loving: Love is the energy that enhances the quality of life in sexual partners and empowers them.
- Responsible: Loving relationships exist in community and give sexual partners an interpersonal history.

New Testament Thinking About the Human Person

Body and Flesh

There is an ambivalence about the body in Christianity in which a positive doctrinal view of the body coexists with moral panic about carnal pleasure. Resolving that depends on getting clear what is actually meant by the 'body', in the New Testament, which is not a straightforward matter (Gooder, 2016). It is particularly important for present purposes to distinguish between body and flesh.

It is a distinction that is really important in St Paul's thinking, but has not been overly emphasized in recent centuries. I believe that a lot of Christian problems about the body fall into place in the light of that distinction. Speaking in very general terms for now, St Paul is rather negative about the flesh, but positive about the body. Without the distinction between flesh and body, some of his negative attitude towards the flesh can be transferred onto the body.

St Paul talks about the flesh (*sarx*) rather than the body (*soma*) when he wants to emphasize what is externally observable. The flesh is also seen as imperfect and subject to death in a way that is not true of the body. Both flesh and spirit, in different ways, have connections with the transcendent. The spirit in humans can connect with transcendent spirit, whereas the flesh of humans is connected with what is imperfect in the transcendent realm (Welker, 2014). Neither body nor soul are seen as having transcendent connections to quite that extent.

The body is potentially spiritually connected in a way that flesh is not, and is open to redemption in a way that flesh is not. Michael Welker (2014) enumerates the various ways in which St Paul takes a positive view of the body. God lives in the body. The body is a place of revelation where one can perceive life and death. Christians are part of the body of Christ and are constituted together as such by sharing the body and blood of Christ in Communion. As Welker says, the body is 'not finally or completely defined by its corporeality', and 'need not be identified with its corporal frailty and finality' (2014, p. 51).

St Paul's view of the human person is dynamic rather than static (Theissen, 2014). He is concerned with prospects and possibilities, and with transformation. What needs to happen with flesh and body are very different. The flesh needs to be subjugated and ultimately discarded. However, body is capable of being interpenetrated with spirit and can be transformed and redeemed. There is no resurrection of the flesh, but there is resurrection of the body. However, that depends crucially on the state of the body and, as St Paul explains in 1 Corinthians 15, it is the spiritually transformed body of Jesus which is resurrected, and which is possible for other bodies as well. We will return to the potential transformation of the body in Chapter 11.

We struggle with this distinction between body and flesh if we imagine that the body is something completely separate from the flesh. We can observe our flesh, but we are puzzled if we look for something else that we can call the 'body'. That would be an example of what the philosopher, Gilbert Ryle, called a 'category mistake' (2000). He uses the example of someone looking at all the colleges and departments of the University, and then asking where the University is, assuming it was something different from what they had already seen. However, the University is not a separate entity; it is a different way of looking at the same things, or a different way of describing and classifying them.

The distinction between anatomy and physiology is somewhat similar to the distinction between flesh and body. Anatomy and physiology are not describing different entities, they are different ways of describing the same body. Anatomy focuses on the observable bits and pieces of our bodies. Physiology takes a more functional approach, looking at how the body works, and what it does.

Biblical Anthropology

For much of the Christian period there has been a prevailing assumption that the human person is composed of body and soul. However, the Bible certainly operates with a much richer view of the human person than just body and soul. The main word in the New Testament that is translated as soul is *psyche*. It is a word that has passed into the English language and it may be better to leave it untranslated. It can mean life, self, or soul. The New Testament makes a significant distinction between psyche and spirit (*pneuma*), a distinction that was gradually lost through the first millennium.

The fourth Chalcedonian Church Council in 867 may have been the point at which the distinction between soul and spirit was finally abandoned in the thinking of the Church (Prokofieff, 2010). That was regrettable, and probably led to a loss of the recognition that there is something genuinely spiritual about human beings, something that can connect with transcendent spirit.

The Jungian psychologist James Hillman develops the distinction between soul and spirit in an interesting way, suggesting that the soul tends to go deep, whereas the spirit tends to soar above things (Hillman, 1998). There is a place for both in personal and spiritual development, but they are different, and it is not helpful to confuse the two. There seem to be two separate instincts in people: one to go deep within ourselves, in what St Teresa of Avila called the 'inner journey', and a second instinct to rise above ourselves and our circumstances and to connect with something above and beyond ourselves. These two instincts are reflected in 'depth psychology' and 'transpersonal psychology'.

There are other words in the Bible that also refer to aspects of the psychological core of personality. The Bible has a much richer concept of the heart (*kardia* in the New Testament) than we have now, and sees it as the seat of much of our thinking, not just our feelings. This can be distinguished from our thoughts and our understanding of things. One word for that in the New Testament is *nous*, which has also passed into the English language.

The Bible seems to recognize the distinction between mind and heart (or head and heart, as we might now say), which has also been important in

much recent thinking about the human person. That distinction maps onto
the growing recognition in psychology that humans, probably uniquely
among species, have two alternative ways of doing central cognition. One
is abstract, rational and linguistic. The other is more affective, embodied and intuitive. In most people rational intelligence is located primarily
on the left side of the brain, and our more intuitive intelligence on the
right side (Watts, 2013b). There has been much discussion recently about
human uniqueness (e.g. Jeeves, 2015). My own approach has emphasized
that what is distinctive about humans is having two ways of doing central
cognition, both head and heart; that is not true of any other species.

It is important to maintain a broad multi-faceted understanding of
the human person that includes biological, social, intellectual, emotional
and spiritual aspects (Watts, 2000b). It seems to me that the Bible maintains such a view. Contemporary theology has had more trouble in doing
so, though there are commendable exceptions such as Edward Farley's
handling of the aspects of human nature relevant to Good and Evil
(Farley, 1990). If each facet of human nature is to be given proper regard,
it is best to avoid making any one of them foundational and trying to
derive the others from it. Such attempts at foundationalism about human
nature are generally unconvincing.

Distinctions and Divisions

There has been an increasing dissatisfaction in recent years about seeing
the human person as composed of body and soul. Sorting out the issues
involves making two different moves at the same time. In part, we need
a more differentiated conceptualization of the human person that goes
beyond the simple two-part schema of body and soul. At the same time,
we need a less sharp division or separation between these different facets
of human personhood.

Body and flesh are not completely different things, but are rather different perspectives, or ways of describing the same person. There are
similar points to be made about all the terms used for the human person
in the Bible: soul, spirit, mind, heart etc. These are not a series of separate
things, each one of which can be located separately. It is closer to how the
Bible uses these terms to say, not that they refer to separate things, but
that each term describes the whole person, but with different emphases
and associations (Richardson, 1950).

Another way of making this point is in terms of the classic philosophical
distinction between denotation and connotation. The various biblical

terms for the human person do not denote completely separate things, but they have very different connotations. Yet another way of making this point, using philosophical terminology developed by Frege, is to say that the terms 'body' and 'flesh' differ in their 'sense' but not in their 'reference'.

Our mental habit of dividing things up into a series of separate things, each one of which we can point to, really belongs to the external physical world, but it causes misunderstanding if it is applied more generally. It does not even really apply in the biological world, which emphasizes how interconnected things are (Watts, 2019c). We talk about our body being composed of things like cells, genes, neurones, etc. in a way that suggests these are separate things, with boundaries between them. However, inside our bodies, things flow into each other. There are gradients around cells rather than walls (Sharma, 2015; Watts and Reiss, 2017). There are no hard edges between one thing and the next. Body and flesh are interconnected; they are not separate from each other. There is a distinction to be made between them, but they cannot be divided from each other.

The philosopher and poet Samuel Taylor Coleridge recognized that a lot of philosophical problems arise from taking distinctions and turning them into divisions (Barfield, 2014, pp. 23–26). Imagining that body and flesh can be separated from each other, or that they refer to separate things, is thus an example of a more general conceptual problem.

For much of the Christian era there has been a tendency to talk about body and soul as though they were separate and distinct things. The same has been true of talk about body and mind. However, in post-war philosophy of mind, there has been a growing recognition that this is a mistake. Gilbert Ryle led the way in suggesting that, though we have mental powers, the mind is not a thing or substance in the same sense as the body (Ryle, 2000). Interestingly, this post-war development in how to use terms like 'mind' brings us back to something much closer to how terms about the human person are used in the Bible. They are not used to refer to separate entities, but for different perspectives on the human person.

Post-war philosophy of mind has influenced how talk about the soul is understood. There has been a tendency to conclude that the 'soul', like mind, is not an entity, separate from the body, and one that can be located in the same way as body can. We have soul qualities and attributes, just as we have mental powers. But it causes confusion to say that we have entities called a 'mind' and a 'soul,' as well as a body (Watts, 2002a).

What has led to the quite widespread view of body and soul being separate? There are two obvious motivations for thinking of the soul as separate from the body. One is the rather negative view of the body that has infected Christian thinking, particularly in late antiquity. The other is the wish to find a plausible way of supporting belief in immortality. Humans don't like to think of death as being the end. Thinking of the soul as sufficiently separate from the body to survive without it seems to be one solution to that problem. I return to that issue in Chapter 11 and discuss what might be involved in a body of flesh being transformed into a spiritual body.

Contemporary Issues

Beyond the Mind–Brain Divide

Most contemporary Christian thinkers who reflect on the nature of the human person are agreed on what extremes they want to avoid, though they are less clear on how to find a path between them. Most want to avoid extreme physicalism, especially if that means eliminating all talk of mind, soul or spirit (or regarding them as just a shorthand for what could be said more accurately in terms of brain processes). Equally, most Christian thinkers don't any longer want to regard the soul or personality as a separate substance or entity, comparable to the physical body. There is general agreement that it is best to avoid strong physicalism and a strong form of substance dualism. We are looking for some middle way.

There has been a significant body of opinion that has wanted to join modern science in espousing some kind of physicalism, but has also looked for a way of avoiding being reductionist about mind, soul and spirit. The question is how to combine physicalism and non-reductionism. One approach is in terms of 'emergentism' – seeing mind as emerging from the physical body but, once it emerges, being able to operate in ways that are not entirely determined by physical laws, so not reducible to them (Clayton and Davies, 2006). An alternative is the 'non-reductive physicalism' advocated by Warren Brown and Nancey Murphy, that is framed in terms of supervenience, a dependent but non-reductive relationship between properties (Brown et al., 1998).

I am not unsympathetic to these proposals. They get us into the right ballpark. However, like some others, I am not convinced that they actually hold together in a coherent way. Among those working on the interface of science and religion, James Jones has been particularly forceful in advancing objections against these tempting solutions to a difficult problem (Jones, 2005). I suggest that embodied cognition points towards an attractive alternative solution to these problems, and one that may be philosophically more defensible.

Both emergentism and non-reductive physicalism are in danger of treating the mind as more separate from the body than it really is. I won't get into complex discussions about the causal influence between the two (whether it is just that the brain affects the mind, or whether the mind can have causal inferences on the body as well). That is because I think that two things have to be more separate from each other than mind and brain are for it to be appropriate to talk at all about one having a causal influence on the other.

Contemporary thinking about embodied cognition and biblical concepts of the human person agree in thinking that mind and soul are intertwined with the body; they are different faces of the same multi-faceted entity. We have an embodied mind, or a soul-infused body. There is no possibility of the two coming apart, or of one having a causal effect on the other.

In thinking about these issues, I find that going to sleep is an instructive example. It makes no sense to talk about the mind going to sleep as a separate process from the brain going to sleep. It is the whole person who goes to sleep, not their mind or brain. It also makes no sense to talk of the mind going to sleep causing the brain to go to sleep, or vice versa. There is a single process of going to sleep which has both mental manifestations (in loss of sense of time and place, and loss of consciousness), and also physical manifestations (picked up through recordings of electrical brain rhythms). However, these are both ways of monitoring and describing a single process of the person going to sleep.

Oliver Davies, in an excellent paper on 'Neuroscience, Self and Jesus Christ' (Davies, 2014), sketches out a sequence that starts with a pre-modern paradigm in which a 'porous' self is at home in an enchanted world, moves through the modern paradigm that sees a distant and controlling relation between self and world, to an integrated paradigm in which the opposition or separation between matter and mind breaks down. As he says, 'although mind and matter are different from one another (and always resistant to the reduction of one to the other) they are now more clearly indivisible' (p. 81).

Embodied cognition leads us back to something close to 'dual-aspect monism'. This sits easily with the multi-aspect monism that is implicit in the biblical understanding of the human person that I sketched out earlier in this chapter. So, from a theological point of view, it is a very congenial resolution of the mind-body problem. It is also attractive for those concerned about doing theology in a way that is credible in the present scientific age. Rather than the uneasy and somewhat unconvincing truce between theology and the science of non-reductive physicalism, it is based on a significant scientific development that has been gathering pace over the last 30 years.

From Individualism to Personhood

Embodied cognition also helps with another significant problem in the conceptualization of the human person. There has been a tendency throughout the modern period to take the individual out of social and relational context, and to assume an abstract individualism that isolates people from their social context. Theology, on the other hand, has become increasingly committed in recent decades to a relational view of the human person, something that has been argued quite powerfully in a variety of ways (Grenz, 2001; Kelsey, 2009; McFadyen, 1990; Zizioulas, 1985).

Scientific psychology, on the other hand, has often seemed to side with abstract individualism, creating a tension between theology and science. However, embodied cognition helps to resolve this problem as well. Embodied cognition has abandoned abstract individualism, and I am here following Léon Turner's exposition of the significance for theological anthropology (Turner, 2013). There is a much fuller discussion in his forthcoming book, *I Am Who I Am.*

One important strand of work has been research on mirror neurones, which shows that when people are paying attention to the actions of another person their own brain activity is the same as it would be if they were performing those same actions themselves (Gallese, 2006). Evan Thompson sees this as underpinning the important human quality of empathy, and sees empathy as fundamentally an embodied phenomenon (Thompson, 2005).

It seems that initially there is no distinction between me and not-me; that is a distinction that is only gradually learned. Indeed, it seems that our sense of who we are, our individuality, arises from our embodiment. We know ourselves as embodied beings who have a particular location in space, and engage with what is around us through our bodies. In similar vein, Antonio Damasio (2000) has argued that what he calls 'the auto-biographical self' is based on our memory of acting in the world. It is our embodiment that gives rise to both our numerical and qualitative distinctness as individual human beings (Harré, 1998).

There has not been much interest so far in historical shifts in the significance of embodiment for the human sense of individuality and personhood. However, the modern period, since the seventeenth century, seems to have been marked by a stronger and more explicit sense of individuality. It seems likely that explicit *assumptions* about individuality in that period were accompanied by a stronger *actual sense* of individuality.

Humans in earlier periods seem to have been less self-conscious about being distinct individuals. For example, in the trance dancing of hunter-gatherer societies that is discussed in the next chapter, it seems likely that the sense of merging with other dancers was stronger than their sense of individuality.

Owen Barfield suggests that the stronger sense of individuality that developed in the seventeenth century was accompanied by a stronger sense of embodiment, i.e. by individuals having a stronger sense of having a body that was theirs, and separate from other bodies. He also sees this sense as having developed slightly earlier in England, an island nation, than in some other places (Barfield, 2012). On this view, it was embodiment that gave rise to a sense of individuality and separateness.

However, we now seem to be living in a time in which that sense of separateness is giving way to a sense of individuals being in relationship. We now feel that we are embedded in a physical and social context in which we are indeed ourselves, but in which we are also always interacting with others. The shift in intellectual assumptions that has taken place in the last 50 years or so is very marked, and seems all pervasive. This three-stage sequence from a lack of self-consciousness about the self, to a strong sense of individuality, and then a sense of personhood and relatedness is similar to the three-stage sequence described by Oliver Davies (2014).

There is a very interesting piece of intellectual history waiting to be undertaken about the connections between the various fields in which this shift to a more contextualized understanding of the human person has been felt. An early herald of this new awareness can be found in John Macmurray's two series of Gifford Lectures given in the 1950s, and especially in his book *Persons in Relation* (Macmurray, 1961).

This new awareness of the contextualization of the human person has been elaborated in many fields. It can be found, for example, in the new emphasis in cognitive psychology on the embodied and embedded nature of human cognition with which we are concerned here, also in the shift in psychoanalysis towards object relations theory, in the shift in theological anthropology to an emphasis on relationality as the key hallmark of human personhood, and in the shift in moral philosophy to a stronger sense of the context in which moral decisions are made and away from an isolated rational decision maker. Iris Murdoch has been especially trenchant in her criticism of the idea that people make choices and set goals in isolation from what is around them (Murdoch, 2013).

I assume that these conspicuous shifts in intellectual discourse are probably accompanied by a shift in actual human consciousness, and that people in their everyday lives are now becoming more conscious of being 'persons in relation'. It is interesting that awareness and embodiment gave rise, first, to a stronger sense of individuality in the seventeenth century. Equally, it seems now to be the interactive nature of our embodied engagement with the world around us that is giving rise to a sense of interconnectedness and interdependence.

As Bishop Stephen Verney has commented, it is one of the great challenges of our time to find a way of holding together the contradictory desires to be individuals and to be part of the collective (Verney, 1976). We seem to want both to develop our individuality and also to merge with others in mass movements. The twentieth century went to both extremes. However, we now seem to be edging towards a stronger sense of *interdependence*, and of being persons in relation. To use Verney's metaphor, we need neither to be solo performers, nor to play on the baton of the maestro, but to improvise together in a co-ordinated way like a jazz ensemble.

There are probably differences between people in how strong a sense of individuality or interconnectedness they have. That may be a significant aspect of the difference between introverts and extroverts. Introverts tend to lead relatively solitary lives that can further strengthen their sense of individuality. Extroverts live out and about, and probably have a stronger sense of living in relationship.

It will also make a difference what activities people engage in most regularly. Most team sportsmen probably have a strong sense of being embodied, and of being embedded in what is around them. A mountaineer will have a strong sense of interacting with the physical environment, whereas in a high-contact team sport like rugby there will be a strong sense of knocking up against the bodies of other people around you and skilfully weaving coordinated actions. An athlete will have a strong sense of testing his personal limits.

Conclusion

We have covered a lot of ground in this chapter, and deliberately so, because I want this book to be devoted largely to religious practices rather than to religious ideas. We began with the striking ambivalence about the body in the Christian tradition, which was partly very positive, but also in some ways very negative. I have suggested we can go some way to resolving that ambivalence in terms of St Paul's distinction between the body and the flesh.

I emphasized that those terms represent different perspectives on the whole person, rather than referring to different and separate components of a person, and that the same is true of the complex network of terms about the human person to be found in the New Testament. We need a broad, comprehensive and multi-faceted way of understanding the human person that makes distinctions between different facets of person-hood without reifying them and turning them into separate components.

I then turned to the contribution that recent ideas about embodied cognition can make to a religious understanding of the human person. I suggested that they provide a way of moving beyond the divide between mind and brain. Though there is a conceptual distinction between mind and brain, I don't consider that they are sufficiently separate from each other for either to have a causal effect on the other.

There are also issues about individuality and personhood. I suggest that both embodied cognition and the present emphasis on relationality and personhood in theological anthropology are manifestations of the broad recognition that has swept across many disciplines in recent decades that human persons are constituted by their embodied relations with others.

3

The Embodied Origins of Religion

One approach to the role of the body and religion is to look at how religion got started. The central claim of this chapter is that religion started with the body. Religion started with embodied practices, and the other aspects of religion came later. In this chapter I set out a view of how and why religion evolved that takes the role of the body seriously.

I am indebted to various people in my approach to this, especially Robin Dunbar, an Oxford anthropologist and evolutionary psychologist (e.g. Dunbar, 2014, 2020, in press) who has developed a theory of the significance of religion in human evolution. Dunbar's view of how and why religion evolved is nested within a broader view of human evolution. For him, religion is not an incidental feature of human evolution; it is crucial to the success of human evolution. He does not press the much-discussed question of whether religion was a by-product of other evolutionary developments, or was adaptive in its own right (Kirkpatrick, 2004), but would be inclined to say that it was both. Léon Turner has published a helpful discussion of the theological and interdisciplinary significance of Dunbar's approach (Turner, in press a).

I am also indebted to Michael Winkelman who has taken a similar approach to the evolution of religion. His textbook, *Supernatural as Natural: A Biocultural Approach to Religion,* is one of the best guides to how religion evolved (Winkelman and Baker, 2008). Robert Bellah (2011) has also provided an account of the evolution of religion that is convergent at the descriptive level with those of Dunbar and Winkelman, though it lacks their biological perspective. I am also building here on my own previous work on the evolution of religion (Watts, 2014, 2017a, 2020).

One of the complications in making the claim that religion started with embodied practices is that it is debatable exactly when the precursors of religion really become 'religion' in the full sense of the word. Religion is a multi-faceted phenomenon as most scholars recognize (Watts and Bretherton, 2017).

Religion started with what people did, moved on to what they felt, and ended up focusing on what they believed. That is the evolutionary sequence. Beliefs are the late developer and emerged only slowly. As we will see, beliefs in 'Big Gods' (Norenzayan, 2013) were much more a feature of the religion of stable settlements than of hunter-gatherer societies. The cognitive side of religion took a long time to develop, and it is debatable how far it needs to develop before we have what can really be called 'religion'.

For something to be indisputably and unequivocally called a 'religion' it probably needs to involve practices, experiences and beliefs. However, those three facets of religion can become dissociated, and you can have just one or two of them. Whether that should properly be called religion is debatable. Some might want to call the embodied practices from which religion evolves 'precursors' of religion, rather than religion itself. I don't have strong views about that semantic issue, though I think it is not unreasonable to refer to embryonic forms of religion as 'religion'.

Embodied Practices

Can embryonic forms of religion be found in non-human animal species? You certainly have something that looks like the seed-corn of religion, though I think myself that it stops well short of something that can properly be called 'religion'. If there is any primate spirituality at all, the best candidate is probably how chimpanzees respond to a waterfall. In *Reason for Hope* Jane Goodall has described how, when chimpanzees in the Kakombe Valley arrive at a particularly striking waterfall, they go into a kind of dance (Goodall and Berman, 2000). Frans de Waal (2013) has also described these primate rain dances. It is as though the animals are worshipping the waterfall, with displays towards it, which involve hurling rocks and branches. There is also often a rhythmic stamping of the feet in the water.

Solar rituals have been observed in some species, such as the wild baboons Malan observed making a special effort to witness the rising and setting of the sun (Malan, 1932). Kohler (1927) observed chimpanzees taking part in a motion pattern based around repetitive rhythmic sounds, similar to the dancing of whirling dervishes. Such synchronized rhythmic movements are characteristic of the primate practices from which religion emerges.

Trance Dancing and its Benefits

It is in the nature of rituals that groups of humans or other animals undertake them together, engaging in the same repetitive, stereotyped behaviour. The trance dancing of early humans was clearly a development of the rituals found in other species, but took things considerably further. One of the key consequences of trance dancing, as Dunbar has pointed out, is the collective release of endorphins.

Dunbar takes as a model of the trance dancing found in hunter-gatherer society the rituals of the !Kung San in Southern Africa. Normally, the women provide the music by singing and clapping, while the men engage in a round dance that continues until, eventually, it induces a trance state (Katz, 1982; Marshall, 2000). Such synchronized rhythmic movement seems to have a powerful effect in giving rise to collective endorphin release.

The collective endorphin release triggered by trance dancing seems to have had three main consequences. First, it gave release from physical pain and contributed to healing of the body. Second, it provided a rapid and very effective way of achieving social bonding, with larger numbers than had previously been possible. Third, it gave rise to transcendent experiences and a sense of the afterlife, as is evident from burial practices. Some might see the latter as the only really 'spiritual' benefit of trance dancing, but I suggest that all three (physical healing, social bonding and transcendence) were closely intertwined, and together constituted the spirituality of hunter-gather societies. All three arose from the embodied practice of trance dancing.

Somewhat similar effects can be observed in effervescent religious rituals, especially in the present day with the rather high-octane religious practices that can be found in countries like Brazil. Highly embodied forms of religion improve social bonding and increase pain tolerance, a measure that is often used to pick up the effects of endorphins (Charles et al., in press).

Healing

Field work in present-day Kalahari (Marshall, 2000) suggests that the motivation for trance dancing is primarily the need for healing in the community. Trance dancing is an intense and exhausting experience for everyone concerned, and is undertaken relatively infrequently. There seems to be a point where the accumulation of pain and illness makes another trance dance necessary. It is the role of the shaman to initiate the trance dance when it is needed.

Routine healing involves rubbing, bleeding and the application of condiments, but trance dancing is of an altogether different order of intensity. Sometimes the healing rite will be used by the healers with each other, to maintain purity. Sometimes it will be used in special curings for particular individuals. However, the paradigmatic use of trance dancing is in the ritual healing dance in which everyone is involved. The healer goes into a trance and purges the whole community of all its ills (Marshall, 2000).

The primary role of the shaman in a hunter-gatherer community is as a healer, and healing seems to be the most common function of a religious specialist in hunter-gatherer societies. James McClenon (2002) suggests that the ability to go into a trance is related to hypnotizability, and that healers were highly suggestible members of the community, chosen for their ability to enter into an altered state of consciousness.

Though hunter-gatherer societies explain healing in terms of supernatural power, it seems that there are also physiological processes involved. This may involve the use of psychedelic substances, but it is also mediated through the endorphin release that is triggered by trance dancing. Endorphins are part of the opioid system, and have powerful analgesic affects. They tune the immune system and reduce vulnerability to infection. They thus have a double significance for healing: they help to prevent disease and also help people to cope with the pain resulting from disease.

Social Bonding and Social Regulation

Endorphins seem to be the social neuropeptide, unlike oxytocin which is much more individualistic in its effects. Endorphins are social in two senses. The most powerful triggers for the release of endorphins involve collective activities. The synchronous movements of eight rowers in a boat are a classic sporting example, and trance dancing also involves similar synchronization (Dunbar, 2014). In addition, endorphins contribute to social bonding and cohesiveness. They build up the experience of being part of a tightly knit group, with all the loyalties and mutual concern that go with that.

Endorphin-producing rituals thus have significant social effects. Collective endorphin release seems to have been a mechanism of social bonding found in humans and other higher primates. Significant time is spent on activities that produce collective endorphin release, and the benefits of that can be seen in social bonding, as well as in healing. Higher primates tend to bond together to form grooming circles. Mutual grooming is a pleasurable and effective way of doing social bonding. However, it is very time-consuming, and is therefore only feasible with a small number of other animals.

This meant that there was a need to develop other ways of social bonding that worked more quickly and with larger numbers. Various physical activities served this purpose, including laughing, singing and dancing. Some of this developed before *homo sapiens*, and Steve Mithen has written at length about the role of singing in Neanderthals (Mithen, 1996). However, dancing seems to have been particularly important in anatomically modern humans. Trance dancing rituals played an important role in human evolution, enabling a significant number of people to bond together rapidly and effectively.

Dunbar has suggested that 150 is the natural limit on the number of people who can bond together in this way. This number, which has come to be known as 'Dunbar's number', is not just of evolutionary significance. There is evidence among those who have studied congregation size that 150 is the natural limit for a single congregation with a single pastor, and that for a church to exceed that number it has to find some restructuring solution (Bretherton and Dunbar, 2020). New churches tend to peak at slightly over 150, show signs of tension, and then fall back slightly.

Different kinds of religion have gone about social regulation in different ways. In evolutionary theories of religion there has been much interest in fear of supernatural punishment (Norenzayan et al., 2016). Social Brain theory sees that as a feature of later, more doctrinal forms of religion, associated with more frequent but less intense rituals. Trance dancing delivers social regulation in a more positive way, through facilitating social bonding. The social effects of shamanic religion associated with trance dancing are mediated through the social bonding that is facilitated by collective endorphin release, whereas the social effects of doctrinal religion are mediated through other processes such as fear of supernatural punishment. The mechanism in the two cases is quite different, though both contribute in different ways to maintaining social cooperation (Watts, 2020).

The evolution of religion arises within complex patterns of co-evolution. Having larger social groupings, with more complex structures, demanded enhanced cognitive capacities (including 'theory of mind' and the ability to intuit what another person is thinking), which in turn demanded larger brains and, in particular, expanded frontal lobes. Humans have exceptionally large brains in relation to the size of their bodies. Dunbar argues that managing the complexity of their larger social networks necessitated larger brains. On this view, brain size, cognitive capacities and social structures developed together. Dunbar's approach to the evolution of religion is one aspect of a systemic process in which the emergence of religion both depends on, and facilitates, other developments.

Transcendent Experiences

Trance dancing was the soil out of which religion emerged, fuelled by endorphin release, and giving rise to various experiences of the spirit world. For the !Kung San, trance dancing induces experiences of both bad spirits (who try to deflect them from finding their way back to the normal world), and good spirits of ancestors (who help them to find their way back). The entrance to the way back is typically described as a narrow entrance to a tunnel that connects the spirit world with the normal world.

It seems to have been a reflection on these exceptional experiences that led to a religious worldview. Interesting issues arise about how to interpret the spiritual experiences of trance dancers. It seems clear that there are biological processes involved, i.e. that there are neural processes involved in experience of good or bad spirits, and that the intensity of the experience is increased by endorphins and other physical factors such as exhaustion.

It is tempting to suggest that if biological factors are involved at all, the whole experience can be explained away in such terms, and dismissed as a mere epiphenomenon of extreme or unusual physical states. That sets up a polarization in which the experiences of trance dancers are seen *either* in biological *or* in spiritual terms. There is a temptation to go for what William James in *Varieties of Religious Experience* called 'medical materialism' (James, 2012) and to argue that, if biological processes are involved at all in giving rise to the experience, there really cannot be anything more going on, and that any suggestion that the experiences are of a spiritual world is pure illusion. Michael Marsh has advanced this kind of argument about near-death experiences (Marsh, 2010), explaining them entirely in biological terms and dismissing the idea that they are visions of heaven and the afterlife.

This imagined opposition between biological explanations and spiritual reality seems to me wrong-headed. Humans, like all other creatures, are embodied; there are biological aspects of all human experiences, including spiritual experiences. Whether there is any reality to the spiritual experiences is a completely different question, and one that is not settled by biological processes being involved. Of course, it is possible that apparently spiritual experiences can be explained entirely in biological terms. However, the fact that biological processes are involved leaves open the possibility that they provide a glimpse of spiritual reality.

Spiritual Participation

Though I want to resist biological reductionism here, neither would I want to assume that there is a completely separate spiritual world which people enter in trance states, and about which they can bring back reports. As Rowan Williams (2019) has pointed out, we misunderstand things if we imagine that pre-modern religious experience involved the kind of knowledge that a detached observer might have of some different world. It is rather that those who have exceptional experiences are *participating* in an expanded reality, and one that they are struggling to make sense of as best they can. They are participating in that expanded reality, rather than studying it as detached observers.

Archaeological evidence of burial practices provides confirmation that by 25–30,000 years ago there was belief in a spirit world to which people went after physical death. Burials in this Upper Palaeolithic period are very different from previous burials. The bodies are laid flat in the earth, rather than just dumped. Red ochre is often used in the burial. People are often buried in groups. Grave goods are buried along with the bodies, to provide people with what they will need in the next world.

There are also cave paintings that date from the same period. It has recently become possible to date cave paintings more accurately; dates vary, but some in France go back 30,000 years. The scenes are often of animals crowded together. There are also often geometric shapes, and stencilled handprints. We cannot be sure why these elaborate paintings were made, and various suggestions have been put forward. They might have been connected with hunting practices, or that they might have been associated with puberty rituals. The most interesting possibility is that they depicted shamanistic experiences of the spirit world arising from trance dancing.

Related Anomalous Experiences

It may be helpful to make a comparison with the unusual spiritual experiences of people in psychotic states such as schizophrenia. There are general grounds for supposing that there is normally a good deal of selection and filtering that determines which cognitive processes reach conscious experience. In schizophrenia those normal filtering processes break down to some extent, resulting in a wider range of sometimes disconcerting experiences reaching consciousness. As I have argued elsewhere (Watts, 2018), the suggestion that the normal cognitive filtering processors break down in schizophrenia is perfectly consistent with the idea that genuine spiritual experiences are occurring.

I grappled with the intersection between neurological and spiritual aspects of unusual experiences in working with someone who had strange and unsettling experiences of presence around him, often touching his body, and with malign intentions (Watts, 2018). Examining the story of how this developed, it seemed clear that the experience arose from a motorcycle accident, and from damage to the brain. However, there was also clear evidence of another psycho-spiritual layer in these experiences. Spiritual healing had an effect, and even entering the church building for a healing service had a remarkable calming effect. How he interpreted the sense of presence seemed much influenced by psycho-socio-spiritual factors that went beyond the neurologically based tendency to sense a presence around him. I concluded that some kind of two-factor theory was needed that included both neurological and psycho-spiritual factors.

It seems likely that there are significant individual differences in the extent to which people have transcendent experiences as a result of practices such as trance dancing. James McClenon (2002) has suggested that hypnotizability is an important factor. The dimension of transliminality that has been discussed in connection with psychotic predisposition to psychotic experiences may also be relevant (Clarke, 2010). Simon Dein has suggested that a sense of self-transcendence is a personality trait with a genetic basis (Dein, 2020).

There may be a good deal of overlap between these various personality dimensions. There may be more different ways of formulating the same thing than different dimensions that can be distinguished from one another. It can be assumed that shamans are people who are particularly prone to transcendent experiences. They presumably have more experience than most of navigating them, both how to come out of them as well as how to enter them. That experience leads them to be selected as a guide for others.

One of the important questions that arises about spiritual experiences in trance states is what contribution they make to other aspects of human evolution, and in particular whether they contribute to healing and social bonding. It might be that healing of the body and experiences of the transcendent are two relatively independent consequences of the altered state of consciousness that arises with trance. However, it seems more likely that a shared experience of the transcendent contributes to, and enhances, the social bonding that is facilitated by trance states. However, it is difficult to find knock-down arguments that settle that question one way or the other.

The Mind-set of Early Humans

I want now to explore the mind-set of humans in the Upper Palaeolithic period who engaged in trance-dancing, burial practices and cave painting. It seems that the mindset of the early humans who engaged in these various practices was probably very different from our own. Things that may seem intuitively obvious to us may not have been obvious to them.

Much the best-known account of the evolution of religion at the present time is that derived from the Cognitive Science of Religion (CSR). There has recently been a softening of some of the more hard-line assumptions of original CSR (e.g. Boyer, 2001; Barrett, 2004; Tremlin, 2010), and a greater willingness to broaden it to integrate other approaches (Norenzayan at al., 2016). However, in its original form, CSR seems to embrace some misleading assumptions about the mind-set associated with early religion.

CSR has been too wedded to a unitary account of what counts as 'religion', and inclined to assume that all religion is essentially the same. There is sometimes a surprising lack of recognition of the extent to which religion has itself evolved. The implicit assumption often seems to be that 'religion', when it first evolved, was essentially the same as it is now in the twenty-first century. However, that is obviously an untenable assumption.

CSR, as its name suggests, is also inclined to see cognition as the core and essence of religion. However, the evidence suggests that religion began with embodied practices. The doctrinal aspects of religion seem to have been one of the later aspects to develop. Almost every anthropologist agrees that the first phase of religion in hunter-gatherer societies (variously called shamanic, imagistic or animistic) was a matter of embodied practices, and that doctrinal religion developed later when stable settlements emerged.

There is also a tendency in CSR to take the individual out of social and relational context, and to consider people in isolation from their surroundings (Turner, in press b). CSR tends to take a disembodied and decontextualized view of the nature of religious cognition. We have come to see religion as an individual private matter but, on the contrary, religion underpinned the collectivity of hunter-gatherer societies.

With the move from hunter-gatherer societies to stable settlements, ritual practices became more frequent, but less intense. There was a shift from the facilitation of social bonding by collective trance dancing to an attempt to regulate free-riders by threat of supernatural punishment. There was also a shift from intuitive and embodied cognition towards a more abstract conceptual form of cognition and the development of religious doctrines.

It seems to me that the modes of cognition associated with trance dancing, cave painting and early burial practices were very different from the cognition found in doctrinal religion in stable settlements. I have suggested that this shift in cognition roughly maps onto the two modes of central cognition that can be found in humans (Watts, 2020). There is an intuitive, embodied mode, associated with the right hemisphere, which seems to have been the mode that hunter-gatherer society largely relied on. That was very different from the more abstract, articulate cognition associated with the left hemisphere which is a later evolutionary development, and which began to be important with the religion of early stable settlements. There was a shift in religious cognition from the highly embodied mode of cognition associated with religion in the trance-dancing period to the more mixed modes (some still highly embodied, but some becoming less embodied) in the more doctrinal religion of early stable settlements.

The Evolution of Consciousness

This evolution in religious thinking reflects a more general evolution in human cognition. Various schemes have been put forward to summarize this. Though they are not identical, there is a good deal of overlap between them. An important source for several recent schemes, such as that of Ken Wilber (2007), is Jean Gebser, whose influential book, *The Ever-Present Origin*, was first published in 1949 but not translated into English until sometime later (Gebser, 1986).

His theory is sometimes taken to be a theory of the *stages* through which consciousness developed but Gebser tries to emphasize that modes of consciousness that develop later do not replace earlier ones but exist alongside them. He calls his five modes archaic, magic, mythical, mental and integral. In broad terms, he charts a development from highly embodied, participatory, undifferentiated modes of consciousness to more detached, intellectual and abstract modes. Lockley (2010) provides a helpful and accessible exposition of Gebser's complex ideas.

Bellah's approach to the evolution of religious thinking (Bellah, 2011) makes use of Merlin Donald's distinction between four types of culture:

episodic, mimetic, mythic, and theoretic. Philip Barnard's scheme is based on the progressive addition of subsystems in his model of Interacting Cognitive Subsystems (Barnard, 2019). Though these schemas have different starting points, and differ in detail, it is remarkable how much convergence there is between them.

The Emerging Distinction Between Natural and Supernatural

Most CSR theorists assume that the world is simply a natural world, and that theism and supernaturalism are false. However, there is nothing in CSR that necessitates this view, as James Jones and others have pointed out (Jones, 2015). The widespread naturalistic assumptions of the twenty-first century are all too often just projected back onto emerging humanity (Watts, 2014). It is too easily assumed that it was obvious to emerging humanity that the natural world was just that, a natural world and nothing more.

However, there are indications from cave art and burial practices that for emerging humanity the world was enchanted, and there was no divide between the natural and the supernatural. It was one world, rather than a dual world, partly natural, partly supernatural. There seems to be a clash between evidence about how emerging humanity saw the world and the claims of CSR theories of religious cognition. CSR tends to project backwards our own naturalistic assumptions and to assume people in hunter-gatherer societies must have recognized, as many people do today, that the natural world was just that, a natural world.

From a CSR perspective, the question arises of what went wrong for religion to get started. Something seems to have gone wrong with the intuitive naturalism that CSR assumes that early humans must have held. CSR then has to invent some kind of 'fall' from naturalism which led to the cognitive mistake that CSR sees religion as being based on. This is sometimes seen as 'domain violation'. It is assumed that emerging humanity had a clear distinction between the animate and inanimate world, and then somehow made the mistake of thinking about the natural world as though it was a living thing, and fell into animism.

Various explanations can be put forward for why this fall took place. However, there remains what seems to me a completely unfounded myth that naturalism has always been obviously correct, and that it was somehow lost or obscured. On the contrary, I suggest that naturalism is almost certainly a late development, and does not at all represent how emerging humanity saw things.

There is a parallel in the evolution of the meanings of words. It is often assumed that words began by being used for things in the natural, physical world. It is further assumed that they later came to be used for experiences through some kind of extrapolation. However, as Owen Barfield (1984) points out, the etymological evidence indicates that words start as double-aspect terms, often referring both to something in the physical domain and something in the psycho-spiritual domain. There is no etymological evidence that emerging humanity started with literal terms and later extended them by metaphor, just as there is no evidence that emerging humanity saw the natural world as purely inanimate and natural, and then imported alien concepts to understand it. There is more about this in Chapter 7.

There is some approximate recapitulation of evolutionary development in child development. Children do not start with conceptual distinctions and lose them. Conceptual development follows something like the path that Jean Piaget sketched out a long time ago from close observation of his own children. He called the main stages pre-operational, concrete operations and formal operations. The conceptual distinctions with which we are concerned here belong to formal operations, and are hard won. It is unlikely that they were obvious to emerging humanity.

There seems to be some recapitulation of the gradual emergence of the distinction between natural and supernatural beings in infants. Using ingenious experiments, Justin Barrett (2012) showed that, up to the age of about four, children seem to assume that everyone knows what really is the case, in the way that God does. It is only later that they recognize the limitations of human knowledge, and that humans only know what they have had the opportunity to learn. The distinction between natural and supernatural beings seems to emerge gradually out of the initial assumptions that everyone has God-like omniscience.

There seems to be some folk record of the emergence of more conceptually differentiated thinking in the story of Adam and Eve eating the fruit of the 'tree of knowledge of good and evil' in Genesis 3. Eating this fruit seems to be a mythological way of speaking about the acquisitions of the capacity for making conceptual distinctions. The distinction between good and evil is the one that is referred to explicitly, but there is another, implicit distinction about how Adam and Eve became more conscious of the distinction between themselves and God, and had to wear something to hide their embarrassment about nakedness. You need to have a capacity for conceptual distinctions before you can feel embarrassment. So, I find Genesis 3 to be a mythological pointer to cognitive aspects of human evolution. It may be myth, but I believe it points to evolutionary realities (Watts, 2002a).

4

The Ascetic Life

This chapter examines ascetic practices in religion, especially in Christianity. I consider the objectives of the ascetic life and ask whether it achieves its objectives. To anticipate, I give qualified support to ascetic practices, as I think there are reasonable grounds for thinking that they probably do broadly achieve what they are intended to achieve.

I also consider the reasons ascetics give for their practices, and their views about how and why ascetic practices work. On this, I am much more critical, and argue that there are widespread misunderstandings in the ascetic literature about why these practices are helpful in the religious life. So, my general conclusion is that asceticism is reasonably effective in achieving its objectives, but that there are often serious misunderstandings about why and how asceticism gets the results it does.

There are various factors that make it difficult to take a calm, balanced and judicious approach to asceticism, and the misleading rhetoric with which it is often advocated is only one of them. Most people feel strongly for or against the ascetic life, and are unable to take a balanced approach. Those engaged in the ascetic life, writing from an insider's perspective, are generally in favour; those looking on from the outside are often sceptical or hostile.

For some time there has been a reaction against asceticism. William Blake (1968) was shocked by it and called it a 'mental rebellion against the Holy Spirit', and 'fit only for a soldier of Satan to perform' (p. 154). In the twentieth century there has been a widespread reaction against ascetic practices. This critique came initially from liberal and modern theology, but it has also come more powerfully from atheistic sources, especially Nietzsche, Freud and Foucault.

For Foucault, asceticism is essentially about ecclesiastical power and control over sexuality. However, he was a subtle thinker who often changed his mind about the details of what he wanted to say, though there are recurrent themes (Jordan, 2015). After Foucault, it is hard to assume that sexuality is simply absent from ascetic life; it is ruthlessly controlled but not absent. It is also hard not to at least consider whether there might be an element of sadomasochism in some ascetic practices (MacKendrick, 1999). There seem to have been some fairly obvious sadomasochistic practices in some ascetics, such as Martin of Tours (Burrus, 2007).

One problem with these critiques is that they are coming from a hostile place, and often show little understanding of what ascetics are trying to do. They are a 'hermeneutic of suspicion' (Ricœur, 1977). Though I think there are criticisms to be made of the ascetic life, the endeavours of ascetics need to be properly understood in their own terms before they are roundly criticized. The critiques also tend to overgeneralize about asceticism and to see it as all essentially the same, whereas I am with Sarah Coakley in wanting to distinguish true asceticism from false repression (Coakley, 2015).

Another problem is that there is a shortage of good literature about the ascetic life. There are 'how to do it' books written by ascetics for those who wish to follow in their footsteps (e.g. Colliander, 1985). Such books may be useful from a devotional point of view, but they are not adequate on their own to understand asceticism. Among older books, Oscar Hardman's *The Ideals of Asceticism* (Hardman, 1924) is impressive, and in many ways remains unsurpassed as a sympathetic but fair and judicious assessment of the ascetic life.

There is also a burgeoning historical and socio-cultural literature on ascetic practices in particular contexts that is producing numerous fascinating case studies of the slightly different forms that ascetic practices take in different situations (e.g. Wimbush and Valantasis, 2002; Valantasis, 2008). However, in my view, such studies don't help much in understanding what is really going on in the ascetic life. They are more interested in differences in the form that asceticism takes in different contexts, rather than what ascetics have in common.

The Psychology of Asceticism

My intention here is to take an interdisciplinary approach to the ascetic life and to consider a psychological and biological perspective on these practices. That brings an outsider's perspective to bear, to complement the insider's perspective of those engaged in the ascetic life, and will lead to a critical re-evaluation of insiders' accounts of asceticism. I bring the ascetic tradition into dialogue with modern psychology.

There is, at best, a somewhat uncomfortable relationship between psychology and asceticism, as even those well-disposed to asceticism would recognize (e.g. Bouyer, 1955; Kugelmann, 2011). Many psychologists assume that the traditional ascetic practices of fasting, sleep deprivation and laceration of the flesh represent a perverted approach to religion, and one that should be discarded.

It might be assumed that any psychological approach to asceticism will inevitably be a 'hermeneutic of suspicion'. Some (e.g. Duffey, 1950) have seen scope for a sympathetic psychological interpretation but, unfortunately, Duffey doesn't show any detailed knowledge of psychology and psychiatry. It has even been suggested that the replacement of asceticism by a more psychological approach to the religious life is one of the key causes of the church's current problems with child abuse (Linacre Institute, 2006), though that seems a naive interpretation of the historical changes involved.

Fortunately, a good cross-disciplinary literature on asceticism is beginning to emerge, including Inbar Graiver's *Asceticism of the Mind* (Graiver, 2018). She focuses particularly on the ascetics of late antiquity who, she suggests, had a more 'porous' mind then we do now, in which they were vulnerable to 'demons' (unwanted intrusive thoughts which they felt were assaulting the body). They soon discovered that trying too hard to eliminate unwanted thoughts actually just makes them even more intrusive.

Graiver draws a parallel with recent work on cognitive control which has reached the same conclusion (Wegner, 1994). There is similar practical advice by the seventeenth-century spiritual adviser Augustine Baker, who recommends that the person should 'divert quietly his mind from them', and 'neglect' them rather than pursue them (Baker, 1964, p. 236). I have earlier pointed out the similarity of that advice to what is found in cognitive therapy (Watts and Williams, 1988).

My approach here has been influenced a good deal by *The Ascetic Mind* (Kroll and Bachrach, 2006), an important collaboration between a historian and a psychiatrist. I see this chapter as also being a sympathetic engagement with asceticism, and approaching it from the perspective of relevant scientific research.

There are at least three reasons for engaging in ascetic practices that deserve sympathetic consideration, and which I examine in turn. It is often claimed that asceticism (i) strengthens capacities for self-regulation, (ii) intensifies religious experience, especially the experience of prayer, and (iii) strengthens religious commitment and the capacity to make sacrifices.

All of these rationales see deprivations and mortifications as a means, not an end in itself. If it is intended that there should be benefits from asceticism, then different ascetic approaches can be assessed for how well they deliver these benefits. However, some traditional ascetic practices seem a rather blunt instrument for achieving their potential benefits, and they might be made more effective with the help of psychology. Ascetic practices are not for everyone, but they can be helpful for some people.

Ascetic Practices and Their Benefits

Those pursuing the ascetic life are committed to putting significant time and effort into mental prayer on a regular basis; that alone is likely to result in a significant enhancement of prayer experience, and a range of other personal benefits. For most ascetics, except hermits, there is also a demanding round of religious services, attended with others committed to the religious life. The effects of that also seem likely to be considerable.

Many monks spend a considerable proportion of the day in prayer, sometimes the majority of their waking hours. The sheer frequency of services makes an impact. If, like the Cistercians, you attend services every 2–3 hours, there is little opportunity to lose religious focus. What people do with the majority of their time is bound to have a huge impact. In a sense, 'we are what we do'. Doing church services collectively means that people are tacitly encouraged by one another, and can be held to account for being present, awake and focused.

However, ascetics have realized that they can go much further if they bring their bodies to bear on the objective of intensifying religious experience. Ascetic practices include both deprivations such as of food and sleep, and self-harming practices such as flagellation. For the ascetic, the religious life is the over-riding priority, if not the only priority. Ascetics are prepared to put their bodies fully at the service of their religious life, in whatever ways will enhance and intensify it.

From the late middle ages, i.e. from around the twelfth century onwards, there seems to have been a close association between the mystical and ascetical paths (Kroll and Bachrach, 2006). Before that time, mystics and ascetics were often different people, though some were both. From the late middle ages onwards, ascetic practices seem to have been used more routinely to intensify mystical experience. Most accounts of ascetic practices include recommendations for eating, sleeping, and laceration of the flesh. I am indebted here to the excellent recent review of Kroll and Bachrach (2006).

Considering food regimes first, an extreme, but perhaps not atypical, regime was that of Guthlac (674–714) who became a solitary hermit in East Anglia. His daily food intake consisted of a 'scrap of barley bread and the small cup of muddy water', taken each day after sunset (Kroll and Bachrach, 2006, p. 85). The best guide to the effects of such extreme fasting comes from a study carried out in Minnesota at the end of World War II by Ancel Keys, using volunteers who had been conscientious objectors during the war (Keys et al., 1950). Severe restriction of food intake led to significant weight loss. Sexual interest and expression were virtually eliminated. There was also considerable emotional instability, depression, irritability etc., and a tendency towards self-centredness and a reluctance to engage in social activities.

The ascetic life also usually involves significant shortage of sleep. Thomas Merton (1949) has provided a modern account of the Cistercian pattern of life, which revolved around the night office at 2am. He retired to bed at 7pm in the winter, and 8pm in the summer. The amount of sleep obviously depended on how quickly he got to sleep. However, it is a sleep pattern that amounts to slight but prolonged sleep deprivation, which would be expected to lead to irritability, a reduced sense of well-being, and loss of vitality and an ability to concentrate It would also increase sensitivity to pain.

There is probably more variability in the methods used for the laceration of the flesh, and in their severity. The medieval example cited by Kroll and Bachrach is Beatrice of Nazareth (1200–1265), who would regularly beat her body 'using sharp twigs and even the prickly branches of the yew tree' (p. 68). She also put sharp yew leaves on her bed with the result that 'scarcely any part of her body remained unscratched by the punctures'.

Such practices would lead to considerable pain. However, they also lead to the release of endogenous opiates such as endorphins. The trance dancing of hunter-gatherers discussed in the last chapter also led to endorphin release, but laceration of the flesh would induce more pain and an even greater rush of endorphins. Flagellation and blood-letting continue among some modern Christians, such as members of Opus Dei who use the discipline on their backs and the cilice on their thighs.

One caveat that needs to be entered here is that, though we know what effect such practices would have on most people, we don't have good information about the effect of the contemplative life on how the body responds to such practices. The contemplative life may lead people to cope better with deprivations of food and sleep, and there are ways in which the religious life could increase pain tolerance. I return to the experience of pain in Chapter 6.

Improving Self-regulation

A key part of the traditional case for asceticism is that it strengthens self-control. For many years, concepts such as 'will-power' were seen just as folk psychology, with no scientific basis. However, in recent years there has been a significant resurgence of strength models of self-control, led by Roy Baumeister (e.g. Baumeister and Tierney, 2012), which offer an alternative to the previously dominant cognitive approach to self-regulation. The strength model of self-control likens it to a muscle that gets stronger with exercise and training. This restates many of the traditional assumptions about self-control that have underpinned the ascetic life. It seems highly likely that the beneficial effects of the ascetic life on will-power could be demonstrated if suitable research was undertaken.

An interesting issue relates to the relative benefits of the relentless, routine application of abstinence and hardship as compared with a harsh response to failures of control, such as the penalties received by a Cistercian novice for talking in choir. It seems likely that a regime of zero tolerance of lapses is beneficial in strengthening self-control in the ascetic life, as it has been in policing in New York and elsewhere. If people think there is a chance of getting away with lapses, it seems they tend to work on the optimistic assumption that they will do so. It introduces a different mind-set if people know that they definitely won't get away with lapses in self-control. The uncompromising nature of the ascetic life again seems likely to be vindicated.

Hardships can no doubt be useful in strengthening self-discipline, and that probably works best when people intensify their ascetic practices as a response to having been lax or wayward. Remorse can easily be superficial, but electing to undertake physical hardships after lapses will ensure that there is learning at the deeper level of embodied cognition.

Another issue, not yet much researched, concerns the relative benefits of verbal and physical approaches to enhancing self-control. Though there are no doubt individual differences, it seems likely that many people show a relative disconnect between thinking and behaviour. If so, physical approaches to enhancing self-regulation may have more impact than verbal ones. Or, rather, the most effective approaches may well be those that integrate physical and conceptual responses to failures and transgressions. The emphasis on physical practices in the ascetic life is entirely consistent with the current trends in psychology that focus on embodied cognition.

Advocates of the strength theory of self-regulation have accumulated a good deal of evidence in support of reserves of will-power becoming depleted by use, like physical energy, and have demonstrated the restorative benefits of giving will-power a rest (Baumeister and Tierney, 2012). For example, there are probably benefits from taking breaks from ascetic practices, such as those on Sundays and Feast Days that have been a traditional part of the ascetic life, so that reserves of will-power can recover from depletion.

The ascetic approach to enhancing the capacity for self-regulation is tough and uncompromising, and therein probably lies part of its appeal for some people. Many people are attracted to tough regimes of physical training, and again the analogy between physical training and training in will power seems apposite. For many people there seems to be something very satisfying in setting yourself tough targets and rising to the challenge of meeting them.

The appeal of ascetic self-discipline is likely to be greatest for those who find self-control difficult. If they find that their normally feeble efforts at self-regulation are significantly enhanced by the adoption of an ascetic life, that will come as a welcome relief. Feeling out of control is never a comfortable experience. For many, the rigours of asceticism are better than feeling out of control.

The attraction of enhanced self-control does not necessarily depend on the assumption that there is anything inherently wrong with the tendencies that are being controlled. That may sometimes be the case as, for example, with those who find themselves sexually attracted to children. However, an enhanced capacity for self-regulation will often be welcome, even when there are no specific moral issues at stake.

Intensifying Experience

Christians who attend Mass or some other church service often fail to obtain any intense religious experience that makes much impact. Of course, powerful religious experiences can occur spontaneously to anyone at any time, and about a third of the population report having had such an experience (Hay, 1982). However, outside such spontaneous experiences, an intensification of religious experience is generally available to those willing to put in time and effort on a regular disciplined basis. It seems that the ascetic life can intensify religious experience, and that can be another key reason for undertaking it.

The majority of research on meditation has been on methods derived from Indian tradition. Silent mental prayer in the Christian tradition has been less well researched, but there is sufficient evidence (e.g. Luhrmann,

2012) that those who put in even just twenty minutes a day on a regular basis can obtain significant personal benefits. Interestingly there is no single method than can deliver this; a variety of approaches to mental prayer seem able to deliver comparable results, though people may differ in what method suits them best.

Though the psychobiology of the ascetic life is not yet fully understood, one key factor in determining the intensity of experience is how physiologically aroused people are. Intense religious practices usually take people to extremes of arousal, in one direction or the other, sometimes combining elements of high and low arousal (d'Aquili and Newberg, 1999). The traditional ascetic ingredients of pain, fasting and sleep deprivation represent a radical assault on the body, and one that is bound to have far-reaching effects on experience. Many ascetics have been prepared to do anything to their bodies if it intensifies religious experience.

Placing religious experience in the context of heroic asceticism is likely not only to intensify such experience, but to change its character. Surrender to the will and purposes of God is often an important strand in mystical experience, but one that is likely to be heightened by the experience of surrendering to the abstinence, pain and fatigue engendered by rigorous asceticism. There is likely to be a merging in the mind of surrender to God and surrender to ascetic practices, each one enhancing the other.

There are resources in Freud to understand how desires connected with sex or power can be redirected in a way that intensifies other experiences, including spiritual ones. Freud was no friend of asceticism, but Sarah Coakley's careful reading of him (Coakley, 2015), including the twists and turns in his theoretical development, shows that Freud can be used to understand how the sublimation of desires can lead to an intensification of spiritual experience.

A key focus in the religious life of many ascetics has been identification with Jesus. That means that the physical burdens of the ascetic life have been particularly used to identify with Jesus in his own sufferings, in the desert and on the cross. The ascetic takes unusually seriously the idea that you cannot hope to share in the joy and resurrection of Jesus unless you first share in his sufferings. The stigmata are one radical manifestation of this identification with Jesus in his sufferings, and a reflection of the vivid identification with Jesus that has often been a feature of the religious life.

I suggest that physical hardships of the ascetic life do most to heighten religious experience when they are used explicitly in conjunction with religious observances. When Jesus refers to fasting in the gospels, he usually couples it with prayer, talking about 'fasting and prayer', implying that he saw them as working together. I suggest that asceticism may work most effectively to heighten religious experience when it is used in conjunction with intensive prayer.

The Cistercian practice of holding one of its major services in the middle of the night, when most people are asleep, is an interesting parallel example of combining sleep deprivation and prayer, and a particularly powerful experience for many Cistercians, i.e. being up praying for the world when the world is asleep. The common practice of keeping a watch with Jesus on the night of his arrest is another example, and a moving experience for many people.

The Stations of the Cross lend themselves to being done in a way that is physically arduous, and can become much more meaningful when done like that. There is nothing particularly arduous about walking the Stations in the usual way. However, one young Christian experimented with keeping the Stations in the gym. Each station was marked by 5 minutes of prayer and reflection, followed by 10 minutes of arduous exercise in a particular part of the gym. His prayerful procession round the gym became increasingly painful towards the end of the three hours. It was a powerful way of commemorating and identifying with Jesus' *Via Dolorosa*, and an example of making demands on the body to heighten religious experience.

Enhancing Commitment

Enduring hardships in the ascetic life can be a helpful test of seriousness of purpose, and can in turn enhance commitment. The relationship between commitment and hardship is bi-directional. Clearly only those who have serious commitment will undertake ascetic hardships. However, I suggest that it goes the other way too, and that undertaking hardships enhances commitment.

The psychological process involved here is cognitive dissonance, first formulated by Leon Festinger in studying the non-fulfilment of the apocalyptic expectations of a Chicago cult (Festinger, 1957). If people undertake ascetic hardships with only moderate commitment a state of dissonance is set up. That can in principle be resolved in one of two ways – either by reducing ascetic practices or by increased commitment. In practice, the latter resolution is often chosen; otherwise the person concerned is left in the uncomfortable position of having endured hardship for no good reason. So, a process arises in which a positive feedback loop is set up between hardship and commitment, each one ratcheting up the other.

For many people a single, strong, over-riding commitment will be deeply satisfying. One of the stressful features of modern life is juggling with multiple commitments, often not knowing where priority ought to be given. The ascetic life resolves all that, with a single intense commitment, and one that is maintained by a sacrificial pattern of behaviour.

In recent years there has been a marked tendency for conservative forms of religion to be the ones that grow (Kelley, 1972). The strong commitment required by an ascetic life is probably one of the factors that makes it attractive, something it shares with other conservative forms of religion, but in a particularly intense form. For those seeking an even stronger religious commitment than they already have, the adoption of an ascetic lifestyle will help them to achieve the single-minded intensity of commitment that they seek.

There may also be attraction for some in making sacrifices. Several things come together here. One is a demonstration of the enhanced capacity for self-regulation that is exemplified in the ascetic life. That may in turn confer an enhanced sense of self-efficacy. Making sacrifices can heighten the sense of identification with Jesus, whose own life involved remarkable sacrifice. For some, at least, making sacrifices will involve a sense of surrender, and perhaps a loosening of over-strong ego boundaries or defences, and a sense of merging into a bigger, supportive spiritual world. Sacrifice can become very appealing.

Finally, the ascetic life will also often involve a gradually increasing sense of commitment to the community in which the ascetic life is developed and practised. The size of this community can be very variable. In some cases, it can be quite large; in other cases, as, for example, with The Little Brothers of Jesus, it could be just one or two other people supporting each other in the religious life. Whatever the size of the community, the ascetic life is probably only sustainable where there are strong (and increasingly strong) commitments between those undertaking it. The ascetic life cannot easily be undertaken in the context of weak or problematic relationships.

It is thus not hard to see how the ascetic life can be appealing. It enhances self-control, intensifies religious experience and enables people to find a single-minded sense of purpose and commitment. In drawing upon both psychology and more traditional religious perspectives to make this point, it may seem as though I am reducing the ascetic life to a matter of psychology, or that I am saying it is undertaken for just personal advantage. However, I am not *reducing* the religious life to psychology in that way. I am rather using the perspectives of psychology and religion in a convergent way to understand better the benefits the ascetic life confers, and why people undertake it.

Secular and Religious Perspectives

For the most part the twentieth century has been puzzled by the ascetic life, and slightly shocked by it. Powerful critiques have been offered of ascetic life, based on Freud's ideas about perversion of sexual desire, and from Foucault in terms of the relationship between power and sex. It is hard to find anyone taking a middle way between either accepting or rejecting these critiques. However, Sarah Coakley in *The New Asceticism* (Coakley, 2015) has shown how to engage with these critiques sensitively, while putting them in a broader context, and resisting the reductionist conclusions that at first glance seem to flow from them. She treads a thoughtful path, relating how Patristic writers like Gregory of Nyssa understood desire to modern debates and scandals about sexuality.

The first thing to be said in response to these critiques is that ascetic practices are very variable. That is the key point that Oscar Hardman makes in the opening chapter of his classic book on asceticism (Hardman, 1924). Asceticism includes legitimate self-discipline as well as excessive forms of bodily purgation. There is a healthy striving for self-development alongside other forms of asceticism that are 'characterized by undue severity, by a false estimate of suffering, or by sheer negativity' (p. 16).

That is a fair point, but it also needs to be recognized that there seem to be very strong tendencies, even temptations, in the ascetic life to go to ever-greater extremes. People either shy away from ascetic self-discipline entirely, or seem to want more and more of it. Many wise spiritual directors find that their role is to restrain people from excesses, rather than to encourage them to be more rigorous.

The question that needs to be asked is why there are these inflationary tendencies in the ascetic life, why do people want to go further and further? There seems to be something addictive about it, and that is not fully explained by the official rationales offered for the ascetic life. Though I have tried to offer a psychologically sophisticated defence of how asceticism achieves its objectives, I also submit that there is more going on which needs to be better understood.

First, I think there is a widespread misunderstanding about the role of the body in asceticism. Much (though not all) of the rhetoric used to explain and advocate asceticism is dualistic. The widespread assumption is that the body drags people down and, if there is to be any salvation for the soul, the body needs to be subjugated. The prevailing assumption is that the body needs to be treated harshly in order to set the spirit free.

I find this dualistic rhetoric intellectually problematic, for the reasons discussed in Chapter 2, which have led to the widespread abandonment of dualism in philosophy and theology since the mid twentieth century. However, I also think that it seriously misdescribes what is going on in the ascetic life. I suggest that the physical rigours and disciplines of asceticism actually involve using the body in a carefully calculated way. The ascetic life is far from being a disembodied form of spirituality. On the contrary, it is highly embodied, and therein lies much of its appeal.

Some ascetic practices can easily become addictive. I think this is more likely to arise with flagellation and physical discipline than with deprivations of food and sleep. The use of a rope discipline on the back, as in contemporary Opus Dei, can easily lead to the breaking of the skin, which in turn produces a rush of endorphins. That is a very intense experience, and can easily become addictive. I think part of the addictiveness of asceticism is an addiction to endorphins.

More generally, in recent decades, there seems to have been a surge of interest in practices of many kinds that Roy Baumeister has called 'escaping the self' (Baumeister, 1991). There are many such practices that have led to widespread addiction in the secular world, including use of alcohol, drugs, and self-harming. The ascetic life also seems likely to lead to an escape from the self that some will find attractive, so it is not surprising if it also becomes addictive.

The practices of some ascetics can become eroticized, leading to quite extreme levels of sexual arousal. Some of the more extreme cases of this sort have been described by Burrus (2007). Some level of eroticization may be quite common in the ascetic life, and another reason why it can become addictive. Some contemplatives have reflected explicitly on the eroticism in their spiritual lives (Slade, 1977).

There are contemporary forms of sexual practice, particularly sado-masochistic or BDSM sex, which can have a striking parallel with traditional religious ascetic practices (MacKendrick, 1999). There is also a small literature on the spirituality associated with BDSM sex (Easton and Hardy, 2004). Mark Jordan (2001) comments on the similarity between the submission of will and intellect required by the Catholic church and sado-masochistic sexual practices. In some cases, there are unmistakable religious overtones in how people conceptualize what they are doing in BDSM sex. It seems that the ascetic spirit is very much alive and has migrated almost unnoticed into the secular world.

Some people engaged in submissive sexuality feel a strong sense of vocation to give themselves in love and service to a chosen mistress or master. They want to prove their devotion by enduring extreme hardship, and to improve themselves by enduring ever more extreme hardships and punishments in their chosen life of service. There can be a fruitful comparison between traditional Christian asceticism and equivalent secular practices. The rhetoric of those engaged in the ascetic life and in BDSM sex can be strikingly similar.

There is nothing very surprising about these observations. The problem is how to interpret them. I don't think it is necessary to draw the conclusion that the ascetic life is nothing but the working out of desires for sex, submission and endorphin-based highs. I suggest rather that, in at least some people, there is an intense desire to form a submissive relationship, a desire that may well have an evolutionary origin. We may also reflect, as Mark Jordan (2001) comments, on how God is present in affliction.

Such relationships can be seen as involving a certain kind of attachment to a being or person who is perceived to be superior (whether God or another human). I suggest that people who have strong instincts of this kind have, in past ages, found fulfilment in the ascetic life but now, in a more sexual secular age, may find fulfilment in BDSM relationships. Unsettling though these issues may be for some, it seems wise to at least acknowledge them; that will lead to better management of religious asceticism.

The Religious Context

The context in which ascetic-type practices occur may make a big difference. The ascetic life often involves a radical reshaping of desire, as Sarah Coakley (2015) points out. Desires of an ascetic kind involve physical and emotional elements, and combine agape and eros. I think that is true of both religious asceticism and its secular counterparts. To understand what is going on in asceticism it is important to move beyond crude dualisms and to recognize the complexity of the desires involved and how they can be reshaped. It may make a huge difference whether the desires are reshaped around God or another human.

Though we know what effect practices of an ascetic kind have on most people, we don't have good information about the effect of the contemplative life on how the body will respond to such practices. For example, those leading a contemplative life may be able to cope better with deprivations of food and sleep. There are good reasons why that might be the case.

First, it is likely to make a big difference whether or not people have chosen to deprive themselves of food and sleep. Potentially aversive experiences are much worse if you have them imposed on you rather than choosing them for yourself. It is a different experience to give yourself an electric shock than to be given one by someone else. It is different to choose not to be employed then to have unemployment forced on you.

One indication that deprivations have different effects on people who have chosen to lead an ascetic life comes from the effects on mood state. Being deprived of food and sleep makes most people irritable. However, there are indications that the mood state of people leading an ascetic life is one of quiet joyfulness rather than irritability. Many people find that deprivation of food and sleep can make it harder to concentrate, but people who have chosen to fast sometimes find it improves concentration (e.g. Sheldrake, 2019).

Deprivations of food and sleep reduce or eliminate sexual interest and activity in most people. For some people that may be a significant reason not to deprive themselves of food and sleep; for others, loss of interest in sex may be welcome, and an important reason for adopting the ascetic life. For others, sexual interest may not go away, but be 'sublimated' in a way that enhances religious life. As Coakley (2015) points out, Freud's view of the sex drive and his concept of 'sublimation' is implicitly sympathetic to asceticism. Looked at from a Freudian perspective, sublimation can be a way of energizing the spiritual life through a channelling of sexual desire. The ascetic is often said not to be learning to have no erotic feelings, but to be focusing their erotic feelings on God.

It may be helpful here to revert to the distinction made in Chapter 2 between flesh and body. There may be important differences in attitude and motivation among people leading the ascetic life. Some have seen their deprivations as punishment of the flesh. Others see their deprivations more positively as contributing to a spiritual transformation of the body. It is likely to make a big difference to the effects of deprivation how people see what they are doing, and whether it is undertaken out of a negative or positive motivation.

There are potential health benefits in food deprivation (Sheldrake, 2019). For example, eating food suppresses release of growth hormone, whereas fasting releases it. Fasting can improve, or even cure, type-2 diabetes, a condition in which the body is so flooded with insulin that cells have become insensitive to it, and the first day or two of fasting often leads to release of toxic substances.

If deprivations are to have positive effects, the scale of them and the pace at which they are introduced is quite important. It takes time for the body to adjust to less food and sleep than is normal. There is a virtuous circle here. Slight deprivations begin the transformation of the body; once that transformation is begun, the body is able to accept and respond positively to greater deprivations. Bodies probably adjust at different rates and, if the results of deprivations are to be positive, it is important that the pace of change should be right for the individual.

Becoming less dependent on food can be experienced as a kind of liberation, with changes in attitudes as well as physiological changes (Wirzba, 2011). Many of us are not very conscious, most of the time, of the sacrifice and death of other creatures that go into our food. Becoming more aware of that can increase gratitude and reduce greed, and make eating more a matter of deliberate choice and less compulsive. The negative consequences of climate change are becoming increasingly evident, leading many people who might not regard themselves as religious to consider the carbon imprint arising from food production. This provides a positive motivation of a new kind for why people might begin to adopt ascetic practices, and to choose a life of reduced food intake.

Some of the same points can also be made about sleep deprivation in the ascetic life. The consequences are no doubt less negative if it is freely chosen rather than imposed. Also, people can probably gradually adjust to a regime of limited sleep in the way that limits the negative consequences. However, as Farré-i-Barril (2012) notes, it is hard to avoid the conflict between the positive claims made for sleep deprivation by ascetics and the scientific evidence for the detrimental effects it usually has. It is possible, though, that the contemplative life results, not just in people being able to manage with less sleep, but in their actually needing less sleep. There are plenty of anecdotal reports of advanced contemplatives who seem to have thrived without much sleep. Needing less sleep gives more time for other things if it can be achieved without the detrimental effect on mood state that normally results from sleep deprivation.

The issues I have begun to explore in the last sections of this chapter are difficult. Secularists will see close parallels between the practices of ascetics and similar practices that are found in secular contexts, and will offer an entirely secular account of what is going on in asceticism. In contrast, ascetics will dismiss secular parallels as of no relevance at all to what they are doing. I suggest that secular parallels and critiques raise significant issues that should be taken seriously.

However, I am also happy to entertain the possibility that the religious context makes a very significant difference to the ascetic life. If that is so (and I suspect it is), there is a further question about exactly what it is about the religious life that transforms asceticism. One obvious possibility is that framing ascetic practices as part of the service of God puts them into a different frame of meaning, and meanings have pervasive effects. Another related possibility is that ascetic practices have different effects in those who are seriously engaged in a contemplative life. These tend to go together, but they don't always. There could be an atheist whose ascetic-type practices were not seen as the service of God, but who spent significant time each day in mindfulness or some other kind of meditation. Whether a religious context actually changes asceticism and, if so, how that comes about, will require much further exploration.

5

Extreme Spirituality as 'Flow' Experience

In 2008 Pete Owen-Jones, an Anglican priest, presented a series of three television films on the BBC called *Extreme Pilgrim*. The choice of title for the series is interesting in itself. 'Extreme' is a good buzzword; it arouses interest. There is also currently much interest in pilgrimage, so 'extreme pilgrim' was likely to pull in a good number of viewers. In fact, the series won the *Radio Times* Readers Award for Best Religious Documentary, and led to a spin-off book, *Letters from an Extreme Pilgrim* (Owen-Jones, 2010).

In the first film, Owen-Jones went to the Buddhist monastery in Central China where martial arts were developed. There he was given a punishing regime of meditation and physical exercise. He struggled with that, and also with what he saw as the commercial development of the monastery as a centre of martial arts. He retreated to a mountain temple where he lived in isolation and began to feel stillness of mind, and to obtain a level of Zen.

In the second film he went to India and engaged with a Hindu pilgrimage to the River Ganges that drew people from all over India. He also spent time with wandering holy men. and searched for a guru who would explain their way of life. Towards the end of the film he travelled to the foothills of the Himalayas where he lived for a time in a cave, seeking solitude.

In the third film he went to Egypt to learn about the Desert Fathers, especially St Anthony of the Desert. He travelled into the desert, to the monastery of St Anthony, where he spent time with the Coptic monks. One of them introduced him to one of their caves, where Owen-Jones lived in solitude for 21 days. There was a pattern in all three films of Owen-Jones struggling with religious communities and regimes, but finding the rigours of life as a hermit more rewarding.

In this chapter I look at several examples of what I am calling 'extreme spirituality'. One of its interesting features is that it spans the religious and non-religious domains. I look at the rare and exclusively religious phenomenon of serpent handling, an extreme practice by any standards, but one that happens to be very well researched. At the other end of the spectrum I look at extreme sports, which I suggest are not just analogous to extreme religious practices, but actually function as a quasi-spirituality in their own right. In between, there are phenomena such as pilgrimage and fire-walking that span the religious and non-religious domains.

Extreme spirituality is in some ways like asceticism, but in other ways different. It is not driven by the sense of guilt and unworthiness often found in ascetics, or by a felt need for punishment of the body. However, some of the positive motivations for extreme spirituality are similar to those for the ascetic life. Those engaged in extreme spirituality, as much as any ascetic monk, often see themselves engaged in the triumph of the will over weaknesses of mind and body, and engaged in an intense form of personal enhancement. Those positive objectives are similar, though in secular forms of extreme spirituality there is a more open recognition of the pleasure and satisfaction of meeting the demands of highly rigorous training.

There is currently not a great deal of interest in practising extreme asceticism in explicitly religious settings, with the exception of conservative Catholic groups like Opus Dei. However, that may not mean that asceticism is in decline. It seems to have migrated across into contexts that are not explicitly religious, where it is alive and well and increasingly popular. There are a number of aspects of religion where this is currently happening. For example, there is currently not much interest in angels in mainline religious Christian denominations, but there is a rapidly growing interest in angels in the secular world.

Fire-walking and Serpent-handling

Fire-walking

Fire-walking is one of the most extreme spiritual practices. In most religions, there are demonstrations of how holy men can be exposed to fire without burning. Usually this is attributed to the protection of the gods, or the saints. It is relatively rare in Christianity but can be found in villages in northern Greece, as part of a three-day celebration in honour of St Constantine and St Helen (Xygalatas, 2012). It has also migrated into the new age movement, as illustrated by the work of Burkan (2016) and McClenon (2002), both of whom have played significant roles in training secular fire-walkers.

The first question that is often asked is whether or not it is a miracle that people can walk over fire and not burn. It is certainly remarkable and 'wondrous', but there are scientific considerations that make it understandable. There are various factors that are relevant. Fire-walkers normally walk on wood, which is a poor conductor of heat, reducing the heat that is transmitted from the burning embers to the feet. The blood circulating in the feet also reduces their conductivity. There are also elements of skill in exactly how you walk, and successful fire-walking is to some extent an acrobatic feat. You certainly need to keep walking rather than stand still, but it seems to help to walk slowly and evenly; walking too quickly can result in pushing the feet into the embers and causing blisters.

State of mind is also important and James McClenon (2002) has concluded that successful fire-walkers are usually people who are quite easily hypnotized, and often enter a kind of trance state. Preparation for fire-walking seems to be important, and McClenon uses a combination of meditation and drumming that goes on for several hours. The social element is also important, and it is easier to get into a state that protects you from burning as part of a group of people than on your own. However, it is not simply 'mind-over-matter'. There are biological factors as well, including increased blood flow.

My general view about miracles (and this is something I return to in Chapter 10 about healing of the body), is that it is a mistake to see miracles as events for which there is no conceivable ordinary explanation. Miraculous events like fire-walking are exceptional, and arise in the context of faith. However, they also arise in the context of a lawful and orderly creation that religious people see as coming from God. There is no reason to suppose that God would set aside the orderliness of his creation in order to bring about events within it. I suggest that there is nothing incompatible in seeing an extraordinary event like fire-walking as being of religious significance, but also looking for the processes within creation that make it possible.

However, the question I am more interested in here is *why* people do fire-walking, and what benefits it brings them. I have not done fire-walking myself, and it seems a very bold and dangerous thing to do. There are some fire-walkers who manage to do it without getting blisters, but a good proportion burn themselves and get blisters that can take several weeks to heal. There must be compelling reasons for doing something so dangerous.

According to Burkan (2016), there are various benefits from fire-walking. The first arises from the fact that the fire is dangerous and scary. Walking over it is an exercise in overcoming fear. There is probably an elation that comes from successfully overcoming the fear of the fire. There may also be a belief that overcoming fear in this one particular context will give you a general ability to overcome fear that will transfer to other situations. Burkan claims that fire-walking overcomes fear by teaching you to pay attention differently. His point is that we have choices about what we pay attention to. We can pay attention to our heads, which may be telling us to panic; *or* we can pay attention to our feet in a matter-of-fact, mindful kind of way, noticing that they are very hot, but that they are not burning. Fire-walking is a kind of training in mindful attention.

Burkan also emphasizes the importance of expectations, or 'faith' in fire-walking. How successful people are at fire-walking depends on whether or not they *expect* to be able to do it successfully. Believing that you can do it makes a significant contribution to actually being able to do it. Once you see something as possible, it actually becomes possible, or at least more possible. Finally, Burkan suggests that fire-walking is a training in purposeful action. You take stock of where you are and where you want to go. You create a plan, and then you do what you have decided to do.

James McClenon (2002) would frame things slightly differently. As he sees it, the main requirement for doing fire-walking successfully is to go into some kind of trance or hypnotized state. Fire-walking challenges you to do this successfully. If you don't, you get burned. The long period of preparation for fire-walking, including meditation and drumming that McClenon arranges for fire-walkers, is designed precisely to enable them to get into that state of mind, so they can do fire-walking without getting blistered.

There is also, no doubt, a remarkable sense of personal achievement. Doing something so difficult and dangerous successfully results in fire-walkers being highly regarded by other fire-walkers. There is both a personal sense of achievement, and a sense of social acceptance; it serves as a kind of rite of passage. Dimitris Xygalatas (2012) interprets this in terms of 'costly signalling' theory. Fire-walking is a very costly way of securing acceptance in a social group. According to this theory, it is precisely the costliness of it that makes it such an effective way of demonstrating your commitment to the fire-walking community. That in turn gives a very welcome sense of achievement when you are accepted into a fire-walking community.

There also seems to be a remarkable degree of social bonding in a group of people who engage in fire-walking. They support one another in getting into the necessary kind of trance states, and support one another in overcoming fear. The extreme challenge that fire-walking presents leads to an extraordinary degree of social bonding of which there are clear physiological markers. These include the collective release of endorphins that must have characterized the trance dancing of early humans. Extremely challenging rituals such as fire-walking generate very high levels of physiological arousal, which in turn give rise to exceptional social bonding. The community bonding that occurs is illustrated by the synchronized heart rhythms that are sometimes found in a group of fire-walkers (Konvalinka et al., 2011)

Fire-walking seems to afford something akin to a 'flow' experience. The concept of 'flow' experiences was introduced by the psychologist Csikszentmihalyi, and the title of his first book, *Beyond Boredom and Anxiety* (Csikszentmihalyi, 1975) brilliantly encapsulates why flow experiences are appealing. He gives as examples of flow experiences the work of a surgeon or concert pianist, which is so demanding that they require completely focused attention.

The total concentration and experience of absorption and flow that fire-walking provides may be part of its appeal for those engaging in it. Fire-walking leaves no mental space to think about what you are doing, as those doing it are too focused on the immediate challenge. Cognition is completely integrated with what is being enacted physically. Some religious practices seem designed to lead to the adoption of a cognitive style in which thought processes are so integrated with embodiment that cognition becomes tacit and implicit, and the familiar sense of separation between body and mind disappears.

Serpent-handling

The serpent-handling that occurs in some churches in the Appalachian mountains in the USA (Hood and Williamson, 2008) represents another extreme religious practice. Serpent-handling is more dangerous than fire-walking. It is thought that around 90 people have died from snakebites in serpent-handling churches and, in any church where the practice occurs regularly, there are people with missing fingers etc. that have arisen from snakebites. The danger involved focuses even more sharply the question of why people engage in such extreme practices.

At the heart of serpent-handling there is an element of obedience that is not found in fire-walking. Serpent-handling seems to be found exclusively in the context of religious belief. Snake-handling churches take very seriously the five marks of the Holy Spirit listed at the end of St Mark's Gospel, of which handling serpents is one. For members of such churches, it is the decisive test of their obedience to the will of God whether they are able to overcome their fears of snakes and handle them. Once it is seen as a struggle between the will of God and human fear, it is inevitable that the perceived will of God will win out for a committed believer, whatever the dangers.

As with fire-walking, there are both individual and social aspects of obedience in serpent-handling. If Christians in serpent-handling churches are to think well of themselves as committed Christians, it is essential that they should take part in serpent-handling. It is equally as important for their standing within the believing community that they should prove themselves in the sight of others by handling serpents.

Many also emphasize the importance of being 'anointed' to handle snakes, i.e. empowered by the Holy Spirit to do so. Some snake handlers, but not all, think that being able to handle snakes safely is only made possible through anointing by the Holy Spirit, and that to handle serpents without that anointing would be dangerous. So handling serpents safely is a public demonstration of being anointed by the Holy Spirit, and further demonstrates the faith of the serpent handler.

The question of what changes psychologically when serpent-handlers are anointed is an interesting one. There is one study in which Liston Pack, a notable serpent-handler, agreed to be videotaped and to have EEG brain-recordings made while in his anointed state (Hood et al., 2018). The anointing was detectable in the recordings, with a sudden change in brain waves from alpha to beta. The recordings confirmed that a religious experience was taking place, though it was more similar to hypnosis than to meditation.

There are also important cognitive aspects of serpent-handling. The extreme danger involved requires that the handler be very focused and single-minded. Any mind-wandering is a luxury that cannot be afforded. There is also no scope for reflective thinking about serpent-handling. The culture in which serpent-handling occurs is a notably non-intellectual one, and the reflections on the serpent-handling of practitioners are generally not very sophisticated or richly conceptualized. Serpent-handling is so obviously a test of trust, courage and obedience that there is no need to reflect explicitly on those things. The cognition involved is enacted rather than mentated. The serpent itself has to be the all-consuming focus of attention, and the attention to it has some of the features of mindfulness. Serpent-handling seems to be another example of a religious flow-experience.

Pilgrimage

Pilgrimage is one of the most important and interesting enactive religious practices and has an important historic place in almost every major religion. For example, every good Muslim aims to go to Mecca at some point. Christians go on pilgrimage to the Holy Land, or to places like Santiago de Compostela. Something akin to a pilgrimage can be formalized into a procession that occurs in a place of religious observance. For example, Christians walk in procession with palms as they commemorate the entry of Jesus into Jerusalem, or they move in procession around a church, through the Stations of the Cross, as they commemorate Jesus' walk from Jerusalem to Golgotha where he was crucified. There is growing scholarly interest in pilgrimage, from both a social science (Dubisch and Winkelman, 2005) and a theological (Bartholomew and Hughes, 2004) point of view.

Rupert Sheldrake (2018) suggests that pilgrimage has its origin in the migrations of human societies, and of other species, before people began to live in settlements. Annual migrations often follow particular routes, and sometimes these routes included striking natural features such as rock, water or whatever. There continue to be some pilgrimages to places of striking natural beauty, but pilgrimage is now often made to places of religious significance, and often to impressive buildings. Pilgrimage has captured the popular imagination.

There seems to have been a gradual development from a religious focus on natural features that have been given religious significance to places and buildings that have been deliberately created to have religious significance (Watts, 2019b). Places of pilgrimage are often believed to be sites of particularly important revelations, or of miracles. The relationship between the site and the building is a complex one. Grand pilgrimage churches like the cathedral at Santiago de Compostela were built because there were already large numbers of pilgrims gathering there, but the building presumably enhanced the significance of the site and led to even more pilgrims.

There have been controversies over pilgrimages. Within Christianity, pilgrimage has always been an important part of the Catholic tradition, but the sixteenth-century Reformers such as Luther tried to stamp out pilgrimages as being unnecessary and unscriptural. Sometimes atheistic authorities have also tried to stamp pilgrimages out. However, pilgrimage has been remarkably resilient, and currently more people than ever are going on pilgrimage. The pilgrimage to Santiago has become particularly popular, especially after the publication of Walter Starkey's *Road to*

Santiago. Over 300,000 pilgrims now walk to Santiago each year. That is very striking, particularly at a time when many religious practices are in decline.

Santiago is also a popular tourist destination, and there has been much discussion about the relationship between pilgrimage and tourism (Swatos and Tomasi, 2002). It is very striking that places of religious significance are often popular tourist destinations. It is one of the facts that gives the lie to the claim that the society in which we live now is a secular one, in any straightforward sense. As one of my friends likes to quip, there has been no decline in people going to churches; it's just that they don't attend when church services are running. They now go to churches as tourists.

Why do people go on pilgrimages? Pilgrimage provides an extended break from the normal demands of life, and substitutes its own different requirements. The demanding physical process of walking engenders its own state of mindfulness. The walk becomes a symbol of a personal or spiritual journey, seeking healing or transformation of some kind; the embodied practice of walking becomes intertwined with thoughts, feelings and devotions.

The long walk to a place such as Santiago is physically tiring to the point of exhaustion. Feet become sore and blistered, and it becomes a severe test of physical endurance. The physical demands of pilgrimage justify calling it a form of extreme spirituality. Cognition and embodiment weave together, each supporting the other. The sense of following in the steps of many others who have walked the same path can lead to a transpersonal experience, and a sense of sharing an extended mind with other pilgrims.

The reasons for undertaking it are complex and diverse, and there is no simple division into those whose motivation is or is not religious. Farias et al. (2019) found that almost 20 per cent of their sample of pilgrims to Santiago described themselves as atheists. It is striking that so many atheists choose to engage in such a physically demanding religious practice, despite their lack of religious motivation. Interestingly, atheists had more individualistic motivation for pilgrimage than religious pilgrims. Farias suggests that the motivation for undertaking a pilgrimage to Santiago is to explore the transcendent, including both vertical (supernatural) and horizontal (natural) aspects of transcendence.

Farias also compared pilgrimage to Christian sites such as Lourdes with pilgrimage to pagan sites such as Stonehenge. Religious community motivations were obviously higher for those making a pilgrimage to Christian sites, whereas sensation-seeking and closeness to nature were more important reasons for pilgrimage to pagan sites. The emotions of pilgrims to Christian sites were more positive than those of pilgrims to pagan sites. However, it would be a mistake to draw too sharp a distinction between religious and non-religious pilgrims. There may often be a spiritual motivation for pilgrimage among those who are not explicitly religious. It seems that natural features and buildings are a significant feature of the motivation for many pilgrims, whether they are religious or not.

Pilgrimage can serve a variety of relational and community building purposes, outside the explicitly religious or spiritual objectives. Jansen and Notermans (2012) suggest, for example, that pilgrimage can facilitate sexual emancipation; it can also consolidate a sense of national identity among migrants, and enable people to form new religious identities in a shifting religious context. They speak of how the old pilgrimage routes can offer 'inspirational opportunities for making new journeys'. Pilgrimage can provide the opportunity for sexual seduction and the formation of new intimate relationships.

There are also psychological benefits from pilgrimage. Morris (1982) reports that levels of anxiety and depression tend to be lower when on pilgrimage. This is not too surprising, and Sheldrake (2018) notes several features of a pilgrimage that are known to be helpful in terms of psychological benefits. Walking itself has psychological benefits. So does exercise, especially when taken in fresh air and green spaces. Pilgrimage involves purposeful activity, that is influenced by the hopes and expectations of the pilgrims.

Victor Turner (1979) suggested that the relentless physical demands of a pilgrimage, together with the sense of purpose provided by the endpoint and the support of the pilgrimage community, combine to make it a very powerful 'flow' experience. Turner suggests that there are six features of pilgrimage which make it a flow experience: experience of merging action and awareness; the centring of attention on the limited stimulus fields; loss of ego; the pilgrim finding himself not in control of his actions and the environment; non-contradictory demands for action; and having no need to have goals or reward outside the pilgrimage itself.

The outer journey of the pilgrimage often seems to symbolize an inner journey. The demands of the outer journey seem to facilitate the inner work that the person needs to undertake, whether that is a journey to the transcendent, a search for mental or physical healing, or a time of reappraisal that may lead to a new direction in life (Coleman and Elsner, 1995).

Secular Quasi-spiritualities

Extreme religious practices are only one kind of the extreme practices that are found in various domains in present-day society. 'Extreme' currently seems fashionable in many different domains, and it is possible that the reasons why people engage in extreme religious practices are much the same as those for which they engage in extreme practices in other domains.

Sport as Spirituality

Extreme sport is the most interesting example of an extreme practice that is not generally thought of as being spiritual, but it actually seems to have many of the hallmarks of a spiritual practice. It may, in effect, be a kind of spiritual practice, even though there is no explicitly religious or spiritual rationale. Sport is not often considered to be a spiritual practice, but it is one of the seven spiritual practices that Rupert Sheldrake discusses in *Ways to Go Beyond* (Sheldrake, 2019). There has also been a good deal of recent theological interest in sport (Dailey, 2018; Harvey, 2014; Smith, 2010).

The analogy between athletic training and the requirements of committed religious life is an old one, and goes back at least to St Paul. There is also a present-day literature on 'spiritual fitness' which develops this analogy (e.g. Tomlin, 2006). It seems that sporting activity might be not just analogous to religious life, but that it could actually constitute a form of spirituality in itself.

For many sports spectators/supporters, sport seems to function as a quasi-religion. Support for a football club or whatever becomes what gives meaning and purpose to life, and the weekly match is analogous to church attendance. However, for those who *participate* in sporting activities, sport can become a quasi-spirituality in a fuller way. That is what I focus on here.

In sport, many participants push their bodies hard, often to increasing extremes. Sports training is often quite painful; that is one of the things that connects it with the ascetic life in religion. The appetite for pain and discipline that was a feature of the ascetic life in the late middle ages has not gone away. It is alive and well, but is now more likely to be found in sport than in religion. Physiologically, endorphins seem to play a role in both. Much sports training consists of regular rhythmic movements, which are ideal for triggering release of endorphins. Flagellation until the skin breaks is equally likely to trigger release of endorphins. Through various different routes, endorphins seem to be the spiritual neuropeptide.

Sporting activity also absorbs the mind and gives release from the seemingly endless, inconsequential thought processes that dog many people. In that respect, extreme sport seems to be yet another 'flow' experience. Many sporting activities require skill and complete focus, even when they are not physically demanding. A top snooker player needs to be completely focused as they pot the ball, and a good break at snooker can probably become a flow experience.

Learning to still the mind through meditation is the classic approach. However, a workout in the gym, or a long run, can do it in a different way, with the combination of the hypnotic effect of regular movement and physical fatigue. It can serve a role similar to meditation in stilling the mind. A sporty release from mind-wandering can be very satisfying, and become almost addictive. It is striking that many people who run regularly say that, when they are tired, going for a run actually refreshes them, despite the considerable physical demands that it makes.

The more extreme the sport, the better the release it gives. Extremes of skill, extremes of speed, extremes of the expenditure of physical energy can all, in slightly different ways, contribute to the quasi-spiritual experience that sport can give. Sport, like the ascetic life, is an effective way of delivering what Roy Baumeister calls 'escape from the self' (Baumeister, 1991). The exercise of skill also gives relief from mind-wandering in a somewhat different way, as it becomes a flow experience.

One of the interesting points of connection between sport and spirituality is the sense of grace and empowerment that people often feel in sporting activity. Religious people often have a strong sense that their religion requires them to stop trying to do things in their own strength, and instead just let the grace of God work through them. Buddhism has its own distinctive and powerful way of formulating that experience of surrender and an abandonment of ego control.

There have been many books about sport that extol the virtues of playing the inner (or natural) game of this or that, for example a tennis player who stops trying to work out how best to respond to an oncoming ball and instead, just allows the experience of the natural game of tennis to flow through him and guide his movements. That experience of empowerment through surrender is clearly a kind of spiritual experience, and it seems it enables people to actually play better (Gallwey, 2015).

Some sports people pursue an ideal body through sporting activity and work-out, among other things (Dutton, 1995). The perfectly developed body becomes the ultimate goal, and the pursuit of it justifies any sacrifice in terms of time, effort and even pain. Sometimes people just want to know themselves that they are achieving their ideal body; sometimes they want their body to be appreciated by others. Whichever, development of the body is pursued with quasi-religious devotion.

Sporting activities often give rise to altered states of consciousness, to experiences which, if they occurred in a religious context, would undoubtedly be regarded as important religious experiences and moments of revelation. Michael Murphy's *The Future of The Body* (Murphy, 1992) is the best guide to such quasi-religious experiences in the context of sports and other physical activities. He identifies various features of sport that make it a transformative practice, including sustained and focused attention, the relinquishment of limiting psychological patterns, and new ways of integrating mind and body.

Spiritual but not Religious

The popularity of extreme sport may be part of the spirituality of those who see themselves as 'spiritual but not religious', an increasingly significant group in the contemporary spiritual landscape. Recent decades have seen a progressive movement away from conventional forms of religion, especially away from church attendance. This process, often misleadingly referred to as 'secularization', disguises the fact that some aspects of spirituality are very much alive, though many people would now identify themselves as 'spiritual but not religious'.

There are many ostensibly secular activities that in practice function as secular spiritualities. In two recent books, Rupert Sheldrake has surveyed fourteen of these (Sheldrake, 2018, 2019). Sheldrake has an interesting threefold classification of spiritual activities as involving a sense of returning to base, a reframing that allows for a more enlightened way of seeing things, or an activity that brings a dynamic sense of energy and empowerment. Some sports involve more than one of these. He draws an analogy between these three forms of spirituality and the three persons of the Trinity.

The spirituality that is experienced in sport is clearly of the latter kind, a dynamic empowerment through activity that is akin to pentecostal religion. It requires considerable expenditure of physical energy to achieve the release from humdrum ordinary life, and the sense of energy and empowerment, that extreme sport gives. You have to give your all, but you receive the 'kingdom'. The parallels with spirituality in a religious context are very striking.

There are probably other activities that place extreme demands on people which, like sport, sometimes give rise to spiritual experience, though sport is the best example. The extreme demands sometimes made by military service probably function in a similar way and deliver really intense bonding with comrades that ex-service people hanker after for the rest of their lives. Military-style extreme training is held up as a way of learning survival skills for ordinary life (Hudson, 2019). The world of business makes regular use of demanding physical challenges as a way of delivering team bonding and improving motivation, leadership qualities and coping skills.

The spiritual experiences that arise in sport and other activities involving extreme physical demands are still a relatively unexplored field in the study of spirituality. However, it raises many interesting questions for those who want to understand the spiritual life, and deserves more attention than it has so far received. It seems likely that the reason why people engage in extreme practices is often spiritual, in a broad sense, regardless of whether or not the context and framework is explicitly religious.

6

Attending to Our Bodies

In the last two chapters I have explored two different ways of relating to our bodies in the spiritual life, and in this chapter I explore a third approach to the body.

The ascetic life seems to rest on fundamentally dualistic assumptions. It sees the religious life as a matter of mind and spirit, and the physical body as a potential distraction and handicap. The ascetic treats the body in ways that will allow the person to transcend it. It is an attitude that was summed up by St Francis, who called his body an 'ass' that needed harsh treatment. The slogan, 'I have a body, but I am not my body', which forms a key tenet of the psychosynthesis developed by Roberto Assagioli is in a similar vein (Assagioli, 1993). In asceticism and psychosynthesis, in different ways, the body is disowned.

The extreme spirituality that we considered in the last chapter switches things around and sees the spiritual life as essentially a matter of physical performance, involving feats that are sometimes athletic and require great skill, and which all involve bravery and courage. Extreme spirituality focuses completely on the performance in hand, whether fire-walking, serpent-handling, mountaineering, or whatever. Such performances can give rise to intense spiritual experience. There is usually no discursive thinking in such performances; the person's intentions are performed rather than mentated.

This chapter explores a gentler and kinder way of living with the body in the spiritual life, one in which people get to know their bodies better, become more attentive to them and aware of them. It is an approach that leads people to be very conscious of how mind and body interact in everything they do. It is a kind of spiritual life in which people learn to attend to their bodies, to live well with them, and inhabit them better.

The best route into this third way of using the body in the spiritual life is through forms of meditation that focus on the body. In the long run, that leads to a different way of living with the body in the spiritual life, one that is all-pervasive and goes beyond meditation. Later in the chapter I explore some of the ways in which people may become unhappy with their bodies, and the role of religion and spirituality in coping with that.

Meditation

There are countless different ways of meditating and there is now a rich scientific literature on meditation (West, 2016). There are two widely used approaches: one focuses mainly on words or sounds, the other focuses on the body. The sound-based approach stems from Hinduism and has been popularized as 'Transcendental Meditation' (TM). Its benefits are well-established (Benson, 2001), though it is less clear that it has any specific benefits over other methods of relaxation. The sound that a particular meditator uses in TM is usually meaningless in itself. However, through constant use in the context of meditation, it acquires significance and probably becomes the stimulus to which relaxation is a kind of conditioned reflex response.

Repeated use of a meaningless syllable achieves what experimental psychology has termed 'articulatory suppression' (Baddeley, 2007), i.e. people are rendered unable to actually think any words. Short-term memory often makes use of an 'articulatory loop' in which we hear mentally what we want to remember. The repetition of a meaningless syllable to block the articulatory loop has made a useful contribution to the experimental investigation of short-term memory. Some time ago, I began to explore, with colleagues, its potential as a treatment for insomnia (Levey et al., 1991)

Christianity has also made extensive use of mantra-based meditation, as in the approach of the World Community for Christian Meditation, founded by John Main and now led by Lawrence Freeman. Here, the words chosen are of spiritual significance. However, as in TM, it is important to have a single regular focus which, through practice, takes the person into a meditative state. The most extensively used mantra in Christianity is the Jesus Prayer, 'Lord Jesus Christ, Son of God, have mercy on me, a sinner'. It comes from the East and has been increasingly taken up in the West (Barrington-Ward, 2011). It combines a regularly used mantra with a focus on the breath, as the first part is associated with breathing in, and the second half with breathing out.

The main body-focused form of meditation in Hinduism is yoga. Yoga is practised, not so much to give rise to specific thoughts, as to induce a mode of cognition in which thoughts become implicit in the practice of yoga, and are integrated with it. It is 'enacted cognition'. A sense of an integrated relationship between mind and body is evident in the principles that underpin the practice of yoga (Goldberg, 2005), and there has been growing interest in how embodied cognition theory can provide a framework for understanding the benefits of yoga (e.g. Francis and Beemer, 2019). It promises to be a fruitful dialogue, and could be added to the psychological research questions about yoga that deserve exploration (Gerbag, 2008; Nevrin, 2008; Watts, 2000a).

Mindfulness

Body-based methods of meditation have also been developed in Buddhism, and have been disseminated in the secular West as mindfulness. The therapeutic benefits of mindfulness have been widely recognized and it currently has the unique status of being a spiritual practice of religious origins that has been accepted in the UK by the National Institute for Clinical Excellence (NICE) as an effective treatment for depression. However, there are those who think that the scientific evidence is not as conclusive as is sometimes claimed (Farias and Wikholm, 2015). I want now to explore the approach to the body that is illustrated by body-focused mindfulness. I am much indebted here to my former colleague Mark Williams, a very effective teacher of mindfulness, whose approach is in turn indebted to John Kabat-Zinn's enormously influential book *Full Catastrophe Living* (Kabat-Zinn, 2013). Of course, I am not here to teach mindfulness. If people want to learn mindfulness, they should go elsewhere, for example to *Mindfulness: A Practical Guide to Finding Peace in a Frantic World* (Williams and Penman, 2011). My primary focus is not on how to *do* mindfulness, but on understanding the way of relating to the body that mindfulness illustrates.

In this book I am taking a predominantly Christian approach to religion, partly because it is what I know about. Mindfulness, on the other hand, comes from the Buddhist tradition. I have no problem about that, and I argue that the approach to the body represented by mindfulness is compatible with the Christian tradition. However, the fact is that Buddhism has concentrated more on body-focused meditation than most other religious traditions, and it is helpful to learn from that.

The basic principle of mindfulness is to focus entirely on sensory experience and to avoid conceptual, discursive thought; or to put it another way, to focus entirely on what you are experiencing in the present moment and avoid any thoughts about what you are trying to achieve. Kabat-Zinn says it is 'paying attention in a particular way: on purpose, in the present moment, and non-judgementally' (Kabat-Zinn, 2013, p. 4). For many people, this focus on your present sensory experiences feels liberating and calming; focusing on immediate sensation provides a respite from reflective, evaluative thinking.

It seems to be especially helpful to focus on bodily sensations, but the principles of focusing on present sensory experience can be introduced in other ways. One common exercise uses a raisin (Williams and Penman, 2011), and takes participants through various stages of holding a raisin in their hands, seeing how it really looks, touching it, smelling it, holding it up to their lips, tasting, swallowing, and finally feeling it in their stomach. The exercise needs to be taken slowly, lingering over each stage, and practising focusing entirely on current sensation.

The principles can also be illustrated by some old research conducted by Arthur Deikman (1990). The participants in his research went to a quiet, subdued room in which there was nothing but a blue vase. They were asked to concentrate on the vase in itself and to avoid thinking *about* it, and just to focus on the vase 'as it exists in itself'. After each session, participants were interviewed about their experiences.

Many reported that the colour became more intense and luminous. Some felt that they were merging with the vase or that it was radiating heat. Time passed quickly, and they became totally absorbed in the present moment. Deikman saw these experiences as an analogue of mystical experience. They seemed to be analogous to the experiences reported by those who use Tibetan exercises that focus on visual objects. Deikman also drew an analogy with some of the experiences reported in the Christian mystical classic, *The Cloud of Unknowing*.

Though it is possible to take a mindful approach to any object, it seems to work well to focus on the body, especially the breath. Breathing is something that every living person does continuously, and it has become a focus of spiritual practice in most religious traditions. Breathing is a continuous, rhythmic process that is always available as an alternative focus of attention to conceptual thinking. In meditation, people learn to focus on their breath in an unusual way, according it more objective attention than is usually the case, while avoiding discursive or evaluative thought about it.

A classic introductory exercise has involved a person lying on their back and feeling their abdominal wall rise and fall as breath comes in and out. They might put their hands on their abdomen to help focus attention there. With practice, people can attend to their breath in any position, focusing on the changing sensations from one moment to another. The mind is likely to wander, of course. Participants are advised not to be concerned if that happens; just to notice it and to gently bring attention back to their breath.

Another widely used exercise involves a scan of the body. You lie on your back and focus your attention on how your body is feeling, moving the spotlight of your attention from one place to another, usually starting with the abdomen, then bringing your attention down to the legs, feet and toes, and scanning each part of body in turn in the same way. The art is to avoid any evaluation of how you feeling, and just to focus attention entirely on what you are experiencing.

Why Focus on the Body?

If you want to focus on present-moment sensations, and to avoid discursive thoughts or thoughts about what you are trying to achieve, it works well to focus on the body (Williams et al., 2015). Focusing on the body keeps you in the present moment, as it is difficult to focus on past or future body sensations. Also, experience of the body is more direct and unmediated than experiences involving more external sensory modes such as vision or hearing. Interpretive thought processes are an almost inevitable part of external sensory experience. That is much less true of experiences of the body.

It seems that perception can operate either in a relatively objective or relatively subjective mode. Schachtel (1959) makes a distinction between 'allocentric' (or outer) and 'autocentric' (or inner) modes of perception. Some senses, such as the outer senses of vision or hearing, are usually objective; others, such as the inner senses of taste, smell and proprioception, are more subjective. The outer senses can be digitalized and simulated online, but that is not so far possible with the inner senses.

Rudolph Steiner (1971) suggested that the inner senses are subjective in a double sense. One is that we experience the inner senses as coming to us, whereas with the outer senses we feel we are reaching out to the external world. The other is that the inner senses are more affected by our personal state and how we are feeling. To some extent, a single sense can be used in different modes, and the focus on breath in mindfulness seems to involve treating what is usually an inner sense as though it were an outer one. Attending to breathing seems able to move people to a mode of cognition in which sensation and cognition are integrated rather than separate.

Focusing on the body and breath may also be helpful because it leads to a more embodied mode of cognition. The human brain, more than that of any other species, is different on the left and right sides. The non-dominant hemisphere, for most people on the right-hand side, is much better connected with the whole body than the so-called dominant hemisphere, usually on the left. So, a focus on bodily experience leads people to use the right-brain rather than the left-brain. That leads them to a mode of cognition that is intuitive, relational, and affective, and away from abstract, conceptual thought. That is another important anatomical reason why focusing on the body helps to make the shift from conceptual thought to sensory experience. I say more about this embodied mode of cognition in the next chapter.

Williams et al. (2015) suggest various other reasons why focusing on the body can be helpful in making this mental shift from the conceptual to the experiential. The body can provide information about the mind and give early warning of mood shifts. It gives people a place from which they can see their thoughts in a more detached way, and can notice the feeling associated with their thoughts and actions. It makes them aware of the tipping point where feelings are likely to lead to action.

Christianity and Mindfulness

As mindfulness has become increasingly popular, there has been a good deal of discussion in Christian circles about whether a technique that comes from Buddhism is appropriate for Christians. There are now several books placing the practice of mindfulness in a Christian context (Oden, 2017; Stead, 2016; Tyler, 2018), but the best discussion of the relationship between mindfulness and Christianity is probably in *Being Mindful, Being Christian* (Bretherton et al., 2016)

The case for mindfulness in Christian theology rests on the assumption that God is mindful (e.g. Psalm 8.4). The Hebrew word that is translated as 'mindful' can mean various things, such as 'remember', 'keep in mind', 'call to mind', 'be concerned about' etc. (Bretherton et al., 2016). There is a quality of attention in God's stance towards his creation that corresponds to mindfulness. The stories about Jesus in the gospels portray Jesus as mindful. In St Luke's Gospel, for example, Jesus is mindful of Zaccheus wanting to see him (Luke 19.5). When Jesus is on the cross, the thief beside him ask Jesus to 'remember' him, i.e. be mindful of him (Luke 23.42).

As well as the quality of attention associated with God, and exemplified in Jesus, Bretherton et al. (2016) suggest that virtues such as trust, gratitude, having a beginner's mind, not worrying, being attentive, and being non-judgemental are found in both Christianity and mindfulness. Jesus encourages people to treat God as utterly trustworthy, to be grateful to God for everything that they receive, to have the mindset of little children, to avoid worry, to notice what is going on in the people around them and in nature, and to avoid being judgemental. These are virtues that Jesus teaches, and which are cultivated by mindfulness.

The ancient Christian tradition of praying with breath in the Jesus prayer focuses attention on the breath. It often uses the ceaseless rhythm of breathing to enfold the Christian in a stream of prayer so that, even when they are not explicitly praying, breathing has spiritual connotations for them, and breathing itself becomes a kind of prayer.

There is also, of course, a rich Christian mystical tradition which has, in countless different ways, provided paths towards the stillness of the body and mind. Mindfulness is itself one of a family of different meditation techniques that are slightly different from each other. Within the Christian spiritual toolkit, there are many ways of praying and meditating that are part of the same family, and which lead to the same place.

There has recently been much interest in 'interoception', the integrated totality of sensory information that people need in order to maintain desired physiological states (Tsakiris and de Preester, 2018). It is a complex and multi-faceted concept and there is still much discussion going on about how best to conceptualize and classify it. However, there seems at least to be an important distinction between the objective accuracy of body perceptions, which is most commonly measured by the accuracy of people's perceptions of their heart rate, and other more subjective aspects of body awareness that can be measured by a questionnaire.

Many psychological disorders, especially emotional disorders, are characterized by poor body awareness (Tsakiris and Critchley, 2016), though it is hard to know quite what is cause and effect here, and it seems that emotional recovery is accompanied by improved body awareness; it may even be that improving body awareness would lead to emotional improvement. There are some people who seem to be relatively unaware of their feelings and have little emotional language. That is sometimes called 'alexithymia', literally 'no words for feelings'. That emotional disconnection seems to be accompanied by a somatic disconnection that leaves people relatively unaware of their bodies as well as unaware of their feelings. The two things seem to be linked (Taylor et al., 1999).

Given that mindfulness involves careful attention to sensory experience, it might be expected that mindfulness would improve interoceptive awareness (Beharrell, 2019; Farb et al., 2015; Gibson, 2019). Indeed, it has been suggested that the reason why mindfulness is helpful might be that it improves interoception. However, both mindfulness and interoception are complex multi-faceted concepts, and the story of the connection between them is not simple. For example, different mindfulness exercises seem to have slightly different effects. Focusing on the breath is found to be relaxing by most people, whereas the body scan exercise can sometimes produce a disconcerting body awareness.

So far, there is little evidence that mindfulness, or indeed any other kind of interoceptive training, produces improved accuracy in heart rate awareness. However, mindfulness training does seem to produce improvement in questionnaire measures of body awareness. There is also evidence of mindfulness and related meditation techniques producing lasting changes in the parts of the brain that are associated with proprioception, or awareness of body sensations (Bretherton et al., 2016; Jones, 2019).

There is a kind of spirituality which takes the body seriously, recognizing its wisdom and intelligence. As Rowan Williams comments, interoception is not a straightforward information-gathering exercise. It is indeed a form of knowledge, but a participatory one that is focused on 'coping successfully with the givenness of what we are and where we are' (Williams, 2019, p. 1040).

Pain

The most common therapeutic application of mindfulness is probably in the treatment of emotional disorders of depression or anxiety (e.g. Williams et al., 2007). However, I want to focus here on its role in the treatment of chronic pain. Pain is a complex phenomenon involving a network of physical, cognitive and affective elements. Certainly, the amount of pain a particular person experiences is affected by psychological factors as much as by physical factors such as the amount of tissue damage.

An early attempt to integrate the physical and psychological aspects of pain in a single theory was the so-called 'gate' theory of pain developed by Melzack and Wall (1996). Theories of pain have become more complex since then, but the gate theory was an important milestone in recognizing the importance of cognitive and affective elements as well as physical factors in pain. Given the importance of psychological interpretive and emotional factors in pain, it is not surprising that there is scope for religious faith to affect the amount of pain that people experience (Coakley and Shelemay, 2007).

Religion has often provided a framework for making sense of pain (Koenig et al., 2012; Numbers and Amundsen, 1986). Many religious people have believed that pain works for their spiritual good, if they are receptive to God's guidance. If doctors can provide relief from pain, that can be seen as a blessing that comes from God but not one that should be completely relied upon. You don't have to agree with such interpretive frameworks to recognize that having an interpretive framework at all can make the pain more bearable. Hinduism has had a rather different view of pain from most other religions and sees pain as an illusion, a view that has been inherited by the Christian Science movement. That view of pain is, of course, an interpretative framework in itself.

For religion to ameliorate pain, it seems that you need a background framework of religious belief, but it also helps to have some religious image on which you can focus in the immediate situation. Wiech et al. (2008) studied both atheists and nuns, and presented them with either religious or secular images while they were subjected to pain induction. The nuns felt less pain, but only when seeing a religious image. Only the *combination* of religious beliefs and a religious image seemed to alleviate the pain. This alleviation of pain was found to be associated with increased activity in a particular area of the brain, the right ventrolateral prefrontal cortex.

Mindfulness has for some time been used in the treatment of chronic pain, and with encouraging results (Burch and Penman, 2013). In some ways it is paradoxical that mindfulness, which involves closer attention to sensory experience, should be helpful in alleviating pain. It presumably does so by helping people to separate out the physical sensations they are experiencing from the distress and discomfort that normally surround them. Mindfulness affects pain in a range of different ways in the short-term (Zeidan and Vago, 2016), but the longer-term benefits may be more dependent on the affective aspects of pain.

A variety of meditative interventions have been used in the treatment of pain, apart from mindfulness, with generally encouraging results (Koenig et al., 2012), especially in studies that have looked at the benefits derived from a spiritual intervention. It seems that almost any kind of meditation training can be helpful. So far, it does not seem that there is any particular benefit in mindfulness over other spiritual practices such as yoga. However, in one of the most interesting studies so far, Wachholtz and Pargament (2008) compared spiritual meditation, secular meditation and relaxation in people with chronic migraine headaches. Those who practised spiritual meditation experienced a greater decrease in their headaches than those using the other procedures; secular meditation did not work so well.

Body Dissatisfaction and Deterioration

I now turn to some of the ways in which people are unhappily aware of the limitations of their bodies, and the role of religion and spirituality in coping with that.

Many people are unhappy with their bodies. There is now a good deal of research on body dissatisfaction, which seems a widespread phenomenon. Dissatisfaction with the body often focuses, in the young, on how the body falls short of the physical appearance they desire. Body ideals differ between the sexes, and there is also quite a lot of individual variation. The most common pattern is that girls want to be slim, especially in the waist, whereas young men often want to be muscular and developed. However, these are by no means universal preferences and people can have many different body ideals. People can be dissatisfied with their height, with their manual skills and co-ordination, and much else.

People can have negative attitudes to their sexuality and be disturbed by their own sexual desires. As we saw in Chapter 2, there has been a good deal of moral panic about the body. People sometimes feel that their bodily impulses and desires can lead them astray. That was prominent in the early Christian centuries; it is less common now, but it has not gone away. It is probably felt most strongly in people of homosexual disposition who sometimes hate their sexual orientation. Indeed, they can come to hate their sexuality so completely that they wish they were still pre-pubertal. Such people often gravitate into religious circles, and can find some consolation in the religious condemnation of homosexuality.

There can also be 'gender dysphoria', a very specific form of body dissatisfaction in which people feel they have the body of the wrong sex. The distress caused by gender dysphoria can often be very intense and troubling. It is a complex phenomenon (Watts, 2002b) and there does not seem to be any universally correct approach. Gender realignment surgery can provide relief for some people, but it is not universally successful, and is sometimes a disappointment. People who are unhappy with the gender of their bodies tend to have a very black-and-white view of gender, and regard their private sense of what gender they are as definitive. In contrast, I would be inclined to emphasize the complexity of gender, and that the various facets of gender are not always aligned.

A spiritual life of some kind can be helpful in rebalancing an excessive focus on the body, and can put preoccupation with the body in broader perspective. One approach that seems promising is an approach to mindfulness that is focused on compassion or loving kindness (Gilbert, 2010). There is evidence that body dissatisfaction is reduced by a brief course in compassion-focused meditation (Albertson et al., 2014). That involves elements such as taking a more caring and understanding attitude towards the self, recognizing that all people are imperfect and make mistakes, and becoming aware of one's own painful experiences in a balanced way.

Shaun Gallagher (2006) has made a helpful distinction between body *image* and body *schema*. Body image is more concerned with the externally observable aspects of the body and focuses on how the body appears to other people, as well as how we regard ourselves. Dissatisfaction with the shape or development of the body is an aspect of body image. However, in this chapter, I am more concerned with body *schema*, i.e. with our awareness of the internal processes of our bodies. Awareness of body image is a kind of distal perception, whereas interoceptive awareness of our body is much more proximal. There is a fascinating but still under-explored psychology of how people experience their bodies (Schilder, 1950).

Failings of the Body

Rather different issues arise around the failings of the body that come with illness and old age. It may become difficult to walk quickly or confidently, or even to maintain balance. People may find they are becoming incontinent. Sight and hearing may begin to fail, and there may be reduced grip or physical strength. All such failings are potentially distressing, and it is no easy matter to handle them psychologically in a way that avoids one becoming exasperated with oneself.

Older people are quite likely to be religious, which makes it important to consider the role of religion in handling the failings of old age. The greater religiosity of older people seems to be partly a generational effect, i.e. successive generations are becoming less religious. However, it also seems to be partly an ageing effect, in that people become more religious as they get older, particularly in retirement, when they have more time. There is now a large literature on spirituality in older people (e.g. Jewell, 2004; Johnson and Walker, 2016). Those involved in the care of the elderly are often more comfortable in focusing on what they regard as the spiritual life of older people, rather than on confessional forms of religion. However, there seems to be a mismatch here, as the elderly themselves are actually more religious, not just more spiritual in a rather general way (McFadden, 2013).

Religion affects attitudes to the ageing process. This is well illustrated by ageing in Catholic nuns (Corwin, 2012). Nuns age remarkably well, with good mental and physical health, and longevity. In that sense, they are objectively a model of successful ageing. However, the rhetoric that surrounds the successful ageing paradigm advocates people taking control of their ageing process. Catholic nuns achieve successful ageing, but with a very different ideological framework based more on graceful acceptance than on taking personal control of their ageing.

There are particular issues associated with the growing cognitive deterioration often associated with ageing, and found in more extreme form in people suffering from dementia or brain tumours, or similar neurological conditions (Coles and Collicutt, 2019). Cognitive deterioration affects *how* one can be religious. It does not in itself prevent religious attendance, though it may affect the quality of engagement with church services. There seems to be some reassurance for many elderly people in continuing with religious attendance, even if they are less engaged than they used to be; just as there is reassurance in continuing to spend time looking at a newspaper, even if not much content is being processed. Private prayer is probably the aspect of religion that is most affected by cognitive deterioration. Conversational prayer, in which people talk with God, may be particularly challenging. On the other hand, more ritualistic prayer, in which set prayers are recited, will be less affected by cognitive deterioration.

There are more subtle issues that arise in people who are experiencing severe neurological problems, perhaps through a brain tumour. Though I am not aware of formal research on this, there seems to be a lot of variation between people. My limited personal experience suggests that in some cases the personality and spirit of a person can be remarkably preserved, despite considerable neurological and cognitive deterioration, whereas in other people the personality becomes eclipsed much sooner. If people have had a really deep spiritual life their spiritual personality seems able to withstand neurological deterioration for a surprisingly long time, even though their spiritual life may have to take a different form.

Particular issues arise for people with bodies that are no longer able to regulate themselves in the usual way. People with diabetes may be dependent on insulin injections. A more extreme example is people with kidney failure who need regular dialysis. It is clearly unsettling to have a body that is no longer able to regulate itself normally. Some people cope with this better than others, of course, but it can easily lead to a build-up of anger and resentment at dependence on regular medical interventions, and a longing for the autonomy that comes with a self-regulating body.

There is now a growing body of research on patients with chronic kidney disease that shows that religion and spirituality are helpful in coping with the considerable psychological issues presented by the need for regular dialysis (Bragazzi and Puente, 2013). Religion and spirituality seem both to provide psycho-social support, and to provide people with coping strategies. Interestingly, religion is positively correlated with survival among kidney dialysis patients. This is just one example of the significant role that religion and spirituality can play in how people attend to their bodies in many health conditions.

7

Embodiment: Postures and Meanings

In this chapter I want to go more fully into the new ideas about the embodied nature of cognition that I introduced in Chapter 1. Recent work on embodied cognition (e.g. Shapiro, 2019; Varela et al., 2017) has emphasized that we are embodied creatures, and that what we do with our bodies makes a big difference to our perceptions, judgements and experiences. The embodied cognition perspective can be used to understand better the contribution made by the physical aspects of religious and spiritual practices. In turn, studying embodied cognition in religion promises to contribute to our general scientific understanding of how embodied cognition works.

This chapter mainly considers the role of body language, posture and gesture in prayer and liturgy, drawing on embodied cognition to help us to understand the significance of how the body is used in religious rituals and other spiritual practices. Towards the end of the chapter I discuss how most of our language, perhaps especially spiritual language, makes use of metaphors that implicitly refer to the body, even if we are sometimes not conscious of the embodied language we use.

One of the core strands of evidence in support of embodied cognition is that body posture affects thoughts, judgements and mood (e.g. Teske, 2013). For example, smiling and nodding tend to lead to positive affect, while slumping and pushing away lead to negative affect. I now consider the impact of the postures and gestures adopted in religious practices. In both public and private religious practices people use their bodies in a deliberate and explicit way that is likely to impact on their thoughts and feelings.

Posture and Gesture

Many collective religious practices make use of physical movement. Even where there is no physical activity involved, posture is often important. Though religion is often thought to be a 'spiritual' matter, there is probably no domain of human life in which people make such delib-erate and extensive use of embodiment and several recent books on religion have included a chapter on the body (e.g. Cave and Norris, 2012; Fuller, 2008; McGuire, 2008; Steinberg, 2012; Washburn, 2003). Cally Hammond has recently provided an excellent historical survey on the use of posture in prayer and liturgy (Hammond, 2015).

Religious traditions reflect an awareness of how people's thoughts and experiences are affected by what they are doing with their bodies, even though that has not generally been formulated in scientific terms. How-ever, there has been increasing interest in the implications for religion of recent scientific work on the body (e.g. Barsalou et al., 2005; Jones, 2019; Soliman et al., 2015; Van Cappellen and Edwards, 2021).

Posture

How people are affected by religious practices is likely to depend on whether they stand, sit or kneel. Receptive postures such as kneeling make people more willing to adopt religious teachings or inner prompt-ings (Barsalou et al., 2004). Kneeling is a submissive posture and is likely to induce a submissive attitude. Posture influences thought processes in a way that is similar to the influence of mood. It is well established that low mood leads to more negative thoughts and memories (e.g. Teasdale and Barnard, 1993). In a similar way, a submissive posture leads to submissive and religious thoughts.

There is now evidence for the effects of posture on religious thinking. For example, Ransom and Alicke (2013) found that religious people were more likely to judge events as miraculous if they were kneeling rather than sitting. Similarly, Fuller and Montgomery (2015) found that people reported high levels of religiosity if they adopted a low-power posture than if they were in an upward and expansive high-power posture. These are just the beginnings of research on how posture affects religiosity. There is scope for much fuller investigation of how this works (Van Cappellen and Edwards, 2021).

The complication is that there is no one-to-one link between posture and mood, for example between kneeling and receptiveness. Kneeling can express a spirit of penitence and regret, which is not quite the same as receptivity and submission. Also, kneeling is not the universal posture of prayer. In fact, there are considerable variations between religions in the positions that people adopt while praying. This will be surveyed in more detail by Sara Savage in her Appendix to this book.

Though Christians often kneel, Jews often stand with uplifted hands, and Muslims prostrate themselves. Hindus adopt the lotus position in yoga, and Buddhists often bow before sacred objects. All these are submissive postures. It is interesting that, despite the similarity in the devotional postures adopted in different religions, there are also significant differences. There may also be subtle differences in the devotional cognitions in different religions, just as there are subtle differences between religions in the nature of religious experience (Katz, 1978). Different devotional postures in different religions may give rise to slightly different religious experiences.

Though there is some scope for movement in religious postures, movement is often very constrained. It is also notable that movement is normally in the vertical rather than the horizontal axis. Edwin Straus, in his influential essay on body symbolism (Straus, 1966), suggests that the vertical axis is concerned primarily with authority and submission, whereas the horizontal axis, which is generally avoided in devotional postures, is concerned with reaching out to the world and acting in it.

It is an interesting question whether the postures adopted in religious practices always have the same psychological effects, or whether the effects depend on context and circumstances. Van Cappellen and Edwards (2021) suggest that some aspects of posture and facial expression have direct physiological and psychological effects. However, other effects depend on the meaning and significance attached to postures in a particular cultural context (e.g. Tsai et al., 2013). Intentions are also relevant. Kneeling may be more likely to lead to an attitude of receptiveness if the person who kneels *intends* to be receptive. It may also be relevant whether people attend to their posture in a deliberate and 'mindful' way.

Devotional postures seem to be an expression of both receptivity and submission, but they also serve to further support those attitudes. A cycle is thus set up in which an attitude is expressed in bodily posture, and the bodily posture in turn reinforces the attitude. Memory also contributes to this process. As people adopt devotional postures, those postures are likely to evoke previous occasions when the same postures have been adopted, which in turn re-evokes devotional cognitions. There is thus a to-and-fro between posture and cognition. This may be one of the reasons why many religious people find it helpful always to use the same postures. Revisiting familiar postures such as kneeling re-evokes the thoughts that have been associated with those postures in the past.

Embodied practices sometimes carry meaning and significance implicitly within themselves, rather than influencing conscious thoughts that can be clearly distinguished from those bodily practices. Religion seems

to provide richer examples of cognition being integrated with bodily practices than most other areas of human life. Religious life involves postures
and gestures which become so saturated with meaning that the meanings
do not need to be made conscious or explicit.

Gesture

Many religious practices involve gestures. It seems likely that, in evolution,
thoughts were initially communicated through gesture and intonation
rather than through language (McGilchrist, 2009, Chapter 3). Thought
seems to have preceded language in evolution, indicating that cognition
does not require linguistic expression, and that embodied 'cognition' can
include non-linguistic, gestural ways of communicating thoughts and
intentions.

Religious rituals may constitute one of the most important survivals of
gestural communication in the modern world. Many embodied religious
practices involve a display or communication of some kind, which is consistent with evolutionary theories that emphasize the signalling functions
of religion (e.g. Purzycki et al., 2014). Christianity makes much use of
the extended arm and open hand in gestures of giving, as when a priest
gives a blessing, or holds his or her open hands over bread and wine at
the Eucharist.

One very particular gesture that occurs in a religious context is laying hands on the head of another person. In the Christian tradition, for
example, it is used by a bishop at confirmation and ordination, and by
a priest in healing rituals. The hands represent a channel of grace; the
laying on of hands is often accompanied by speech, but may be done
silently. There is probably a range of views about why hands are used
in this way, and what effects they have. Some probably see it as merely
symbolic while others see it as efficacious in some way.

The use of hands in religious healing may have antecedents in the
grooming behaviour of primates (Gilbert and Gilbert, 2011). Physical
contact can have measurable physiological effects and can trigger release
of endorphins. There is more going on here than just a richly significant
gesture. Physical contact between primates is not merely symbolic; there
are direct physiological effects. However, in humans there is an extra
layer of symbolic meaning and cultural interpretation.

Improvisation and Coordination

Sometimes very exact instructions are given about the posture or sequence of postures that should be adopted in religious rituals. Following these requirements precisely can become a mark of religious respect, and people can take great pride in doing so. In other religious traditions, more freedom is allowed in bodily expression, though within a basic framework. The experience is then more like jazz improvisation than like musicians playing from a score; it is like a singer and accompanist performing together with slight adaptations of tempo and rhythm that are not prescribed but which they feel together. Where bodily postures and movements are used in that way, it avoids what Erikson (1977) called 'ritual excess'. Body movements become able to express what people are actually feeling, as well as a basic attitude of receptivity and compliance.

Improvisation

Though religions have often prescribed the postures that should be adopted in prayer or worship, there has recently been a movement towards greater freedom in how the body is used, and people are encouraged to use the body imaginatively. Vennard (1998) discusses creative uses of the body in prayer. Similarly, Savage (2001) says that if she is depressed she might flop down or curl up. She might also reach out to Christ by reaching for a symbol such as an icon or cross. Her postures can also connect with the focus of intercessions. So, if praying for someone buried in an earthquake, she might lie down on the floor and imagine tonnes of rubble over her.

There are now prayer manuals that include recommended postures for particular prayers. For example, Pagitt and Prill (2005) offer a set of 30 different prayers for specific goals, each with an appropriate prayer posture. For example, looking up might go with a prayer of hopefulness; a body hug might go with prayer for an end to loneliness; deliberate breathing might go with a prayer of forgiveness etc. Some of these linkages probably work better than others; the more natural and instinctive they are, the better they are likely to work. Actors have well developed skills for expressing inner states in body language (Marshall, 2001) and some of this could be used in improvised body prayer. This approach to prayer is predicated on the basic assumption of embodied cognition theory, that cognitions are influenced by body postures and activity.

This kind of creative approach to the use of the body in prayer is parallel to how the body is used in some forms of therapy, suggesting that a rich dialogue could be developed about use of the body in the two contexts. Gestalt therapy, in particular, has a long history of work with the body. So far, there has been only a limited amount of work on religion from the perspective of gestalt therapy (e.g. Walker, 1971), and it has not focused specifically on ways of using the body in therapy and religious practice.

Externally-focused Prayer and Icon Prayer

It may be surprising to include praying with icons in the context of embodiment, but icon prayer is actually a highly embodied form of prayer (Forest, 2008). People often close their eyes when they pray, which leads to a retreat into a private, inner space. However, when people pray with icons, they keep their eyes open and are more connected with what is around them. The reason for closing eyes is presumably to avoid distraction. However, the icon provides an external object on which to focus, which also avoids distraction. It is similar to how people sometimes use a candle in prayer or meditation: it similarly provides a constant focus, but one that is also always changing slightly, which helps to hold attention.

In Catholic and Anglo-Catholic churches there is also devotion to the Blessed Sacrament in the service of Benediction, when the bread in which Christ is believed to be present is held up for veneration. It is a service at which the boundary between the worshipper and the host becomes quite thin. Adoration streams from the worshipper, and the worshippers feel that they are receiving something very important from the presence of Christ in the sacrament.

The host is in some ways above and beyond the worshipper, but also a presence to which the worshipper can draw very close through an act of reverence. There are probably deep developmental roots to this kind of eyes-open devotional prayer which go back to the early days of infancy, with the infant gazing into the eyes of the mother while sucking on the breast. The mood is well captured in the last verse of 'My God, How Wonderful Thou art', by the nineteenth-century Catholic hymnist, Frederick William Faber:

Father of Jesus, Love divine, what rapture will it be
prostrate before thy throne to lie, and gaze and gaze on thee!

In icon prayer there is also a sense of connection with the person who made the icon. Making an icon is felt to be very different from painting a picture. It is a spiritual act in itself, accompanied by prayer. People who pray with icons often have a strong sense that they are praying with the person who made the icon. The icon provides a physical medium of connection with the maker of the icon, rather as a tomb can provide a sense of connection with a deceased person.

In icon prayer there is also a sense of engaging with the icon as one might engage with a living body. Gaze is important. It is not just that the person praying with the icon gazes at it; the icon is often experienced as looking at the person who prays. Someone who prays with an icon of Jesus may feel not only that they are looking at Jesus, but also that Jesus is looking at them. The icon is often made with the direction of gaze in mind, to facilitate this experience.

Dance and Coordination

Religious rituals also often involve coordinated physical movements, such as dancing. Group dances are common at Jewish weddings and other social occasions. Dance has had a chequered history in the Christian church (Davies, 1984). It was largely forbidden as a form of worship by the early Church, partly because of its associations in Greek culture with sensuality and mystery rites. Although dance in the Church has continued to appear at a grass-roots level at various points throughout the centuries, notably in the Middle Ages with various dances and mystery plays, there have been repeated campaigns against it.

Dance is an integral and especially important part of Christian worship in Africa (Elochukwu, 1996). The Pentecostal revival, especially among African-Americans, represents another major shift, with movement and dance being a normal part of Pentecostal and Charismatic services. Charismatic Christians make particular use of physical freedom, lifting their hands in worship. The 'charismatic hop' is a joyful jigging up and down, moving from one leg to another. There are often quite strong feelings about dance in worship, either for or against. Not many people are indifferent about it.

Synchronized movements take place in many religions. Orthodox Jews sway in unison while praying. In some Christian churches, the whole congregation genuflects together, or makes the sign of the cross at the same point in the service. At Muslim prayers, all face in the same direction, adopting an identical posture, and prostrate themselves together.

Sometimes many people perform the same action in a synchronized way; at other times there is a reciprocal interaction between people, as in the giving and receiving of a blessing. Coordinated actions express the sense of being members of a collective religious body, and coordinated actions in turn play a role in developing that sense.

Sometimes coordinated body movements arise from everyone following the same instructions. However, embodied cognition theory (e.g. Thompson, 2007), offers another perspective on this coordination, and might see it as arising out of an intuitive 'inter-subjectivity', something to which I return in the next chapter. Synchronized ritual movement represents a remarkable integration of mental, physical and social facets of human functioning (Schüler, 2012). As we noted in Chapter 5, participants in fire-walking rituals show coordinated patterns of heart-rate (Konvalinka et al., 2011).

There is a strong element of co-ordination in dance, but it clearly does not arise from everyone following the same instructions; it often arises from imitation and from intuitive coordination. Coordinating dance movements with those around you is likely to increase a sense of empathy and bonding. As noted in Chapter 2, empathy is thought to be mediated by mirror neurons that allow people to coordinate motor actions in unison with others, and which may be important in religion (Gallese, 2006; Wilson, 2011). The coordinated actions of a praying or worshipping community may reflect an empathic bond between them, and help to strengthen that bond further. The same parts of the brain are involved in both empathy and imitation.

In many religious rituals there appears to be an intuitive sensory–motor coordination. Motor coordination can both reflect, and help to foster, an extended mind. Synchronized dance movements are also likely to lead to collective endorphin release, as with the trance dancing of early humans. The strong feelings people have about dance in worship may depend on whether people want that strong sense of bonding, or whether they definitely do not want it!

Language and Embodiment

Many of our concepts are also shaped by our physical interaction with the world and reflect embodied metaphors (Lakoff, 2003). Since the seventeenth century it has often been assumed that we know the world best by standing back from it. I believe that assumption is mistaken, and that it is linked to a mistake about how the meanings of words developed.

It is often supposed that words started with literal meanings, and that the meaning of words is clearest when we stick to their literal meanings. As a view of the origins of language this seems to be simply a mistake. One relevant line of evidence comes from etymology, the study of the history of the meanings of particular words. If words began with the natural meanings, you would expect to find that, as you traced back the meanings of words, they became increasingly literal; metaphors would be later extensions of their meanings. However, as Owen Barfield (1984) has pointed out, the opposite is the case.

As you trace the meanings of words back, you find that they become more figurative; literal meanings are later derivations from earlier figurative ones. Tracing back the meanings of words leads you into a figurative consciousness in which concepts of the world are intertwined with concepts of your own experience. The two are different sides of the same coin. We are led back into a world that philosophers might call 'dual-aspect monism'.

The most likely scenario is that humanity started with poorly differentiated thinking and a lack of sharp conceptual distinctions, and that their words reflected that lack of differentiation. I suggest that a more differentiated way of thinking is a later development. It seems that conceptual distinctions emerge only slowly, and with some difficulty. Distinctions like that between humanity and God, natural and supernatural, inanimate and animate, are all quite advanced distinctions, and are not obvious or easy.

It is striking that Hebrew thinking characteristically involves double-aspect thinking. Most, if not all, of the core concepts of the Old Testament involve a double-aspect conceptualization of the world. For example, wind, breath and spirit are different aspects of the same thing. Heart is both a part of the body, but also a centre of human feeling and understanding. Jesus continues this double-aspect thinking. The Aramaic language which he spoke, like Hebrew, is shot through with double-aspect concepts.

This makes the thinking of Jesus very difficult to translate into modern language. There has been much concern in the last 50 years about moving from the potentially obscure English Bibles written a few centuries ago to modern language translations. However, there has been much less discussion of the more fundamental problem of rendering the double-aspect Aramaic/Hebrew thought of Jesus into languages like Greek and English that operate much less with double-aspect concepts.

Jesus seems to have thought in a holistic way, always linking mind and body, matter and spirit. If you try to render such thinking into a language that lacks suitable double-aspect concepts, you repeatedly have to go for just one half of the meaning, and neglect the other. That is fundamentally misleading. It may be that we need a paraphrase to show the rich network of meanings that are being implied. Neil Douglas-Klotz (2001) has engaged in the interesting and challenging task of trying to understand the Aramaic thinking behind our Greek gospels, and has then rendered that into a modern English paraphrase.

The double-aspect linkages that we find in languages like Hebrew and Aramaic are not arbitrary. The psychologist Solomon Asch (1958) has looked at a range of historically independent languages, and found that they all have the same linkages between their meanings. That implies that those linkages were discovered rather than invented, just as it is often suggested that mathematics is something we have discovered rather than made up, something in the mind of God (Polkinghorne, 1998). The fact that historically independent languages have the same linkages between physical and inner meanings suggests that they reflect how earlier humans actually saw things, and are not just some inventive use of words. It seems that these double-aspect linkages in our language reflects some deep reality rather than being a human invention.

Linkages between religious words and posture seem to be deeply ingrained in religious concepts. It is possible to demonstrate that in contemporary research. For example, God and heaven are thought of as 'up', and the Devil and hell are thought of as 'down'. These linkages seem to be more than arbitrary conventions. Meier at al. (2007) found that the words 'God' and 'Devil' were processed more quickly and easily if presented visually in a location (up or down) that was congruent with the word. Similarly, Chasteen et al. (2010) found that presenting words connected with God in the upper and right regions of a display screen led to faster detection of signals.

Using Words Meditatively

The most radical theological programme for getting rid of the embodied linkages that pervade religious thinking was Rudolf Bultmann's programme of demythologization (Bultmann, 1958). He aimed to exorcize all these confusing linkages and metaphors from religious language, and to find a way in which we could say exactly and literally what we meant to say. With hindsight, that seems to have been a misconceived ambition that misunderstood both the nature of cognition in general, and the religious mindset in particular.

Rather than trying to move towards some literal and abstract religious language, I suggest that it would be better to recognize the embodied origins and significance of religious language, and to find ways of using it more effectively, so that it speaks to people more deeply. There is currently much interest in forms of meditation, like mindfulness, which avoid words altogether and focus on the body. Also, as noted in the last chapter, there are forms of meditation that use words repetitively, as a kind of mantra. However, there is scope for a way of using words in meditation that doesn't just get lost in discursive thought, but uses them in a way that connects better with our experiential, embodied, affective intelligence.

Friedrich Rittelmeyer (1969) makes some helpful suggestions about how people can meditate on a word such as 'love' in a way that makes the word come alive within them. One approach is through memories of times when they feel they have met love in its highest form. We can 'look at such an experience, seeing only the nature of the love, the spirit of the love which revealed itself' (p.14). This leads to an understanding of love that is rooted in specific episodes and in experience.

Another suggestion is to ponder the words of St John in the New Testament, such as 'God is love, and he who dwells in love, dwells in God, and God in him' (1 John 4.16). Rittelmeyer suggests we can ponder 'how this word shines out in the soul of the disciple John as a great revelation' (p. 14), and how it was actually felt by him. People can also ponder what words like 'love' and 'peace' meant to people on whom they made a deep spiritual impression. Yet another suggestion of Rittelmeyer's is for people to imagine themselves at the end of the earth's development in the company of a multitude of people who have experienced the secret of love in its highest form.

Yet another possibility is for people to actually *hear* a word like 'love' spoken to them, in their mind's ear, rather than just thinking it silently. If people imagine actually hearing a word it activates many of the same pathways in the brain as if they really hear it. Rittelmeyer suggests that we can imagine the word being spoken to us 'from all the breadths of the world, from all the heights of heaven' (p. 15). That may help people to hear the word 'love' spoken, not by themselves or another human being, but by the Word, the *Logos*, who is presented in the Prologue of St John's gospel as one of the faces of God. The word 'love' then makes a different kind of impact.

We noted above some of the postures and gestures that have been suggested for particular prayers (Pagitt and Prill, 2005). It is possible, similarly, to make physical movements, either observably or in imagination, that connect with the words on which people are meditating. This can become like using a sign-language in meditation as they ponder words of deep spiritual significance. Words that are heard in that kind of embodied way will make a different kind of impact, and speak to our embodied intelligence.

Rittelmeyer's suggestions for how to meditate on a word such as 'love' show a remarkable practical and intuitive grasp of the principles of embodied cognition. His material was first circulated in 1928, but his approach might have been derived from recent work on embodied cognition. It would not be difficult to do scientific research on the way of using words that he suggests. There might well be a distinctive pattern of brain activity associated with this kind of word-based meditation.

Human Embodied Intelligence

Human cognition is highly embodied, but it seems to me that some human cognition is more embodied than others (Watts, 2013a). Religion is an arena in which humans make particular use of their capacity for embodied thinking.

As already noted, humans are unique in having two different modes of central cognition. One very explicit scientific formulation of this is Philip Barnard's work on the human cognitive architecture, which sets out its evolution from a simple four-subsystem architecture in earlier primates to the nine-subsystem architecture of humans (Teasdale and Barnard, 1993). Before humans, there was just one general-purpose subsystem for central cognition. The crucial development with humans is that humans have two alternative modes of central cognition. I think this is the best way of formulating what is distinctive about human intelligence. One of our central subsystems, what Barnard calls the 'implicational' subsystem, is intuitive and relational. The other, which he calls the 'propositional' subsystem, is more abstract and linguistic.

One interesting point for present purposes is that body state feeds directly into the implicational modes of cognition, but body has no comparable direct route into propositional cognition. To put it simply, implicational or intuitive cognition is embodied, but our more abstract, linguistic cognition is much less embodied. I think this is an important point and one that has generally been neglected in work on embodied cognition (Watts, 2013a). There is abundant evidence that embodied cognition is very important in humans. However, in a sense, it has been the distinctive achievement of humans to develop a mode of cognition that is relatively independent of embodiment.

It is also important that our embodied intelligence is much more affective. It speaks to our feelings and mood-state in a way that our more abstract intelligence does not. The religious person would aspire rather to a mood of calm, quiet joy. The intuitive, embodied mind is also more relational and socially embedded than our abstract intelligence, which enables people to relate to 'God' as well as to other people (Clarke, 2008).

Another way of approaching this is in terms of the two hemispheres of the brain, as Iain McGilchrist has done in his magisterial book, *The Master and his Emissary* (McGilchrist, 2009). The contrast that Philip Barnard makes between implicational and propositional cognition is parallel to the distinction McGilchrist makes between right brain and left brain cognition (though the neuropsychological mapping of Barnard's subsystems is not quite so simple). The distinctive abstract and linguistic mode of cognition that humans have developed, one relatively independent of embodiment, has been based on a development of the so-called 'dominant' hemisphere of the brain which, in most people, is the left brain. In humans the left and right brains are more different from each other than in other related species. Interestingly, as McGilchrist (2009) points out, there is less interconnection between the two halves of the brain in humans than in our primate ancestors. We seem to have developed the two hemispheres of the brain in a way that gives us two alternative modes of cognition.

McGilchrist is concerned about the extent to which western civilization has come to depend in recent centuries on our abstract linguistic intelligence. In his history of western consciousness in the recent centuries, he describes some pushback against this, for example in the romantic movement. However, the big story is the onward march of the dominance of the so-called 'dominant' hemisphere. Even things like art and religion that might have rebalanced things have often been refashioned in a left-hemisphere way; religious literalism and fundamentalism are an obvious example of that. Religion provides an opportunity for humans to make full use of their capacity for embodied, intuitive cognition (Watts, 2013b), which is arguably one of the ways it makes an important contribution to the flourishing and continuing development of humans.

There sometimes seems to be a misunderstanding about the relation between embodied cognition and human distinctiveness. Wentzel Van Huyssteen (2013) emphasizes that the embodied nature of cognition is crucial to human empathy and imagination. That is true up to a point. However, it is not embodiment that is distinctive about human cognition. On the contrary, our intuitive, relational, embodied mode of cognition is what we have in common with our primate ancestors. It is our abstract linguistic intelligence that is new in human beings, and it is the combination of the two modes of cognition that enables us to take empathy to new levels.

Having both modes of cognition has enabled humans to develop their embodied cognition in important new ways. Art and religion arise from a fruitful interaction between the two modes of human cognition. The to-and-fro between embodied and relatively disembodied modes of consciousness has enabled humans both to relate to the world in an embodied way, but also to reflect on what they may know, using their new and distinctive abstract intelligence. It is part of the skill of using our minds and bodies to best effect in religious practices that we draw wisely and effectively on our highly embodied mind, but also on our more abstract, less embodied mind, and harness them together.

8

Enacting Liturgy

In this chapter I explore the sacramental approach to religion; not just the primary Christian sacraments of Baptism and the Eucharist, but the more general sacramental mindset or disposition from which these particular sacraments arise. This is an under-developed topic in theology, though there are some useful pointers in the theological literature. However, I believe that we now have the scientific resources to understand the significance of the sacramental approach to religion better than ever before. There is an opportunity for an exciting synthesis of sacramental theology and the new scientific understanding of embodied minds.

There are recent developments in cognitive psychology which make it timely to be developing the psychology of sacramentalism as a human characteristic, and that is what I try to do here. I continue to explore the implications for religion of the '4Es' approach to cognition (e.g. Anderson, 2003; Newen et al., 2018). As we have already seen, embodied cognition theorists assume that cognition is embodied, enactive, embedded and extended (the four Es). The last chapter focused on embodiment, how the movements and postures adopted in religious practices are likely to influence religious thoughts and dispositions, and how the meanings of religious words reflect their embodied origins. Now, in this chapter, I look at how it is enacted, embedded and extended and apply that particularly to understanding what is going on when the sacraments are enacted.

Enactive, Embedded and Extended Cognition

Enactive Mind

Religious cognition involves actions or performances that provide a framework for religious cognition, or sometimes actually constitute an implicit form of religious cognition. Religious understandings arise from what people *do*. The enactive approach to cognition similarly makes a break with seeing cognition as involving a representation of the world and instead grounds it in the interactions between a person and the environment. Classic formulations of the enactive approach are *The Embodied Mind* (Varela et al., 2017), *Mind in Life* (Thompson, 2007) and *Ecology of the Mind* (Fuchs, 2017). There are also helpful collections of essays extending the enactive approach (e.g. Stewart et al., 2010; Durt et al., 2017).

The enactive approach to understanding finds one of its classic expressions in the sacraments, though so far there has been hardly any mention of sacramentalism in the scientific literature on the enactive approach to cognition. The Eucharist is something people *do*, and it is only through actually doing the liturgy that its participants arrive at any kind of enhanced understanding. People build up their religious understanding through enacting the liturgy together. Religious practices such as the Eucharist are active performances, and the cognition that supports them is integrated with those active practices.

The religious mind understands the value of 'faith', which is the antithesis of a detached, objective view of the world. Faith understands the value of being engaged and committed. Faith, far from being an obstacle to understanding in the world, can actually be a prerequisite for understanding it. People know the world through faith. As Thomas Aquinas puts it in one of his hymns, 'Faith alone the true heart waketh, to behold the mystery'. Science often imagines that it has abandoned a faith-based approach, but I suggest it uses a faith-based understanding of the world almost as much as religion, though the faith is in science and scientistic assumptions.

The idea that we know the world through committed engagement sits uneasily with the cherished assumption of modernity, that we know the world best through being detached about it, and that objective knowledge of the world depends on that kind of detachment. It has been assumed that we have to stand back and examine the world as onlookers (Davy, 1958). The idea of science, as it has been conceived since the so-called scientific revolution of the seventeenth century, depends on what the theologian Nicholas Lash has called a 'spectorial' consciousness (Lash, 1995). The core assumption is that we know the world best if we stand back from it. Only then can we know the world as it really is in itself, rather than in a way that is distorted by our interaction with it.

The enactivist approach to cognition says that the ideal of detached knowledge of the world is a fantasy. It is just not how things actually work. It is a tribute to the integrity of science that scientific investigation of cognition has led to the abandonment of the idea that there is a world that we can study by being detached from it. So, if religious people emphasize the importance of committed engagement, they are no longer arguing against science, they are saying something with which science increasingly agrees, even though it has got there by a different route.

Some of the classic scientific evidence that has led to this comes from the study of visual perception. Seeing what is around us is *not* like taking photographs of the world and passing them to some kind of inner person (or homunculus) deep within us. On the contrary, seeing is a process in which we are actively engaged. The optical tract is *not* all sensory input; it is full of motor pathways with which we actively shape our visual perception of the world (Hubel, 1988). Visual perception is not a two-stage process in which we first collect visual data and then make sense of it. The visual data itself gives us what the influential psychologist James Gibson calls 'affordances' (Gibson, 1977), which arise from our interaction with the world and allow us to respond to it in a way that is largely automatic.

Cognitive science has increasingly abandoned the idea that knowledge depends on representing the world in our minds. Science has, of course, always been interactional in that it understands that knowledge arises from getting practical, from conducting experiments. However, science has often combined that experimentalism with the ideal of detached objective knowledge, without noticing that they are very uneasy bed-fellows. Scientists have tried to build abstract laws of nature from the practical knowledge that comes from experiments, but it is an uneasy transition (Cartwright, 1983). From the knowledge of the world that we obtain through interacting with it, we imagine we are building an abstract concept of the world as it exists in itself, independent of our engagement with it. We further assume that we have representation of that world in our own heads.

This is an anti-religious idea. This idea of a world that we know is independent of ourselves was called 'idolatry' by Owen Barfield, in the subtitle of his classic book, *Saving the Appearances: A Study in Idolatry* (Barfield, 1957). This idea of the world as independent of *us* is often linked with the idea that the world is independent of *God*, i.e. that the world is a freestanding separate entity. It is because of that linkage that it is helpful, from a religious point of view, to abandon the idea that we can know the world best by standing back from it. The new enactive view of cognition leads to the abandonment of the naturalistic assumptions about the world that have been one of the major philosophical obstacles to religious faith.

The alternative view, exemplified in enacting liturgy, is that we know the world by *participating* in it. It is what Michael Polanyi (1997) called 'personal knowing'. It is a kind of knowing that, far from requiring detachment, requires personal engagement. Through participating in liturgy people build a sense of spiritual community and of divine presence from what they are doing. The sense of divine presence arises from, and is embedded within, active engagement and participation (Corwin and Erikson-Davies, 2020).

Embedded Mind

Human cognition is also embedded in our network of social contacts; we reach an understanding of things in conjunction with others, not as isolated individuals. It has been another of the mistakes of modernity to exaggerate the extent to which individuals are isolated. In fact, all of us are very much creatures of the context in which we live. As John Donne, Dean of St Paul's in the early seventeenth century, put it, 'no man is an island'. Owen Barfield suggests that the sense of individuality may have been particularly strong in the British, an island nation, and that they may have fallen prey more than most to the idea that we are all just separate individuals (Barfield, 2012). It is a view that reached its apotheosis in Margaret Thatcher's famous remark that 'there is no such thing as society'.

The widespread emphasis on the individual has affected our view of how morality works. There is a tendency to see morality in terms of the moral decisions made by a series of isolated individuals. The philosopher and novelist Iris Murdoch (2013) has been a particularly trenchant critic of this view. Morality is learned by living it, as Warren Brown has pointed out (Brown and Reimer, 2013). For example, L'Arche communities can be places where morality is *learned*, a kind of moral laboratory, or training ground in morality.

As we saw in Chapter 2, theologians have recently been emphasizing the essentially relational character of human beings (e.g., White, 1996). It seems that humans are made for relationships, and find fulfilment, if at all, in relationships with others. That is often said to be an echo of the essentially relational nature of God, as the Godhead is constituted by the relationships between Father, Son and Spirit (Grenz, 2001). Even hermits, who choose a life of isolation, are often quite embedded in the communities that support them.

How we think is shaped by our language, and language is something that belongs to society; it is not an individual creation. Languages differ according to how different people live, and we tend to have a more finely differentiated language for the things that are important in own context. Inuit people are said to have many different words for snow. We make sense of experience in terms of the patterns of thought in our society. Even a pathbreaking religious genius like Jesus of Nazareth, who has been called a 'spiritual mutation' (Theissen, 1984), clearly thought in ways that were very much shaped by his language and culture.

There are indications that Jesus reached for the Psalms to make sense of key experiences. He seems to have made sense of his baptism in terms of the verse in Psalms about being the Son of God (Psalm 2.7), and he explicitly used the opening of Psalm 22, 'My God, my God, why hast thou forsaken me' on the cross. The extent to which Jesus' thinking was shaped by the Psalms is beautifully conveyed in Clive Sansom's poem 'John' (Sansom, 1956), articulating John's perception of Jesus as he hangs on the cross: 'I search the Psalms – Those Psalms of David that delighted him ...'

Doing things together is particularly important in shaping our sense of being members of a social group rather than isolated individuals, even if that awareness remains tacit and implicit, rather than being fully articulated in language. We saw in Chapter 3 how significant it is that only humans do trance dancing together. It seems to have done more than anything else to bond them into community. Present-day religion often makes use of doing things together. For example, requiring Jehovah's Witnesses to do door-knocking in pairs is likely to make a significant contribution to forming new witnesses into a community.

Oratory can play an important role in building a community. The large numbers of people who listened to Adolf Hitler in Germany were formed into a national community by their experience of listening to him together in large crowds. Something similar happens with outstanding religious preachers, like Billy Graham. It is an important part of the experience of listening to a Charismatic preacher that people don't listen to him alone, but with others, and that builds a sense of belonging.

Religious communities are sometimes built by developing a story or narrative of who and what they are. For many years I have been associated with Coventry Cathedral. The medieval cathedral was bombed in 1940, and subsequently a new cathedral was built, opening in 1962. Under the leadership of Provost Bill Williams the community at the rebuilt cathedral dedicated itself to international reconciliation, with a strong sense of their collective identity as the people whose cathedral was bombed and rebuilt, and whose task it was to work for reconciliation throughout the world. That was a powerful collective narrative that gave the whole community a collective identity.

Many religious practices are embedded in social contexts, and make use of cognition that is socially embedded. For sacramental Christians, doing the Eucharist together on a regular basis is a community-building experience. The Eucharist arises, of course, from Jesus being in community with his twelve disciples on the last evening before his crucifixion. Some Christian traditions insist on it being done in community. The Church of England, for example, insists that, for a service of Holy Communion to take place, there must be two or three people present. From that perspective, the Roman Catholic practice of a priest saying Mass on his own is an aberration.

Among those scientifically concerned with embodied cognition the psychiatrist and philosopher Thomas Fuchs is unusual in having considered its implications for religious rituals, for example in his work on collective body memories (Fuchs, 2017). Cultural practices such as rituals, including the Eucharist, involve culturally determined embodied practices which become a carrier of cultural memory. They serve both to regulate social interaction within a group, and to help the group to cope with difficult situations by placing them in a broader framework of meaning. Many rituals explicitly serve as a commemoration of a past event as, for example, the Eucharist serves as a memorial of the Last Supper of Jesus. By re-enacting the Eucharist, often in a highly stylized way, the community keeps the collective memory alive and strengthens its collective identity.

Another scientific framework for understanding the significance of repeated collective enactments such as the Eucharist is Rupert Sheldrake's theory of 'morphic fields' (Sheldrake, 1988; Watts, 2011b). From this theoretical perspective the countless enactments of the Eucharist that have now taken place will have built up a very strong morphic field for the Eucharist. Each further enactment of the Eucharist will be shaped by that morphic field and will, in turn, contributes to it. There is a sense in which this leads to a connection of those who participate in each and every Eucharist with all those who have ever enacted the Eucharist.

Extended Mind

The mind is not confined within the skin but is also *extended* beyond the body. This is undoubtedly the most controversial of the four 'E's, and the one about which there is most dispute. Even those who subscribe to it mean different things by it. This is not the place to try and sort out all the different ways in which cognition might be said to be 'extended'.

However, the common thread is that they are challenging the assumption that a person's intelligence has to be entirely within their skin.

Intelligence arises from our interaction with the world and there is a valid sense in which human intelligence is located as much in that interaction as in our heads. Some have formulated a 'parity' principle, that all understandings that help us to perform intelligently are equally part of our cognition, whether they are located inside or outside the body (Clark and Chalmers, 1998). 'We' are not defined by our bodies, by what is within the skin. There is a grey area beyond the skin where aspects of our intelligence can equally be found. It is hard to say exactly where human cognition is to be located, but there seems good reason to abandon the idea that it is to be found entirely within people's heads or within their skins.

There is a helpful analogy with the concept of the 'transitional' that has been developed by Donald Winnicott within psychoanalysis (Winnicott, 1971). He was a paediatrician who became fascinated by how infants play in their cots. He noticed how an external object such as a toy or piece of blanket was sometimes appropriated by an infant to the extent that it almost became part of the infant. Such transitional objects were not quite internal, but neither were they any longer wholly external. Winnicott said they were in a 'transitional' space, and were 'inside, outside, at the border'. Human cognition often seems, in a similar way, to be at the border between internal and external, and not always to be in the head. Our understanding of the world around us is often practical. It arises at the border between us and what we like to think of as the 'external' world.

For many psychological theorists, there is an axiomatic assumption that the individual is primary. On that assumption, coordinated bodily movements can be understood as arising out of a series of individuals all engaged in mutual imitation. However, the 'extended' mind can be formulated as a kind of supra-individual collective mind in which individuals participate, achieving co-ordination by doing so. Wilfred Trotter's concept of the group mind underlying the 'herd instinct' was an early exploration, developed early in the twentieth century, of such a concept (Trotter, 1953).

In western civilization in the last few centuries people have often thought in very atomistic ways. We have seen the world as composed of a series of separate things, and that assumption of separateness has become very entrenched. The idea of external cognition challenges the idea that the social world is composed entirely of a series of separate people. There is a sense in which there is a lot of grey area, or transitional space, that is at the interaction between people, rather than the entirely within any one of them.

There is a helpful analogy with the human body. We tend to think of the body as composed of a lot of separate little things, such as cells, with walls between one cell and another. However, there is not really any wall around a cell; it is more a matter of gradients, as one cell merges into another (Sharma, 2015). The human body is characterized by continuous interdependence, rather than a series of completely separate bits. Society is similarly constituted by a plenitude of interactions rather than a set of isolated individuals.

A particular challenge to the idea that cognition is entirely in the heads of each individual person comes from highly co-ordinated group activities such as a flock of birds flying in formation, or eight rowers in a boat. The intelligence that allows such coordination does not seem to be located entirely in the heads of each individual person but, in some sense, in their collective space, and in the interactions between them.

Rupert Sheldrake's concept of morphic fields and extended mind provides one way of making sense of this (Sheldrake, 2011; Watts, 2011b), though Sheldrake is more concerned with the extended reach of the individual mind than with a supra-individual mind. I cannot myself see any strong metaphysical or ideological objections to a concept of supra-individual mind, though it is not necessary to postulate it in order to explain synchronization in religious and other contexts. C. G. Jung's 'collective unconscious' seems to be supra-individual, or at least can be read in that way, especially in his later writings.

In Christianity, there is a strong strand of thought that recognizes mutual indwelling between God and ourselves. This thinking has its roots in the farewell discourses of St John's Gospel, and is summed up in the Eucharistic prayer that 'we may evermore dwell in him, and he in us'. It is also reflected in St Paul's thinking about a body of Christians being like a human body, and the relationships between them being like the relationships between the different parts of a single body (1 Corinthians 12). The halo that is often depicted around a saint in Christian art is analogous to the grey area beyond the skin where some of our cognition seems to be located.

Sacramentalism

I now connect this understanding of cognition as being embodied, enacted, embedded and extended more explicitly with religious meaning-making and with sacramentalism. Humans have been said to be the 'believing primate' (Schloss and Murray, 2010). I don't disagree with that, but it puts the emphasis too exclusively on what humans *think* about things, or what propositions they sign up to. In making a similar point about belief being the essential characteristic of humans, Fuentes (2020) emphasizes that the kind of belief he has in mind is passionate commitment to ideas, not detached assent to propositions. My point is that religion is at least as much about what people *do* as about what they *believe*; or rather it is about the significance that they attach to what they do. The core of religion is to be found in the interaction of believing and doing, rather than in either of them separately.

A similar point is often made about 'faith'. Faith is not just about what you hold to be true: it is also about how you lead your life, about what Maslow calls your 'master motives' (Maslow, 1954), about 'where you are coming from', about basic attitudes. In the language of the Baptism service, it is not just about what do you believe *about* Christ, it is about turning *to* Christ.

Sacramentalism arises from the general tendency that humans have to develop a framework of meaning that makes sense of things. We look for core values, purposes and significances which enable us to place the myriad of confusing events in our lives in some broader framework. Humans seem to need meanings (Baumeister, 1991), and meanings are at the heart of religion. In religion we find not just the kind of meaning-making that characterizes many areas of human life, but a broader approach that Crystal Park has called the search for 'global meaning' (Park, 2010).

Meaning-making often takes a narrative form; it is about telling a story. The way we make sense of things seeks to place confusing individual events within a broader narrative. Religion is particularly helpful in meaning-making because it provides us with a comprehensive and sweeping narrative about the purposes of God, within which we can place particular events in our lives. Humans seem to operate with a nested hierarchy of narratives: individual, relational, and community narratives, all of which can be nested within an even broader narrative about the purposes of God, which is the most comprehensive of all.

Signs and Symbols

Rowan Williams elucidates the sacramental mentality in terms of the human capacity to make signs. He sees sacraments like the Eucharist as arising from the human disposition to make signs (Williams, 1999). However, the sign-making tendency of humans is of much broader significance than the classic sacraments of the church. For example, Rowan Williams also takes a sacramental approach to sexual ethics (Williams, 2014). He notes that sexual ethics are often framed in terms of either following rules, or being nice to people; his question is whether there is anything distinctively Christian about either of these. His own approach to sexual ethics, which reflects his sacramentalism, is to raise the question of what we are prepared to allow a particular sexual act to signify.

Paul Tillich raises similar issues in his use of the word 'symbol' (Tillich, 1957), which is central to his theology, and which he distinguishes from mere 'signs'. Symbols partake of the reality to which they point, and they transcend the distinction between subject and object. Humans know symbols by participating in them. In these various ways, symbolic understanding is more fundamentally participatory than just using signs, which have a more arbitrary relationship to what they point towards and can be treated in a detached way. Using terminology in this way, sacraments are not a matter of mere sign-making, but involve participating in symbols.

Christians have a strong belief that Christ is present when the Eucharist is enacted. However, it is not entirely clear *where* that presence should be located. There is sometimes a tendency to locate it, rather atomistically, in the consecrated bread and wine, but that seems to be too localized an approach (Williams, 1982). The Christian tradition understands Christ to be present in the enactment of the Eucharist in many different ways, not exclusively in bread and wine.

It would also be misleading to see Christ as present just in the minds of each individual participant in the Eucharist. There seems, rather, to be a sense in which Christ is present, diffusely but comprehensively, in the various individuals present, in their collective identity, in their actions, and in the elements of bread and wine. It is perhaps something such as this that is being pointed to in the words attributed to Jesus in the Gospels, 'where two or three are gathered in my name, I am there among them' (Matthew 18.20).

There are many different ways of enacting the Eucharist, and how it is enacted affects the meaning that is collectively attached to it. The Christian Eucharist has many meanings. It is a kind of ambiguous image, like the one that can be seen either as a vase or as two people facing each other. The Eucharist is sufficiently wide and rich in its psychological resonance that people can find different things in it, according to what they need. In that, it is also like psychotherapy. A therapist may behave in much the same way with very different clients, but an essentially common procedure can help different people with different problems. I particularly want to emphasize here that the *meaning* of the Eucharist is much influenced by exactly how people *do* it.

Eucharist and Mystery

Experienced in one way, the Eucharist speaks powerfully to people who have a strong sense of unworthiness (Murphy, 1979). A formal and traditional celebration of the Eucharist begins with an entrance procession in which the sanctuary party, like the worshipper with a sense of unworthiness, begins as far from the altar as possible. As the rite unfolds, the priest approaches the altar and begins the celebration of the Eucharist. A key moment in the Eucharist, experienced in this way, is the confession and absolution, which speak explicitly to the worshipper's sense of unworthiness. It is a mood that is captured with powerful effect in the Prayer of Humble Access in the 1662 Prayer Book of the Church of England, that begins, 'We do not presume to come to this thy table, O merciful Lord, trusting in our own righteousness, but in thy manifold and great mercies ...'

The crowning moment in enabling the transformation of a sense of unworthiness is when the worshippers themselves draw near to the altar rail and, through the holy gifts of bread and wine, receive the living presence of God, who might otherwise have stood over them in unforgiving judgement. For someone with a prevailing sense of unworthiness, the regular experience of such a Eucharistic rite can be powerful and transforming. As with funeral rites, the Eucharist needs to connect with and evoke the sense of unworthiness, but it also needs to provide the resources that enable that sense of unworthiness to be transformed.

The psychological power of the traditional eastward-facing Eucharist lies partly in the fact that it affirms and connects with the sense of unworthiness before it leads to its alleviation. This is analogous to the way in which a good funeral service needs to connect with grief before moving on to its transformation. Roger Grainger (2004) argues that the religious ritual needs to transmit an explicit message about unworthiness, to rule out any ideas of 'the possibility of communicating with God on our own terms' (p. 75). Though union with God is regularly offered at the Eucharist, it destroys the psychology of the Eucharist if that union is taken too much for granted. As Grainger also comments, people ought never to be able 'to accept the truth of their union with Christ without surprise', or 'without a sense of the impossibility of that which has taken place by faith' (p. 71).

If the Eucharist is to transform the sense of unworthiness, there are implications for how it should be conducted. It is of central importance that the worshipper should have a powerful sense of the transcendent majesty and mystery of God. That both chimes in with the initial sense of unworthiness, but also makes the experience of union with God through the sacrament all the more powerful. In turn, for there to be a powerful sense of transcendent majesty, there must be good opportunities for projection. I am not, of course, suggesting that God is merely a projection, just that mechanisms of projection are important in how God is apprehended. In psychotherapy, projection on to the therapist is equally important (in the form of 'transference'), but that does not imply that the therapist is a mere projection.

For transference to operate effectively in psychotherapy, psychotherapists need to maintain as much anonymity as possible, so as to make themselves a blank screen for the client's projection. Similarly, if the worshipper is to have a powerful sense of the majesty of God, it is important for the priest not to obstruct that by being too intrusively personal. If the psychology of the Eucharist is to operate in this way, it is important for the priest to face east, towards the altar, so that his face is normally not visible.

Eucharist and Community

However, there are other ways of doing the Eucharist that emphasize community, as when the priest faces the people. When westward-facing celebrations of the Eucharist became the norm in Roman Catholic and Anglican churches during the second half of the twentieth century, it was probably not sufficiently appreciated what powerful psychological ramifications the change had. It seems likely that, for many worshippers, westward-facing celebrations of the Eucharist changed the sense of mystery that had been at the heart of their Eucharistic devotions. As Corwin found in her work with Catholic nuns, a different way of doing the Mass seems to have led to a different way of framing beliefs (Corwin, 2012).

Though westward-facings celebrations can be as transformative as eastward-facing ones, the psychology is quite different. The focus has shifted from approaching union with a transcendent God to being a full and accepted member of the worshipping community that is enacting the Eucharist together. This can be particularly powerful psychologically when the Eucharistic community gathers round in a circle, and it can work best in a home or an outdoor setting.

There are also implications for how the sacrament is administered. It facilitates the sense of union with a transcendent God for the worshipper to walk reverently towards the altar rail and to kneel to receive the sacrament from a priest. In contrast, when the focus shifts to the Eucharist as the shared act of the believing community, it can be equally powerful, in a different way, for the sacrament to be passed from one lay person to another, with each person both receiving it and passing it on to their neighbour.

There is a danger that contemporary westward-facing forms of Eucharist, which emphasize its community aspect, fail to connect with any sense of unworthiness, though there are different aspects to the sense of unworthiness. Whereas a traditional eastward-facing Eucharist focuses on unworthiness before God, a modern westward-facing Eucharist can focus on unworthiness in relation to others. However, each way of enacting the Eucharist can connect with both. Even where the primary focus is on approaching a mysterious God from a position of unworthiness, that is balanced by a sense of the congregation moving together along the same journey towards union with Christ. Equally, a Eucharist that brings a strong sense of acceptance by the worshipping community can also mediate a sense of acceptance by God.

9

Emotions and their Expression

This chapter is about emotion, recognizing that, whatever else we may want to say about emotions, they have a strong bodily component. I consider both the religious perspective on human emotions, and the role of emotions in religious life. Emotions play an important role in religion, and provide a way of integrating mind and body. Much religious thinking is affective, a form of 'hot cognition'. Religious meanings are often 'felt meanings' rather than being narrowly intellectual. Religious thinking seems to draw to an unusual degree on the more embodied cognition of the right hemisphere.

Emotions provide an embodied perspective from which much religious doctrine can be approached, especially in areas of doctrine concerned with human salvation; an embodied approach to doctrine could be developed taking human emotions as a starting point. An approach to theology that is abstract and intellectual is likely to miss how a more embodied approach to religion can contribute to personal transformation. There is a wide range of emotions that are important in religion, especially self-conscious emotions such as pride, guilt and shame.

Emotions have been a point of continuity in my career as a psychologist, which now spans over half a century. On religious perspectives on emotions, I am much indebted to Thomas Dixon, with whom I worked closely while he was writing his admirable book, *From Passions to Emotions: The Creation of a Secular Psychological Category* (Dixon, 2003). Samuel Powell has provided a helpful survey of Christian attitudes to emotion (Powell, 2016).

Facets of Emotion

There are two troublesome issues in the history of Western approaches to emotion: first, what is the relationship between reason and emotion; second, what is the relation of emotion to the body. There is no consensus about either.

Reason and Emotion

The distinction between reason and emotion goes back to Plato and classical philosophy. In as far as Christianity has taken sides in the debate about the value of reason and emotion, it has tended to be on the side of reason. Often the 'Image of God' in human nature has been seen as consisting of reason rather than emotion. God has been seen as the supreme intelligence, but 'impassible', i.e. not blown around by the emotions of the moment. There has also been a moral concern about the consequences of humans being too much in the grip of their passions.

However, the Christian tradition is quite mixed on all this. There are existentialist thinkers like Pascal and Kierkegaard who have understood the value of emotion in human life. There is also the slightly earlier tradition of Quietism in Christian thought and practice. That influenced Christian theologians like Jonathan Edwards, whose book on 'Religious Affections' is one of the classics of Western thought about emotion (Edwards, 1959), and also Friedrich Schleiermacher, who sought to ground faith in God in the feeling of absolute dependence (Schleiermacher, 1988).

In recent decades there has been a significant shift in thinking on these matters, with a new tendency among philosophers to emphasize the rationality of emotions (e.g., de Sousa, 1987), and a parallel emphasis in psychology on cognition and emotion being intertwined (e.g., Power and Dalgleish, 1997). Part of my own contribution was to be the founding editor of the journal *Cognition and Emotion* in 1984.

One source of confusion here is that 'emotion' is a broad category, and includes very different things. Some forms of emotion contribute to intelligent understanding; others divert us from such understanding. As Thomas Dixon has pointed out, the concept of emotions has only been used so pervasively since around the mid nineteenth century (Dixon, 2003). It is largely a secular category, adopted by an emerging secular psychology.

Earlier religious theorists like Jonathan Edwards (1959) made a distinction between passions and affections. Passions are more violent; affections are gentler and calmer. Passions can make it more difficult to understand accurately what is going on. On the contrary, attending to our affections can aid such understanding. In the nineteenth century passions and affections were put together to form a new secular category of emotions. The word was not new, but it was used more widely and in a new way (Dixon, 2003). However, with hindsight, that may have been a mistake, and psychology has needed to rediscover a distinction, rather like that between passions and affections.

One arena in which it is generally recognized that emotions aid understanding is psychotherapy. Therapists are trained to attend to their feelings about their clients, through what is known as 'counter-transference'. The therapist's own feelings about a client can be a useful guide to what is going on with the client, in addition to listening to their words and observing their body language. The new emphasis in psychology on 'emotional intelligence' is another aspect of that recognition of the cognitive significance of emotions (Goleman, 1995). Emotions are crucial to understanding what is going on in the world and responding to it intelligently.

Emotions and the Body

The relation of emotions to the body also has a complicated history. Emotions manifest themselves in a variety of ways. There are slightly different ways of formulating this, but most people would recognize that emotions are manifest in people's physiological reactions, in their observable behaviour, in their subjective feelings or mood state, and in their thought processes (e.g., Rachman, 1978). Normally, an emotion is apparent in all of these ways, though there are some interesting cases where emotions are apparent in some ways but not others. For example, people who work in bomb disposal don't display emotional behaviour, though there may be other signs of emotion.

In the latter part of the nineteenth century there was an attempt to establish an approach to emotions in which the bodily aspects of emotion were regarded as primary. There was nothing new about recognizing the physical component of emotions; it was the primacy that was attached to it that was new. Interestingly, when the concept of 'emotion' was developed in a new way in the nineteenth century, it was within philosophy. Dixon attributes this new concept to the Edinburgh philosopher Thomas Brown, in lectures given between 1810 and 1820 (Dixon, 2003). Later in the nineteenth century, others developed a predominantly biological approach to this new general concept of emotions, in which key contributions were Darwin's book, *The Expression of the Emotions in Man and Animals,* first published in 1872 (Darwin, 2009), and an important paper by William James on 'What is an Emotion?' (James, 1884).

Darwin's focus of interest was on the facial expression of emotions, and particularly on certain basic emotions having the same facial expression in different species. Darwin's approach has been systematized by his present-day advocate, Paul Ekman, who argues that there is a set of basic emotions that is found in a range of different species and in all human cultures, and which have the same facial expressions (Ekman, 2003). There has been a lot of vigorous debate about Ekman's position. Historians of emotion generally take very strong issue with Paul Ekman (e.g., Plamper, 2015). They argue that he seriously underestimates the extent to which emotions are shaped by language and cultural context (Harré, 1986).

My own view (Watts, 2019a) is that Ekman's view is too extreme and simplistic, but that there is something in it. It is indeed helpful to make a distinction between relatively basic emotions and more secondary emotions. Basic emotions show a greater degree of cross-cultural uniformity. They are also found in infants at an earlier age, and seem to require a less developed self-concept. Secondary emotions are more variable across cultures and between individuals and are more shaped by cognitive processes.

I am inclined to agree with Ekman that there are very basic differences between anger, fear, sadness and disgust. These have strong biological roots, and are not just matters of contextual interpretation. It is one of the interesting features of emotions that there seems to be a broader range of negative emotions than positive ones: emotions that very often arise when things are going wrong and we need rapidly to regroup and change direction. Emotions tend to arise at junctions in plans and goals, and sweep over us in a way that facilitates a rapid and comprehensive change in direction.

There is a case for some kind of two-factor theory of emotion, with a basic level of emotion that is largely biological and relatively independent of culture and context, and another level that is much more interpretive, and which shows a great deal of contextual sensitivity. A two-factor theory of emotion was originally advanced by Stanley Schachter, with the simple idea that *how much* emotion you feel is determined by physiological processes like levels of adrenaline, and *which* emotion you feel is determined by context. The philosopher of religion, Wayne Proudfoot, discussed the implications of Schachter's view of emotional experience for a similar two-factor theory of religious experience (Proudfoot, 1985)

Though Schachter's two-factor theory has largely been abandoned as too simplistic, a more subtle version of it has been advanced by Lisa Feldman Barrett (2006). James Jones (2019) has discussed its implications for the understanding of religion. Barrett's view is that there is a basic level called 'affect' which is largely physiological, and another more cognitive level that is needed before we have what can properly be called 'emotions'. Barrett, like Schachter, thinks that the affect level determines how much emotion people experience, and also whether the emotions arising from it are positive or negative.

Debates about the role of physiological process in emotion were originally focused on William James' influential 1884 paper claiming that emotions are really just interpretations of physiological processes. It was a very simple theory that gave little room for cultural context or individual cognitive interpretation. James received a good deal of push-back against his theory, and ten years later was obliged to publish a revised version that made many concessions to his critics. James' revised theory made so many concessions that it was almost a retraction (Dixon, 2003).

His problem was that the new umbrella category of 'emotion' lumped too many different things together; he was trying to advance a simple mono-causal theory of a complex, multi-faceted phenomenon. It would now be generally agreed that there is more to emotion than it being just a way of describing physiological processes. The body is a very important part of emotional experience, but it is not the whole story.

The recent development of the embodied cognition paradigm has provided fresh insights into the role of embodiment in emotions, and especially in the very persistent emotions found in emotional disorders (Gjelsvik et al., 2018). It has been recognized for some time that in a condition such as depression there seems to be a to-and-fro between an inarticulate negative mood state and more explicit and articulate negative thoughts (Teasdale and Barnard, 1993).

It now seems that part of what happens in inarticulate mood states is that patterns of embodied activity are triggered which arise from, and are consistent with, a particular mood state. These may not take the form of observable activity, and may just be incipient reactions or what Barsalou et al. (2005) call 'simulations'. The activation of these emotionally charged internal embodied reactions can be upsetting for the person concerned and can entrench a negative mood state.

Gjelsvik et al. (2018) suggest a further complication, that in order to avoid this upsetting effect there is a tendency to retreat into a very abstract and over-generalized mode of cognition which in depression exaggerates how appallingly bleak everything is. Because in depression nothing is specified with any precision, it is not really challenged by any empirical considerations, and so takes on a life of its own. In these various ways, internal embodied processes seem to play a significant role in the maintenance of persistent dysfunctional emotions.

Subjective Aspects of Emotion

There seems to have been a historical change in the importance of different components of emotion, with a movement away from the older emphasis on the behavioural expression of emotions towards a growing concentration on subjective feelings. The main indication of this comes from significant changes in what was meant by words for emotions. Owen Barfield, in his brilliant and fascinating attempt to construct a history of changes in human thinking and consciousness from when and how words changed their meanings (Barfield, 1953), suggests that there was a particularly significant period of change in how emotion words were used following the 1660 restoration of the monarchy in England.

He claims that a new language for talking about the interior life developed quite rapidly. Various existing words were hijacked and put to new uses. Before that time, the word 'emotion' was used of material objects, not people. Talk of a person 'emoting' was an extension of established talk about things emoting. Something similar is true of the word 'depression'. Both words became part of the new language for interiority. Various other words changed their meanings. 'Fear' came to refer to an emotional state, as it does now, whereas previously it had referred to a sudden and unexpected event. Similarly, 'sad' came to mean 'unhappy', as it does now, rather than 'sated' or 'heavy'. Talk of a 'sad cake' is a rare survival of an older usage of what is now an emotion word.

The new meanings of these words are now so well established that it takes some excavation to realize that they go back only 350 years. There were words before that period for what we would now call emotions, but those words focused on the external effects or moral significance of emotions, not really on inner feelings. It seems that before the late seventeenth century, emotions were primarily a matter of moral behaviour rather than of inner feeling. The development of a new sense of the interiority of emotions was a very significant one.

The new sense of interiority, that Barfield convincingly argues was developed in the latter half of the seventeenth century, had far-reaching implications for religion. It led to a growing emphasis on the interior, subjective aspects of religion, something which became very marked by the middle of the nineteenth century, with a new sense of religion being an essentially private matter. By the end of the nineteenth century, it was natural for William James to define religion as 'the feelings, acts, and experiences of individual men in their solitude' (James, 2012, p. 31). Three hundred years earlier, no one would have thought to define religion like that.

Social Aspects of Emotion

However, this should not be allowed to disguise the fact that emotions take place in a social context. There are two different things here that can easily be conflated. The new emphasis of the last 350 years on the private, subjective aspects of emotions can lead people to think mistakenly that emotions occur in isolated individuals, and to neglect their social context. However, there is nothing incompatible in recognizing the importance of *both* private experience *and* social context. It is important to recognize the significance of the new emphasis on subjective aspects of emotion, but also to recognize that emotions are embodied and socially embedded.

Recent work on the sociology of religious emotions (e.g. Asma, 2018; Davies, 2011; Riis and Woodhead, 2010) has helped to restore the balance, and to emphasize again the importance of the social context in which religious emotions occur. There is also a related literature on the social history of religious emotions (Corrigan, 2004; Corrigan, 2016) and the place of emotions in the Christian tradition generally (Coakley, 2012), and in particular religious movements such as Puritanism (Ryrie and Schwanda, 2016).

Sociologists of religion are right that emotions are not a purely individual matter. The society and community in which they occur are important too. Riis and Woodhead emphasize that the emotions of individuals are shaped in part by the 'emotional regime' of the society of which they are part (Riis and Woodhead, 2010). It is probably the case that religious regimes carry a particular authority and have unusual power to shape the emotions of individuals.

Religions use a wide variety of methods to maintain emotional regimes. Physical religious objects can arouse strong emotional reactions, as do religious rituals. The locations and buildings associated with religions can have emotional significance too (Watts, 2019b). There is a to-and-fro between self and society in which the emotions of individuals are much influenced by the emotional regime of the society as a whole, and the emotional reactions of individuals help to maintain the emotional regime of the society. There is, of course, no single religious emotional regime. Even a single religion, like Christianity, can give rise to a variety of different emotional regimes.

One of the important questions about emotional regimes is whether they affect people's actual emotional experience, or just what emotions they aspire to. Affect valuation theory makes the important distinction between ideal and actual emotions, and finds that cultures, including religions, have implications for emotional ideals more than for actual emotional experience. It seems possible that religions affect what emotional aspirations people have, but don't have much impact on what emotions they actually experience (Tsai et al., 2013). Recent work on the sociology of emotion, interesting though it is, does not seem to have investigated how the emotional regimes of societies affect actual emotional experience.

Specific Emotions

Though it is probably correct that there are no emotions that are unique to religion, there are certainly emotions in which religion has taken a particular interest, and which have an important place in religious emotional regimes. There are emotions that are characteristic of religion, perhaps even essential to it, even if they can be found in other contexts. Religion seems to represent a particular deployment of emotions that are to be found much more generally. Just as there are no emotions specific to religion, there are probably also no emotions that do not have a place in religious life of some kind or other.

Douglas Davies (2011) provides a helpful survey of emotions that are important in religion. The religious interest in emotions is often concerned with transformation. So, for example, religion often takes a particular interest in guilt and its transformation through forgiveness, in the transformation of grief through funeral rites, and in the role of religious beliefs in the transformation of despair and desolation into hope.

It will be best now to pursue the question of the role of emotion in religious life in relation to a few specific emotions. Awe, wonder and reverence are at the heart of religious devotion; the shedding of tears can be a kind of spiritual practice in itself; the transformation of shame and guilt is at the heart of the religious project; and religious people have shared in the wider moral concern about anger and aggression.

Awe and Wonder

Positive emotions, though not unique to religion, play a particularly important role in religion. For example, love is a romantic emotion, but it is also true to say that love for God, and the sense of being loved by God, plays a crucial role in religion. Hope arises in many difficult circumstances, and religions have powerful resources for engendering hope, which can then contribute to the transformation of individuals and society. Compassion arises in secular contexts, but can also take on particular religious significance, especially in Buddhism.

I focus here particularly on awe and wonder, which can be important in how people respond to the natural world and to works of art, but which also plays a crucial role in religion. Feelings of awe lead people in a spiritual direction (Van Cappellen and Saroglou, 2012). Wonder may also have a useful role in science (de Cruz, 2020). However, scientists can probably do worthwhile science without a sense of awe and wonder, but you probably can't be religious without a sense of awe and wonder (or, if you can, it is some strange and distorted kind of religion in which it is rather obvious that those concerned are tone deaf for religion). Though awe may be essential to religion, it may not be the only thing for which wonder is necessary; it is probably necessary for art as well.

'Reverence' is another interesting member of this family of emotions. Robert Solomon (2002) suggests that awe is relatively passive whereas reverence is associated with more active engagement, and responsibility toward what one reveres. There is also a stronger tendency in reverence than in awe to recognize moral and spiritual greatness. Reverence is probably the most religious of these three terms, but is still not an emotion that is uniquely religious.

Wonder contributes to information and wisdom (Midgley, 1991). Awe and wonder are what de Cruz (2020) calls 'epistemic emotions'; i.e. they are involved in knowledge. Theologians might add that they are also apophatic emotions, i.e. they take us into realms of experience that we cannot describe adequately in words. Reverence requires us humbly to set aside what we imagine we know in order to understand more. Science *can* do that, though it is more inclined to build on what it knows. Religion, I suggest, has a better understanding of the epistemic benefits of awe and reverence.

Keltner and Haidt (2003) see awe as arising from relationships of social dominance. It is a theory that has been influential but, on one key thing, it seems almost certainly wrong. Awe seems to arise less in the context of social relations than in relation to nature. It seems most unlikely that awe and wonder always arise in the context of relations of social dominance.

I suggest that a more promising lead for a scientific theory of awe and wonder would be McGilchrist's theory of the relationship between the two hemispheres of the brain, set out in *The Master and his Emissary* (McGilchrist, 2009). Awe and wonder are characteristic of states arising from the non-dominant hemisphere, where there is a strong sense of the other. They are epistemic in the sense of giving rise to an orientation to understand. However, awe and wonder seek knowledge in a way that shows positive regard, is intuitive rather than articulate, and is humble and modest in its assessment of how much it understands. I think that gets us off on the right lines if we want a scientific theory of awe and wonder.

Rudolf Steiner writes movingly about the role in the spiritual life of cultivating what he calls 'positiveness', a predisposition to recognize and respond to the good, true and beautiful, wherever one finds them (Steiner, 2004). These feelings can bring you up short, make you catch your breath, and help you to set aside limited understandings in favour of a glimpse of something bigger. He sees that predisposition as essential to the epistemic path that meditation opens up. Steiner saw that as important, not only in a spiritual path, but also sometimes as a feature of scientific work, such as exemplified in the scientific work of Goethe (Bortoft, 1996), which Steiner much admired.

Finally, there are issues about how awe and wonder relate to the evolution of consciousness. I can draw some extrapolations about that from Owen Barfield (1957). It seems likely that awe and wonder arose as part of an animistic consciousness that personalized nature. However, animism has faded, and I suspect that awe and wonder have changed as a consequence. They probably now arise in a new and more deliberate way that is less instinctive. The Romantic movement can be seen as a deliberate attempt to cultivate that kind of awe and wonder.

Tears and Grief

There are many references to tears in the stories about Jesus in the Christian gospels. In Luke's version of the Beatitudes, Jesus blesses those who weep. On several occasions Jesus reassures people in grief with the words, 'do not weep'. There is much weeping at the tomb of Lazarus, and Jesus himself weeps there. Jesus' feet are anointed with the tears of an unnamed woman. Jesus weeps over Jerusalem. Peter weeps over his betrayal of Jesus (an event set to music most movingly in J. S. Bach's St. Matthew Passion). Mary goes to Jesus' tomb to weep, and is in tears when she finds the tomb empty.

One of the intriguing facts about tears is that only humans shed them (Trimble, 2012; Vingerhoets, 2013). There is currently much reticence about claims of human distinctiveness, but no one seems to be claiming that any other species sheds tears. The human capacity for weeping seems to reflect the distinctive intelligence of humans. The most-favoured psychological theory at present is that tears are a form of social communication.

However, that seems to struggle to handle the fact that there are many cultures in which tears are shed privately, but in which public weeping is discouraged.

It is often thought that Britain is a nation that believes in keeping a stiff upper lip, a nation in which few tears are shed, at least in public. However, in a delightful history of tears in Britain, Thomas Dixon (2015) shows that this is very far from the case, though there may have been oscillations between periods in which there was much weeping and periods in which it was relatively restrained.

Tears occur in a great variety of contexts. They often occur in moments of uncontrollable sadness, but they can also occur when people weep with joy or relief. Dixon divides his book on tears into five sections dealing with piety, enthusiasm, pathos, restraint and feeling, which indicates the range of contexts in which tears have been shed. It is very interesting, for present purposes, that piety is one of the main contexts in which he considers the shedding of tears. He begins with a chapter on the late medieval mystic, Margery Kempe, who was perhaps Britain's most notorious and prolific weeper, constantly in floods of tears.

Dixon also points out that there were marked divergences between Protestant and Catholic versions of Christianity at the end of the sixteenth century regarding tears, with the Catholic tradition favouring public tears, but the Protestant tradition strongly discouraging them. An influential book in establishing the Catholic emotional regime regarding tears was Richard Southwell's *Marie Magdalene's Funeral Teares*, published in 1591. John Dowland, another Catholic, wrote numerous lute songs about tears at about the same time. Differences between religions in their emotional regimes can be an important part of their distinctive identities. The Protestant view that tears ought to be private reflects the gradual privatization of bodily functions, which Norbert Elias (1984) sees as one of the key hallmarks of civilization.

As Dixon points out, weeping is an important part of Catholic religion at several key points. At times there has been a strong tradition of wailing over the corpse of a dead person. In addition, people were encouraged to shed tears over the passion of Christ. Tears have played an important role in devotion to the Blessed Virgin Mary, and they were part of repentance for sins. Furthermore, as Dixon says, for Catholics, tears 'could do things' and 'had real spiritual consequences' (p. 35). Though public weeping is to some extent scripted and follows cultural norms, it would be a mistake to see it as nothing more than a cultural performance. In tears, there is a complex interaction between private experience and public enactment.

Not all tears are the same. Some religious traditions, especially Buddhism and Eastern Christianity, have distinguished between holy tears and tears that are just an expression of personal emotion (Patton and Hawley, 2005). In some ways this is parallel to the distinction that is drawn between righteous anger and other more egotistical forms of anger. Some tears transcend personal unhappiness and are an expression of the person's religious devotion, and contribute to their religious life.

Funerals are the church services at which tears are most often shed publicly. To be helpful to mourners, a funeral needs to do more than connect with the grief; it needs to facilitate its transformation. The principal mourners at a funeral service will normally have experienced and expressed grief on many other occasions, and there is no reason to suppose that simply doing so once more will make a decisive difference. However, the hope is that grief will be experienced in a *different* way in the context of the funeral rite, and in a way that contributes to its transformation.

In a parallel way, a therapist tries to help clients make contact with their personal problems in therapy in a way that will provide them with a unique opportunity to transform their problems by experiencing them in a special context. The first requirement of effective psychotherapy is that there should be emotional engagement, and that contact should be made between the clients' problems and what happens in the consulting room with a therapist. Similarly, for a pastoral rite such as a funeral, for it to be helpful, the grief of those who have been bereaved needs to be brought, in some way, into the funeral service.

Transforming grief at a funeral service depends crucially on providing a framework of meaning within which the grief can be contextualized. It is also facilitated by occurring in a special, consecrated place, with all the associated sacred resonance. In the liturgical work of transforming grief, there are two main pitfalls to be avoided. One is having such a tightly controlled liturgy that there is little opportunity for the mourners to connect with their experience of grief; the other is having a liturgy that is so banal that it does not provide the cognitive and sacramental resources needed for a transformation of grief. Grief needs to be evoked, but the resources for its transformation also needs to be provided.

Shame, Guilt and Disgust

There are obvious reasons why religious emotional regimes are often interested in shame and guilt. Religions are interested in changing behaviour, and self-evaluative emotions like shame and guilt are an important way of achieving that goal. They are closely intertwined with the religious life, and sometimes arise from religious injunctions, so it is not surprising that religions should have a particular focus on managing them.

Stephen Pattison, in his book on shame, puzzles about the fact that the phenomenon described as shame is very heterogeneous, and concludes that there is no more than a family resemblance between different things called shame (Pattison, 2008). I agree about the heterogeneity, but don't find it as puzzling as Pattison does. It falls into place if you apply to shame the kind of two-factor theory of emotion that I have already mentioned. There are core aspects of shame that are almost universal, but many culturally specific elaborations.

There is a primitive, affective level of shame that is highly embodied and only minimally cognitive. I think it is that kind of shame that Silvan Tomkins is describing in his Affect theory (Tomkins, 1963). The instinct to cringe and hide away when shamed is very strong. Even memories of occasions when you have been shamed can give rise to a very strong instinct to hide away in shame. On the other hand, I think that it is also right to classify shame as a self-evaluative emotion (Tracy et al., 2007; Watts, 2016). There is another level of shame that is to be found only later in the developmental sequence (Lewis, 2014), and which depends on an elaborated self-concept. It is probably correct to say that shame is only fully an emotion when there is that cognitive level of self-evaluation, as well as the more primitive level that embodies shame affect.

The distinction between shame and guilt is a complex one (Watts, 2001; Watts, 2016). It is partly that guilt focuses on specific things that have been done wrong, whereas shame reflects a more pervasive sense of unworthiness. However, there is also a sense in which people feel shamed in the presence of others, whereas guilt can be a more private emotion.

There has been concern that religion can foster guilt, and that religion is therefore bad for people psychologically. However, I suggest that this apparent problem is resolved when you make the distinction that Freud makes between neurotic and realistic guilt. It is neurotic guilt that is all-pervasive, often triggered by very minor mistakes, and which is potentially damaging in its psychological effects. Religion has no use for that kind of neurotic guilt. On the contrary, it is interested in the kind of realistic guilt that is an appropriate response to a particular transgression, and which can lead to reform, or 'repentance' as religion calls it. Part of the potential value of confession to a priest is that it can help people make exactly that distinction between neurotic and realistic guilt.

It has often been remarked that there has been an oscillation between shame and guilt cultures in the Christian West (Watts, 2001). Religions have developed fewer resources for the management of shame than for guilt, and that is a conspicuous gap in the armoury of personal liturgies for handling a sense of shame. There is a need to develop powerful and effective ways of reassuring people that they are loved by God despite the deep sense of shame they may feel (Watts and Gulliford, 2004).

Disgust is another very interesting moral emotion in which religion has taken a particular interest. Disgust plays a very significant role in the Hebrew Bible, especially the book of Leviticus in the Torah, which is a very interesting historical document about feelings of disgust. It is interesting that the same language of impurity and disgust is used, both for feelings of aversion and revulsion associated with food impurity and for other unacceptable behaviours that are now regarded as belonging to the moral sphere such as sexual acts (Kazen, 2011). Ruse has commented that there is often still an element of disgust in moral disapproval of homosexuality (Ruse, 1988).

This seems to be another example of the double-aspect linkages between physical and psychosocial meanings that Barfield pointed out are often found in early language (Barfield, 1984). Jonathan Haidt (2012) has suggested that moral usages of disgust are an extension of an older reaction of disgust to substances. However, the fact that the linkages found between physical disgust and moral disgust go back as far as the book of Leviticus calls that into question. The moral sense of disgust in Leviticus is not a modern extension of the meaning of 'disgust'.

Haidt suggests that there are six different foundations for morality of which sanctity/degradation (and the associated language of disgust) is one. Interestingly, there are significant differences between Christian traditions in the extent to which they use this moral system in preaching. Haidt found that it was used more by Baptists than Unitarian preachers (Haidt, 2012, p. 188). Baptist preachers used a wide range of moral frameworks, whereas Unitarian preachers were more selective in what they used.

With disgust, as with shame, there seems to be a strong physical reaction which has the immediacy and power of a reflex, and is akin to nausea. I am not suggesting that this strong physical reaction is independent of culture and religion, just drawing attention to how it feels. However, this very physical disgust reaction can be developed in much more abstract and conceptual ways, as it was by the taste theorists of the eighteenth century such as Ashley-Cooper, the third Earl of Shaftesbury (Firth-Godbehere, 2019).

Anger and Aggression

Anger, more than any other emotion, has caused concern because of its potentially detrimental consequences, both for ourselves and for others. The management of anger is something with which most societies have been concerned in some way or other (e.g. Stearns and Stearns, 1986). However, it would be a mistake to assume that anger is necessarily a problem. It can also be adaptive and helpful. Anger illustrates the problem of how to make the distinction between forms of emotion that can play a constructive role in life, including religious life, and forms of anger that cause problems for ourselves and others.

The potential value of anger is illustrated by the anger of Jesus that is referred to explicitly when people try to keep children away from him, or complain about him healing on the sabbath. There are other occasions when Jesus' anger is evident in his behaviour, as when he disrupts extortionate money-changing activity taking place in the temple courtyard. It seems that Jesus had no compunction about expressing anger, either in words or behaviour. He did not always keep his anger in. What is significant is the kind of things which make Jesus angry. Most would see Jesus' anger as arising in situations where anger is reasonable and justifiable. In comparison, many people may be aware that they get angry in situations where they are thwarted in getting their way. Much anger is probably rather small-minded and childish.

It is interesting that people don't always get angry when they are frustrated. Whether or not frustrations lead to anger is significantly influenced by people's interpretation of the events concerned. Interpretations of other people's intentions are important; we are more likely to get angry when we assume we have been thwarted deliberately than when we think it is accidental.

There is also quite widespread anger at God, as the psychologist Julie Exline has found (Exline et al., 2011). Such anger occurs most commonly after upsetting events like death, illness or natural disaster, though it can also occur after personal disappointments. It is found in a surprisingly wide range of people, including those who love God, and even among atheists. However, it seems unlikely to occur in people who really make no assumptions about God being responsible for the events that have upset them.

Much social concern is focused on the physical expression of anger: when it is and is not acceptable, and how people can regulate angry behaviour. These are difficult issues and many approaches have been tried. In the early centuries of the Christian period, the assumption was that the crucial distinction between acceptable and unacceptable anger depended on who the anger was directed toward (Watts, 2007). For Lactantius, for example, anger was acceptable to the people of lower social standing but not to people of higher social standing. That now seems a very unsatisfactory approach, and one lacking in moral and spiritual sophistication.

There has also been much use of the hydraulic model, in which anger is assumed to be rather like water building up behind the dam, and needing an outlet if it is not to build up to the point where it spills over the top. Making provision for school children to engage in aggressive sports has often been seen as useful from this point of view. The idea is that if they 'get rid' of their aggression on the sports field they will not do so in other circumstances. However, despite the popularity of hydraulic assumptions about anger, there is not much evidence to support them.

In our own society we have developed 'anger management training' (e.g. Bloxham and Gentry, 2010). That includes skills in managing angry thoughts and interpretations of events that lead to anger, physical relaxation training and, crucially, training in the appropriate expression of anger. People who are not good at managing their anger tend to hold it in for too long and then, late in the day, express it in a way that is rather over the top and damages their own interests. Anger management training encourages people to express their anger in moderate well-chosen ways before it builds up too much.

There is much social concern about the physical violence that may result from anger. However, angry people are less likely to be violent than is often supposed. Violence is a relatively rare phenomenon (Averill, 1982). Also, people are unlikely to be violent with strangers who they do not know. If violence occurs, it is most likely to be towards family members. Even though such violence is relatively rare, it is a problem about which society is justifiably concerned.

The physical expression of anger is certainly sometimes problematic. However, it doesn't seem realistic or justifiable to suggest that there should never be physical expressions of anger. The important questions concern what kind of events trigger anger, and how strongly it is expressed. There can be 'righteous' anger that plays a proper role in religious life.

One of the interesting questions about anger is why it occurs. Presumably it developed originally to facilitate self-defence. It can also probably help people to stand up for moral principles, as it does with Jesus. Rudolf Steiner, in an interesting lecture on the 'mission of anger', suggests that one of its functions is to facilitate a sense of individual identity (König, 2006).

10

Healing

The healing of the body is a fundamental Christian aspiration. It is a key feature of the ministry of Jesus, as recorded in the Gospels. It is also an important feature of the work of the present-day church. From this it would be natural to assume that healing of the body has always been an important part of Christian ministry, but that would be wrong.

We first consider the healings of Jesus, and then look at the period since the revival of healing in the mid-nineteenth century. We then look at research on the efficacy of healing, and finally at the processes by which healing might work. Throughout, I keep the perspectives of both religion and science in view, and argue that they are not incompatible. I think that spiritual healing can be effective, but I take that to be a matter of open-minded enquiry, not dogmatic assertion.

Jesus as Healer

Stories of Jesus' miraculous healings are very prominent in the Gospels, and there is little doubt that Jesus was generally thought to be an effective healer. Though not unique among Jews at that time in being a healer, he seems to have been exceptional. Josephus and other non-Christian sources record that Jesus was a 'miracle worker', and they do not dispute that the healings actually occurred (Meggitt, 2011). Current opinion is that there were not many healers in Jesus' time, and that Jesus healed more frequently and efficaciously than others (Henriksen and Sandnes, 2016).

New Testament scholars have sometimes struggled with what to make of Jesus' healings, and with what was actually going on. The prevailing assumption among scholars is that what Jesus did was not simply miraculous, and they have tried to make sense of it in other ways. Various lines of explanation have been explored.

One approach is to suggest that, though Jesus clearly had a reputation for being a healer, his 'healings' did not necessarily involve curing people.

Anthropologists have often made a distinction between 'healing' and 'cure' (Dein, 2019). Cure involves repairing physiological dysfunction. In contrast, healings arise, as Dow (1986) puts it, from building bridges between personal experience, cultural meanings and social relations. However, the distinction between healing and cure is not watertight (Waldram, 2000). Scientific medicine may bring healing as well as cure, and healings such as those of Jesus may actually cure people.

The question about Jesus is essentially whether Jesus cured people, or whether his 'healings' involved some broader and more diffuse benefit that did not necessarily involve cure. Pilch (2000) has argued that Jesus' healings were 'healings' only in a broad sense of the term, and that they did not cure people, but rather enabled them to come to terms with their problems and to find an appropriate way of adjusting to them. Pilch makes much of the claim that people in Jesus' time did not have the concepts of modern medicine. That is certainly true, but it is hard to believe that they could not tell whether or not someone had actually been cured. It seems to me hard to avoid the conclusion that Jesus was believed by his contemporaries to have actually cured people, and that his healings did often result in cure.

Another approach is to emphasize the non-specific or placebo aspects of Jesus' healings. With all kinds of treatments, the expectations of improvement that people have are a significant factor. For example, people's expectations about medication seem to be influenced by the size and colour of the tablet they are taking. Charismatic healers create an expectation that people will get better, and that is undoubtedly a significant factor in their improvement. There were probably placebo factors at work in Jesus' healings (Moerman, 2002), and increasingly so as his reputation as a healer developed. It is making a similar point in different terminology to say the peoples' 'faith' in Jesus was a significant factor in his ability to heal (Theissen, 1983), as Jesus himself recognized. However, it is again difficult to regard this as a completely adequate explanation of Jesus' remarkable effectiveness as a healer.

Yet another suggestion is that Jesus healed people who were suffering from mental illness, or had psychosomatic problems (e.g. Capps, 2008). That assumes that Jesus' healings were primarily psychological, and only secondarily healings of the body. There is some plausibility in this suggestion; some of the problems that Jesus healed may well have been psychosomatic, and his approach to healing may well have involved psychological change. However, it is hard to develop this into a complete and convincing account of the full range of healings reported in the Gospels. There are too many that don't fit, and attempts to claim that the people whom Jesus healed had mental illness are often unconvincing (Cook, 2020); not all the people that Jesus healed can be regarded as cases of mental illness, or as having psychosomatic ailments.

A related approach is that of Stevan Davies (1995) who sees the problems that Jesus healed as arising from demon possession, with some ailments as being conversion disorders that arose from the psychological process of somatization. Davies sees Jesus himself as in some sense 'possessed' by the Holy Spirit, and draws a connection with the Spirit Christology advocated by Geoffrey Lampe (1977). In some ways I find this an attractive approach, and think that Davies is right to emphasize that Jesus was above all a healer. There is a clear connection between this interpretation of Jesus' healings and the approach to healing widely practised in hunter-gatherer societies, discussed in Chapter 3, though Jesus apparently did not need to use trance-dancing to connect with his healing powers. However, Davies' approach is also not entirely convincing as a complete explanation of all Jesus' healings.

Though we can identify various factors which may have contributed to Jesus as a healer, none of them seems an adequate explanation by itself. Even if we assume that they were all at work to some extent, it is still hard to see that they account completely for the remarkable record of Jesus as a healer.

Healings are an important part of the work of Jesus, and also of the early church, as recorded in the Acts of the Apostles. The Christian literature continues to talk about miraculous healings up to the time of Augustine. Discussion of healing is less evident in the later literature (Clayton, 2011), though it doesn't entirely disappear (Porterfield, 2005). An interest in spiritual healing of the body returned only relatively recently, in the mid nineteenth century.

It is an interesting question why healing of the body faded away as it did. Morton Kelsey (1973) suggested that one factor was the shift from Platonic to Aristotelian philosophy. Philip Clayton (2011) suggests that other factors were an increasing focus on internal spiritual matters, and the assumption that, if sin was dealt with, then healing of the body would follow. It might also have been that anointing with oil for healing was found not to be as effective as was hoped, or as healing had apparently been in the Gospels.

The Revival of Spiritual Healing

When healing was revived in the Christian church, it was first more in a series of New Religious Movements than in the established churches. One of the most significant events was the founding of the Church of Christ Scientist by Mary Baker Eddy in 1879, though it is possible to trace some prior influences, including Swedenborg and Emerson. It was also part of the 'New Thought' movement in the USA, which tended to adopt philosophical idealism and to believe in the power of mind over matter.

The revival of interest in healing in the Christian churches occurred at about the same time as scientific medicine developed, in the formative years 1830–80. James Robinson suggests that the 1860s were the years when illness ceased to be a mystery and became a problem that people wanted solved (Robinson, 2014). In this sense the development of scientific medicine and the revival of interest in healing both reflected this new attitude to illness. Though some people such as Eddy thought you had to choose between medicine and spiritual healing, the majority of people were probably open to anything that worked, whether it was healing, scientific medicine or anything else. The same factors influenced the seeking of health improvements through healing and through modern medicine (Williams et al., in press).

As far as churches were concerned, the new interest in healing occurred largely in the Pentecostal and Charismatic fringe of the church, but it was also apparent in the Roman Catholic church. The first apparition at Lourdes of a lady who identified herself as the Immaculate Conception occurred in 1858; by the following year, large numbers of people were visiting Lourdes, seeking healing of the body. Other mainline denominations took up healing later, and often with only a lukewarm approach.

A path-breaking Christian proponent of healing in the UK in the nineteenth century was Edward Irving, a Glasgow pastor whose ministry gave rise to the so-called 'Catholic Apostolic Church', which brought together revivalism, ritualism and apocalyptic thinking in a heady combination (Flegg, 1992). Healing of the body has continued to be a central focus of many New Religious Movements. For example, Mabel Balthrop who led the Panacea Society in Bedford believed that she was the Daughter of God. Whereas the mission of the Son of God had been to save peoples' souls, she saw it as her mission to save peoples' bodies (Shaw, 2011).

Since the revival of interest in spiritual healing in the middle of the nineteenth century, healing has been conducted in a great variety of contexts, some explicitly religious, some not. The fact that broadly similar methods are used in religious and non-religious settings suggests that, in so far as healing is effective at all, it is effective for similar reasons in different settings. Healing prayer is one of those aspects of spirituality that is probably now found as much outside the church as in it.

Charles Bourne and I (2011) considered the similarities and differences between spiritual healing in religious and non-religious settings, examining how it is presented in popular books. Regardless of the context in which they are operating, most healers see themselves as invoking some healing energy or power beyond themselves, and being channels of healing energy rather than a source of healing powers themselves. The differences between religious and non-religious healers seem to be more practical than conceptual. Healing sessions often last longer in non-religious settings, and people are more likely to pay for healing. The healer is more likely to explicitly set out to cure the patient or at least to alleviate symptoms, and there is more often an explicit claim in non-religious settings that healing will be beneficial. An explicitly religious context seems not to be necessary for healing to work, and may not add much to the effectiveness of spiritual healing. Indeed, in churches where healing is undertaken in a perfunctory way, with little expectation of benefit, it may be less effective than in non-religious settings.

The fact that spiritual healing is practised in non-religious settings as well as in religious ones, and may even work better in such settings, might be taken as suggesting that healing is nothing to do with God. However, that is not at all the conclusion that I would draw. Healing can be seen as a fulfilment of God's purposes, whether it comes about through scientific medicine or spiritual healing, and whether healers believe in God and explicitly invoke him, or not. Theologically, there is no reason to think that God is at work only in religious settings.

In the present-day Church of England, many churches now offer prayers for healing but often, it seems, with little explicit expectation that anyone will actually be cured as a result. The official Church of England report, *A Time to Heal* (Church of England, 2000) actually seems to discourage such expectations, and to regard them as naive, though it still encourages churches to offer healing prayer. It displays a curiously ambivalent approach to healing.

Research on the Effectiveness of Healing

There is now a growing body of survey data on prayer for healing (Hood et al., 2018). In the USA the majority of the population believe in healing prayer, and a significant minority report that they have experienced healing as the result of prayer. There is less data in the UK, but recent data from Tearfund indicates that many more people pray than go to church; among those who pray, healing is one of the principal objects of prayer (Tearfund, 2018).

There are, as always, two questions to be asked about something like spiritual healing; the first is *whether* it works, the second is *how* it works. It might seem that these questions are really separate from each other, but in practice they become rather intertwined. People are often reluctant to accept evidence that something like healing really does work unless they can understand *how* it works. Putting it the other way round, if there are good reasons for thinking that something like healing *might* work, it significantly buttresses the belief that it actually does work. There are several relevant lines of evidence.

First, there is now a vast body of evidence, reviewed by Harold Koenig (Koenig et al., 2012), showing that there is generally a positive correlation between religion and health. Admittedly, there are some studies that have failed to find this positive correlation, but the bulk of the evidence is overwhelming. However, the main limitation of this work is that it generally only shows a positive *association* between religion and health, and doesn't show a causal effect. It fails to show that religion actually brings about an improvement in health. The correlation between religion and good health might arise for other reasons. Healthier people might be more likely to be religious. Also, there may be some hidden third variable, like wealth or education, that is associated with both health and religiousness, and gives rise to a correlation between them.

It is not difficult to see how religion might be good for health. Koenig distinguishes three main pathways: behavioural, psychological and social. First, religion is probably associated with various lifestyle factors which are good for health. Religious people probably avoid excessive eating, drinking and smoking, exercise better, and take health advice more seriously. If so, their health will benefit. Second, religion is likely to be associated with various psychological qualities which in turn make for good health. Koenig lists forgiveness, altruism, gratefulness, positive emotions, well-being, quality-of-life, hope and optimism.

Third, religion often provides people with a supportive community. Not all religious communities are as supportive as they might be, but the evidence shows that religion tends to associated with good levels of social support, and social support is in turn good for health. In addition to these three pathways outlined by Koenig, we might also add a cognitive pathway. Religion provides people with a framework of meaning that enables them to make sense of events in their lives. That is also good for health. Raw, unassimilated events that people can make no sense of tend to be bad for health.

Mind and Matter

The next relevant line of evidence concerns studies of the inter-relationship of mind and body, and how far the body of one person can be affected by the intentions and mental processes of another. 'Biopsychokinesis' is the technical word for that. There is a significant and thorough body of research showing that it is possible for intentional mental activity in one person to have a measurable affect on physiological processes in another organism.

Some of the most impressive research was carried out by Bernard Grad with a Hungarian faith healer, Oskar Estabany (Eysenck and Sargent, 1982). One study found that he was able to increase the activity of trypsin, a gut enzyme. Another showed that he could improve the healing of wounds in mice, just by touching their cages. Yet another showed that he could improve the growth of plants by holding sealed flasks which contained the chemical solution in which they would grow. All these experiments were conducted in carefully controlled conditions.

Effects of mental intentions have been demonstrated for bacteria, laboratory animals, and humans. A major review of 131 research studies found a significant effect in almost half of them (Benor, 1993). One of the most careful bodies of research showed that it was possible to affect the skin conductance of a 'receiver' by a 'sender' who was having calming thoughts or intentions (Schlitz, 2011).

Such research is often controversial, and dismissed by many, because they cannot see how such results could possibly be obtained. However, the quality of the research is actually quite impressive, and meets standards that would be accepted in other fields. Eysenck and Sargent (1982) concluded that it was a remarkable body of excellent scientific work, and one that represents a significant challenge to critics and sceptics. The significance of such research for spiritual healing is that, if it is possible to demonstrate in laboratory situations the effects of the mental processes of one person on physiological processes in another, then it is entirely credible that prayers for healing in one person should have significant healing effects on the other.

There are, of course, differences in the two situations. Healing prayer is carried out with an intensity and seriousness of purpose that exceeds anything found in laboratory studies. Also, the physiological effects that are being sought in healing prayer are not just measurable and statistically significant, but big enough to confer real health benefits. Nevertheless, scientific research on biopsychokinesis lends credibility to the claim that there can be healing benefits of what religious people call 'prayer', or more new-age people would call 'channelling'.

Scientific Evidence for Healing Prayer

There have been controlled trials of healing prayer, though there is widespread uneasiness about this body of research (Brown, 2012). One problem is whether healing prayer that is carried out to meet the requirements of a controlled scientific study will have the intensity and genuineness that may be essential for it to be effective. Theological concerns have also been expressed about whether it is appropriate to test the efficacy of prayer in this way. Some see it is as almost blasphemous to be testing the power of God, assuming that is what is at stake.

Some of these studies have claimed positive results, but the largest and most carefully executed research, carried out by Benson and his colleagues at Harvard, failed to show any benefits of prayer (Benson et al., 2006) They studied the effects of intercessory prayer in cardiac patients. Some were prayed for and knew that was happening; some were prayed for but did not know about it; some were in a control group who were not prayed for. Patients who knew that they were being prayed for actually did worse than those who were not prayed for. There was no effect at all in patients who did not know that they were being prayed for.

I would rate such attempts to evaluate intercessory prayer in controlled scientific trials as the least impressive body of evidence for spiritual healing. For me, the main problem with control trials of intercessory prayer is the artificiality of the prayer. I don't object in principle to investigating the effects of prayer, and basic research on psychokinesis suggests that there could be significant effects, even if not strong ones. However, taking healing ministry out of context in this way is never likely to show to best advantage what can be achieved. Much stronger effects are likely to be obtained when healing is carried out in the context of faith, and with direct contact ('proximal intercessory prayer'). For a healer to take part in an experiment is likely to make them somewhat detached and disengaged, which in turn probably makes their healing ministry less effective.

This points to the need for naturalistic studies rather than controlled trials. There is now a significant and promising body of evidence for spiritual healing recorded in religious communities. Within Christianity, spiritual healing is pursued most enthusiastically in Pentecostalism and Roman Catholic churches; there is less serious interest in Anglican and Nonconformist churches. There is also good record-keeping in New Religious Movements such as Christian Science. The most important research of this kind so far is that of Candy Gunther Brown (2012), studying the healing of problems of vision and hearing in Pentecostal ministry. It is a fulfilment of the classic prophecy that 'the eyes of the blind shall be opened, and the ears of the deaf unstopped' (Isaiah 35.5).

There are scientific advantages in studying problems such as vision and hearing. One is that they are relatively unlikely to be psychosomatic. They could in principle be psychological conversion symptoms, but that is relatively rare; most problems of vision and hearing are not psychological in origin. Another advantage is that they are objectively measurable; you can test how well people can see and hear. Another advantage, from a scientific point of view, is that there is very little spontaneous remission of problems of vision and hearing, so there is less scientific need for a control group. It can safely be assumed that a control group would show little change. Of course, in such naturalistic research it is always good practice to consider alternative explanations and to check them out.

Brown (2012) has documented significant improvements in vision and hearing in Pentecostal ministry in separate studies with different healers in Mozambique and Brazil. This is not to claim that a large number of people went from having no vision or hearing to having normal functioning, but there were statistically significant improvements across the range of people studied, and striking improvements in a few. There were also many subjective reports of people experiencing improvements that they felt to be really significant for them, and which had long-term life-changing effects. To my mind, this is much the most convincing evidence so far of the efficacy of healing ministry.

Interestingly, the Pentecostal healers studied in Brown's research say that they get better results in poor countries like Mozambique where there is less focus on modern medicine. I think it is possible that the mind functions in a rather different way in such countries. One way of phrasing this point would be to say that ego boundaries are less strong in such countries. Another formulation would be to say that the non-dominant hemisphere of the brain, normally on the right side, exercises more influence in such cultures. It may be that Western sophistication is a barrier to faith.

Religious Interpretations of Healing

Theology and Science

I turn now to interpretations of spiritual healing as the work of God. I see it as a theological mistake to suggest that God is able to work only through the church, or only through believers. In contrast, I take a theological position which asserts that all creation and all society are enfolded within the life of God, and that God potentiates all efforts to fulfil his purposes, regardless of where and by whom they are undertaken. Probably few Christians would question that, if pressed. However, many do not act as though they endorse it; those who see all society and all creation as God's arena can appear to be radical (Watts, 2015).

Similar issues arise over considering what contribution science can make to understanding spiritual healing, and it may be helpful to clarify the position I am taking about the relationship between scientific and theological accounts of spiritual healing. Healing by God, miraculous healing, is often seen as an alternative to healing that can be explained in natural scientific terms. When the Vatican looks for evidence of miracles to justify canonization, it looks for healings that cannot be explained scientifically. I think that is a mistake.

It depends partly on what you mean by a 'miracle', which is sometimes seen as dependent on an overturning of the laws of nature. However, this is not theologically necessary; it is a way of thinking about miracles that only arose when the laws of nature were defined so tightly that it seemed that God would need to overturn them in order to do anything significant in the world. I think Richard Swinburne gets it right when he says that a miracle is an event of an extraordinary kind, brought about by God, and of religious significance (Swinburne, 1970)

Theologically, it is important to remember that the whole of material creation, including the human body, is taken to be God's creation. On that assumption, if God were to choose to heal someone, there is no reason why God should in some way bypass the natural processes of creation that God himself established, and intervene in some other way to bring about the healing of the human body. It would be natural for God to work through the lawfulness of creation.

My general methodological approach to the relationship between science and religion is to see them as providing complementary perspectives (Watts, 1998). They are describing things from different points of view, within different discourses. They should *not* be seen as alternatives. Both science and religion describe things from a partial point of view, and can't include everything. We often need to look at things from multiple points of view to get a full and rounded understanding of things.

It may be helpful to take another topic in the relationship between science and religion as an example. There is a scientific account of how the world came into being through a big bang, an event in a quantum vacuum; it was followed by a process of inflation, in which the four dimensions of space and time were established, and the values of the four basic physical forces became fixed. There is also a theological account in which creation is attributed to God. I think it is a mistake to take the theological account as an alternative to the scientific account, and to try to press the question of whether creation came about through natural processes that science can investigate, *or* whether it is the work of God. I would say that it is both, and that both accounts have validity of a different kind.

I take the same approach to spiritual healing. Even though healings are exceptional events, I believe it is possible for science to go some way towards elucidating the natural processes by which they come about. I see the scientific understanding of healings as complementing a theological account of them, not replacing it. I suggest that all healing should be seen as falling within the purposes of God, including medicine and surgery. It is a mistake to assume that, if science can explain something, God is not involved. However, there is a special sense in which spiritual practices that are rooted in faith, and explicitly invoke God or some kind of transcendent spiritual energy, are more explicitly and obviously manifestations of God's healing purposes.

There is a religious approach to healing that connects it with the purposes of God. There is also a scientific approach which spells out the pathways within God's creation by which that healing can occur. These two perspectives elucidate different aspects of spiritual healing, and are not in competition with each other. It is not difficult to see the pathways by which spiritual practices might deliver health benefits. Making that clear is helpful for those who are sceptical about spiritual healing. However, if you spell out scientifically the pathways by which spiritual practices might be beneficial, some people are then inclined to interpret things in a reductionist way, and to say that it doesn't count as 'healing', and is nothing to do with God or prayer. I don't draw that reductionist conclusion.

Transcendent Explanations

Spiritual healing is generally assumed to arise from some kind of spiritual influence, power or energy. Traditions vary over which of those terms is preferred, but it is usually assumed that there is some kind of healing power that is outside both the person being healed and the healer. Christianity talks about 'God', and other monotheistic religions have comparable terms. Jesus calls that source of spiritual power his 'Father'. Religious people are likely to personalize and name this transcendent healing power. More secular traditions will probably think about it in impersonal terms, such as healing 'energy'.

Healers generally see themselves as receivers and transmitters of this spiritual energy, or as channels. The task of the healer is to draw on their familiarity and affinity with transcendent energy and to focus it towards the person who is seeking healing. Christian healers align themselves with the healing power of Christ, and usually invoke his healing power explicitly when they heal. The healer's own spiritual development and capacities will be involved in that channelling process. Pentecostal healers may talk about what particular kind of healing they have been 'anointed' for.

In trying to explain how intercessory prayer might work, John Polkinghorne (2007) draws an analogy with the scientific phenomena of a nuclear resonance. Sometimes when elements collide they fuse to form a different element, though such fusion often fails to occur. However, in some cases, there is what is called a 'nuclear resonance' that facilitates that process of fusion. Carbon, essential for life as we know it, is a somewhat improbable element, requiring for its formation the fusion of three helium-4 nuclei in what is known as the 'triple-alpha process'. However, there is a nuclear resonance which is exactly right to facilitate the formation of carbon.

I suggest that this is a helpful model for understanding how spiritual healing might work. The person who wants to be healed could, of course, establish direct contact with transcendent healing energy themselves, however that is described. However, this is challenging for many people. It can facilitate the process if another person helps to link up the transcendent healing power with the person seeking healing. Polkinghorne's analogy with a nuclear resonance seems helpful in providing an analogy for what may be happening in spiritual healing.

Though healers conceptualize the source of healing power in different ways, it is striking that it seems to be almost universal for healers to have a sense of being channels of a healing power that comes from beyond themselves. Indeed, it may be impossible to undertake effective healing without first getting into a receptive mode of consciousness that connects consciously and explicitly with a transcendent source of healing power. It is also striking that healers have a sense of being aligned with the source of healing power; it seems that they need to have a sense of being at ease and at one with the transcendent power if healing is to be possible.

The person being healed is also likely to attribute healing benefits to God (or to the healer, or the healing community). I explored that in the archives of correspondence in the Panacea Society in Bedford (Williams and Watts, 2014). The Society made use of healing water, which people could make at home, following instruction, by immersing in water linen squares which had been prayed over by the leader of the Society and then mailed out. People who felt the benefits of this might attribute them to God, but they could also attribute them to the Society, or to the water. However, there was a marked asymmetry in their attributions; God and the Society were not blamed in the same way for a lack of benefit. It may well potentiate healing for the person prayed for to believe in a transcendent healing source, but it is probably less important that they should do so than it is for the healer to sense that connection.

Scientific Explanations

I want to emphasize that I don't think there is any single answer to the question of *how* healing works. I am operating with a complementary perspectives approach in which each perspective elucidates a different aspect of what is going on in spiritual healing. I think at least three different perspectives are needed. One is religious, which we have just considered; that is concerned with the transcendent source of healing power and how the healer relates to it. There are also scientific explanations. Among these I first consider psychosocial aspects, which includes the context of faith and expectation in which healing takes place. Then I consider how healing is mediated biologically.

Psycho-social Aspects

Healing is often called 'spiritual' healing, and that raises conceptual issues about exactly what is 'spiritual' about it (Watts, 2011a). I am assuming, building on Chapter 2, that there is a distinction between spirit (*pneuma*) and soul (*psyche*). The spirituality of the person seeking healing is involved in the healing process. Being healed is not a purely passive process, like taking medication and waiting for it to work. Someone being healed is normally spiritually involved themselves, actively seeking healing and opening themselves to spiritual power or energy. A person's own spiritual activity can contribute to healing, and they can probably augment the efficacy of the healer's work by being spiritually engaged themselves.

As Csordas points out in his classic study of Catholic charismatic healing (Csordas, 1994) there is close connection between physical and spiritual experiences. Healing rituals produce powerful physical experiences which are fused with a spiritual experience of the power of the healing Christ. For example, when someone falls backwards as they are 'slain with the spirit', they also experience being overwhelmed by divine power. There are double-aspect linkages here, comparable to the historic linkages between physical and psycho-spiritual meanings of words. It seems that, through this fusion of the physical and the spiritual, the body is transformed by spiritual practices. Indeed, healing brings to the fore a somatic mode of attention that is potentially of wider significance (Csordas, 2002).

Sometimes there may be a significant psychological shift in the person seeking healing; and the healing event could be the catalyst for such a shift. By analogy, most people find it very difficult to give up smoking but, sometimes, a significant life event happens in which people simply decide to give up smoking in a way that makes it relatively easy to do so. To take another analogy, psychotherapists discuss the phenomenon of a 'flight into health' (Kinsey, 2011), in which a significant psychological change occurs that results in people moving from a state of illness to a state of health. It is entirely possible that something similar occurs in spiritual healing. It is usually assumed that the flight into health is unstable and doesn't last. However, it is possible that something comparable can occur which *is* stable and enduring.

It probably also makes a significant difference how the person being healed perceives the healer, and what impression the healer makes on them. It seems likely that healing effects are greater when the healer has charisma for the person being healed. It may also be the case that those who are relatively impressionable or suggestible are more likely to experience benefits from spiritual healing. Recovery from illness is massively influenced by non-specific factors, such as the relationship with the doctor, therapist or healer, and by expectations of change (Marchant, 2016). Whatever else may be going on in healing, such factors seem likely to be very important.

LeShan (1980) makes what seems a potentially important distinction between two different kinds of relationship that can occur between the healer and the beneficiary. In one, there is a bond of unity and love between the two, but no specific objectives beyond that. In the other, the healer has objectives and intentions, and explicitly tries to achieve them. There is probably a tendency for the first kind of healing relationship to occur more in religious settings, especially in non-Pentecostal religious settings. So far, there seems to be no empirical investigation comparing the benefits of these two approaches to healing, but it would be an interesting matter to investigate.

Healing can be effective with just a single healer, but in Pentecostal healing there is often a healing community that plays a significant role. Polkinghorne's 'resonance' model of intercessory prayer connects three persons: God, the healer, and the person being prayed for. Matthew Lee et al. (2013) propose a somewhat similar model, though they also include the collaborators of the healer, who form the spiritual community in which healing takes place. There is then a quadrilateral which features God, what Lee et al. call the 'exemplar' (or healer), the exemplar's collaborators, and the beneficiaries.

Together, they form a critical mass that can generate a remarkable constellation of healing energy, with positive feedback between the various participants that can ramp up healing energy to new heights. As Brown (2012) comments, it represents the kind of 'effervescence' that the distinguished French sociologist Emile Durkheim long ago described as a feature of religion. It seems to be significant that the energy involved is a moral and emotional energy, an energy of love, which may have a particular capacity to ramp up in this way. It constitutes what Lee at al. (2013) call the 'diamond' model of Godly Love.

Whether healing is conducted individually, or in a community context, it seems necessary for it to be conducted with some intensity. There needs to be a real concentration of mental effort if any significant healing is to result. If the healing takes place in a spiritual community, there needs to be a palpable, effervescent energy circulating among those involved. It is doubtful whether perfunctory healing prayer, in which those prayed for are simply mentioned, has much impact.

Biological Factors

I now explore how healing benefits might be mediated biologically. In healing, there is almost always some healing *event*, such as prayer for healing or the laying on of hands, which can result in an alleviation of afflictions. There is obviously an important question about the pathways that go from the healing event to the intended benefits. What I say here is necessarily speculative, but I think it is possible to make some reasonable suggestions about what the pathways might be.

The healing event seems likely to have discernible effects on the brain of the person being healed. We need to make use here of the distinction between the different modes of cognition associated with the two sides of the brain, discussed in Chapter 7.

I suggest that the non-dominant hemisphere, usually on the right side, plays a more significant role than the dominant hemisphere in the mediation of healing benefits. There are two reasons for thinking that the non-dominant hemisphere is particularly important in healing. One is that the healing event is likely to be registered primarily at an intuitive and affective level. The other is that the non-dominant hemisphere is much more strongly interconnected with the rest of the body, and so is a more likely candidate for the mediation of a wide range of somatic benefits.

The biological mediation of healing of different problems is likely to proceed through different pathways. However, I suggest that the immune system is probably the single most important pathway, and the prime candidate for research on how healing is mediated. There is now a good body of scientific research on psychoneuroimmunology (PNI) which considers how the immune system is affected by a variety of social, cognitive, emotional and environmental processes. The immune system also has a very wide-ranging influence on many somatic processes (Martin, 1997).

Health problems usually arise, not from a single source, but from an interaction. Infectious diseases are a classic example. I wrote this book during the coronavirus pandemic, and exposure to the virus was obviously one source of the disease. However, many, perhaps most, people who came into contact with the virus developed no symptoms at all; the majority showed only mild symptoms or none at all. It is the immune system that determines how people respond to a virus. Scientific medicine often tends to be focused on pathogenic agents, such as viruses. Healing, in contrast, probably works largely through internal regulatory processes, particularly the immune system.

Cancer works in a similar way (Boivin and Webb, 2011). Once abnormal, cancerous cells develop in the body, they tend to spread, but how much they spread is regulated by the immune system. A weakened immune system makes people more vulnerable to the spread of cancer. Early research on PNI and cancer found that anger is correlated with the spread of cancer, an effect that seems to be mediated through the immune system (Morris et al., 1981). If spiritual healing has any effect on cancer, it will probably be mediated through strengthening of the immune system. There seem to be very few health outcomes that are not influenced to some degree by the immune system.

It seems entirely possible that healing events have a significant impact on someone's immunity. As far as I know there is not yet any direct research on that, but there are various ways in which it could happen. The release of endorphins is probably one. As noted in Chapter 3, synchronized rhythmic movements produce a very strong endorphin effect, and such movements often occur in Pentecostal worship. The effervescence often found in the Pentecostal healing ministry is also likely to result in a significant release of endorphins, which will in turn enhance immunity. One particularly important way in which the immune system can be enhanced is through spiritual practices, which also trigger release of endorphins. We saw in Chapter 3 how the trance dancing that occurred in hunter-gatherer societies triggers endorphin release, and was relied on for healing. Spiritual practices such as meditation can also improve immunity (Househam et al., 2017).

There is also often physical contact in healing. The most common practice is for the healer to place hands on the head of the person being healed. Occasionally, they might place hands on, or close to, the area where there is discomfort. They might also anoint the person with oil, usually on the forehead. Such physical contact is likely to have a significant physiological effect (Gilbert and Gilbert, 2011), which will have an effect on the immune system. There may well be release of endorphins and other endogenous opiates as a result of touch. In the short term, that would increase pain tolerance; but it would also tune the immune system in a way that would have longer-term health benefits.

One interesting physical aspect of healing concerns heat sensitivity. Many people report that healing hands feel strangely warm, even hot (Bromiley and Bromiley, 2001). It may be that some kind of spiritual energy is being channelled through the hands, which is experienced as heat. Also, some healers place their hands over the body of the person they are seeking to heal, using sensitivity to heat to discern where in the body the problem is located. Such heat effects are not at all well understood, though they are something that it would be possible to investigate scientifically.

There are two caveats that I need to make about the possible biological mediation of healing. First, though I think the effects of healing events on the immune system are probably the most important biological pathway by which healing effects are mediated, I am *not* suggesting that it is the only one. We are at still at the foothills of understanding scientifically how healing events can lead to health benefits.

The other caveat is to emphasize that I am *not* trying to say that there is nothing more going on in healing than these biological processes, and that healers are wrong in thinking that they are being channels for some kind of transcendent healing energy. Actually, I think they are right in believing that; I am just talking here about how the benefits of healing are mediated biologically. Once again, I am working with complementary explanatory perspectives. I am not choosing between biological, psycho-social and religious approaches to healing.

The Objectives of Healing

There are three points at which healing can benefit people: (i) prevention, (ii) reduction or elimination of symptoms or disabilities, and (iii) coping and adjustment. It varies from one situation to another where healing will be most helpful, depending on various factors including the particular person, and the nature of their health problems.

Prevention is not much discussed in the literature on spiritual healing, but it seems to me that it is potentially very significant. It is less part of present-day Christianity to pray for protection than it was in some earlier periods. It is a prominent feature of St Patrick's Breastplate, which invokes protection, including for example against 'everyone who meditates injury to me ... against every hostile merciless power which may assail my body and my soul, and against every poison, burning, drowning and death-wound'. That is more comprehensive than any modern insurance policy! Protection against illness could be mediated through the immune system.

Second, healing can bring about alleviation or elimination of symptoms and disabilities. The benefits of healing prayer by others might be mediated through some kind of biopsychokinesis. That might apply to the Pentecostal healing of problems of vision and hearing studied by Candy Gunther Brown (Brown, 2012). There are also many problems that are more obviously psychosomatic that might be alleviated by healing, including pain, digestive problems and so on. We don't have good data on which kind of health problems respond best to healing, but it seems likely that some conditions respond better than others. According to the gospels, Jesus focused on exorcising evil spirits and restoring bodily functioning. What conditions respond to present-day spiritual healing? In the absence of hard data, the answer has to be tentative, but it looks as though the focus in spiritual healing is very different now from what it was with Jesus. My hunch is that pain and psychosomatic conditions are what respond best to healing now.

Third, healing prayer, even where symptoms and disabilities remain unchanged, can improve coping and adjustment. Pain is a good example of this. As was shown in Chapter 6, the amount of pain that people experience is determined to a substantial degree by the central nervous system, not just by tissue damage etc. Healing prayer may also bring about a different attitude to symptoms and discomfort, which in turn leads to a better experience of them. The modern world has become very intolerant of illness and physical discomfort, and such intolerant attitudes can make physical problems much more difficult to bear. With a more accepting attitude, somatic discomfort becomes less intrusive and distressing.

My first job as a clinical psychologist was working in the community psychiatric and rehabilitation service, providing services for people who had a very poor prognosis. I worked with a charismatic and inspirational Consultant Psychiatrist with whom I co-edited my first book (Watts and Bennett, 1983). He had a number of memorable dictums, one of which was 'I treat those I can, but I rehabilitate everyone'. Similarly, healing prayer may cure some people, or at least alleviate their problems, but I suggest that 'healing' can potentially make a significant contribution to the adjustment of everyone.

11

Spiritual Bodies, Apparitions and Visions

In this chapter I move from the healing of the body to the resurrection or spiritualization of the body. My focus is primarily on resurrection bodies, but I also say something about other unusual bodies, apparitions and angelic bodies. It feels a rather lonely business to be writing about the resurrection of the body in a book that is approaching religion in dialogue with science. Theology discusses the resurrection in a variety of ways but, for the most part, it evades the question of whether resurrection of the body can be expected, and how that might actually happen. Resurrection and afterlife are so far beyond ordinary experience that anyone who writes about them needs to do so with due intellectual humility. My stance in this chapter is to engage sympathetically with claims about life beyond death, and to explore their credibility in dialogue with science.

There are ways of talking about the resurrection of Jesus that place the emphasis elsewhere than on his risen body. For example, many have noticed that the risen Jesus appears to his disciples in the form of a human companion, as he did for example on the Emmaus Road. There is often ambiguity about whether Jesus appears through another human being, or in a separate body of his own. However, appearances of the risen Jesus through companions sidestep the nature of Jesus' risen body. Another approach to immortality that sidesteps the nature of a resurrection body is to see eternal life as living on eternally in the memory of God, in a way that allows some possibility of communion with the departed. However, such attempts to handle resurrection all sidestep the resurrection of the *body,* and make no attempt to examine its credibility.

For much of the Christian era there has been a stronger emphasis on the immortal soul than on the resurrection of the body, but there has been a widespread abandonment in recent decades of the view that human beings are composed of body and soul, or personality. The move away from philosophical dualism has made it harder to argue for the afterlife as survival of the soul or personality. However, survey evidence from the social sciences indicates that in the years after World War II there has been a *growth* of belief in the afterlife (Hood et al., 2018). Interestingly,

143

that has happened at the same time as belief in God has been declining. Clearly, in the popular mind, belief in the afterlife is not dependent on belief in God.

As far as I am aware, there has been no detailed investigation of how, in the popular mind, the afterlife is supposed to work, but it is presumably some kind of continued mental or spiritual existence, rather than belief in the resurrection of the body. It is worth noting that there may be a difference between the views of professional philosophers and the general public about the afterlife, and that dualism may be stronger in the general public than in academia.

Christian churches continue to say creeds which affirm belief in the resurrection. The Apostles' Creed affirms belief in the 'resurrection of the body', and the Nicene Creed looks for 'the resurrection of the dead and the life of the world to come'. However, in as far as there is belief in life beyond death in general society, it seems to be belief in some kind of spiritual afterlife rather than the resurrection of the body.

It is not only among theologians that there is a lack of defence of the resurrection of the body. It is also to be found in church leaders as well. I have already mentioned that I wrote this book during the coronavirus pandemic. With thousands dying from coronavirus, you might have thought that church leaders would have taken the opportunity to affirm belief in the resurrection of the body. However, there was a conspicuous silence about that from most mainline church leaders, just as there was silence about the healing of the body. For example, the Archbishop of Canterbury chose to speak on Easter Day 2020 about faith in life *before* death, rather than about the resurrection.

The phrase 'resurrection of the body' may be uttered at funeral services, but my sense is that people mostly don't know quite what is meant by it, nor whether or not they believe it. Sometimes preachers at funerals talk passionately about the resurrection of the body, but I sense that many people just find that embarrassing and inappropriate, and it does not convince anyone. I once attended a funeral service in the so-called 'Christian Community' inspired by Rudolf Steiner. It was unlike any other funeral service I have been to in that everyone present had no doubt whatsoever that the person who had died had passed on to a different mode of spiritual existence. A funeral at which the whole community believed in life beyond death felt completely different from any other funeral that I have attended.

What is a 'Resurrection Body'?

If the idea of resurrection of the body is to be rendered at all credible, it is necessary to get some clarity about what is meant by a 'resurrection body'. The thinker who I find most helpful on this is St Paul, and I start with him (1 Corinthians 15). Paula Gooder (2016) has provided an accessible account of Pauline thinking about the body.

It is helpful to recall the distinction discussed in Chapter 2 between body and flesh. The way St Paul develops that distinction is that some bodies are bodies of flesh and blood, but that does not necessarily apply to all bodies. There can be bodies of flesh, but there are also spiritual bodies. Bodies of flesh are mortal and perishable, whereas spiritual bodies are immortal and imperishable. Spiritual bodies are derived from mortal bodies but are not the same as them. They are the results of the spiritual transformation of the body of flesh and blood. As St Paul puts it, 'we will all be changed' (1 Corinthians 15.52). The question is what is the nature of that change.

It is entirely consistent with the resurrection stories in the gospel to say that the body of the risen Jesus was not an ordinary body of flesh and blood. For one thing, Jesus was not immediately recognizable. Mary, outside the empty tomb, mistook him for the gardener. The two disciples on the Emmaus road had a lengthy conversation with someone who they took to be a stranger before they broke bread with him and, only then, recognized him to be Jesus. Jesus is seen only by those who believe in him, and through the eyes of faith.

Also, according to the gospels, the body of the risen Jesus could come and go in ways that are quite different from what is possible for an ordinary body of flesh and blood. On Easter evening, when the disciples were behind closed doors, Jesus suddenly appears among them, apparently without having come through the door. After 40 days, he takes his leave of them, in some kind of levitation into the sky, something that would not be possible for a body of flesh and blood. So, both St Paul's exposition of the concept of a resurrection body, and the resurrection narratives in the Gospels, agree that the body of the risen Jesus is not an ordinary body, but some different kind of body, what St Paul calls a 'spiritual body'.

Tom Wright has undertaken a very thorough discussion of how resurrection is understood in the New Testament (Wright, 2017), which can be summarized as follows (see White, 2006). Firstly, risen life is embodied. It is not easy to discern exactly what kind of embodiment is envisaged, but it is clearly not just a disembodied soul. Second, the story of our lives will continue beyond death; the death of the body is not the end of the narrative about us. Third, there is an expectation of some kind of place to which we will go, such as the 'many mansions' of which Jesus speaks, even if there are questions about what is meant by such language.

There is a difficult balance to be struck here. The New Testament envisages some kind of body, but one that is so different from anything we know that it is hard to understand what is meant. The result is that, in the Christian tradition, people have sometimes gone to one extreme, envisaging a completely disembodied existence, and sometimes gone to the other extreme and envisaged a body which is very much like those that we have now.

The body of each person changes over time, and there has been a lot of discussion about exactly what the resurrection body of each person will be like. How old will we be, for example? What teeth will we have? I think Candida Moss (2019) is right in saying that discussions of such issues generally says more about the prevailing assumptions about bodies at the time than it does about resurrection bodies. Such speculation about the exact physical features of a resurrection body seems to me to mis-understand what St Paul is trying to say in explaining that a resurrection body will be spiritual, immortal, and imperishable. Such a body will be radically different from our present bodies. It seems implicit that many things that are defined in one way or another in bodies of flesh and blood will remain undefined in spiritual bodies.

Torrance and Steiner

There are two twentieth-century thinkers that I find helpful in grappling with what the resurrection body might be. One is Thomas Torrance, the distinguished Scottish reformed theologian whose magisterial book *Space, Time and Resurrection* (Torrance, 1976) is one of the highpoints of theology in the latter half of the twentieth century. The other is the Austrian clairvoyant, philosopher and polymath, Rudolf Steiner (1861–1925). He was much influenced by theosophy (though he eventually rejected it), and drew on a wide variety of sources, including traditional Hindu wisdom. However, he held a very strong view of the centrality of Christ to the unfolding and transformation of the created order, and the objectivity of the changes that came about through Christ. He was grap-pling with these issues in the years around the First World War (Steiner, 1991), and his ideas have been developed by various people, such as Emil Bock (1955) and Alfred Heidenreich (1969).

I think there is substantial agreement between Steiner and Torrance in general approach, though they differ on the details. Both would no doubt be very surprised to be bracketed with the other, though I think their approaches to the resurrection body are variations on the same theme. Both Torrance and Steiner understand that the resurrection body can only be understood if it is recognized that it depends on some quite fundamental changes, brought about by Christ, which radically change things, conceptually and ontologically. They both understand that there is much more going on in the resurrection of Jesus than his somehow managing to reappear again in a different kind of body. For both of them, the resurrection body of Jesus arises from, and is made possible by, more fundamental changes, though they formulate those fundamental changes rather differently.

Torrance formulates things in terms of Jesus changing the nature of space and time through his resurrection. The Resurrection happens within space and time; it can be dated within history. However, for Torrance, the more significant thing is that the resurrection represents a transformation of space and time by Christ. He sees this, not as a setting aside of space and time, but as *redeeming* space and time. He particularly emphasizes the transformation of time, with eternity breaking in on historical time. The Resurrection happens at a particular date in history, but it also transforms time so that the resurrection becomes a continuous event. There is a healing of the relationship between the mode of reality that is within space and time and the mode that is unconstrained by it.

Torrance thinks that this led Christian thinkers in the early centuries to work out a new understanding of the nature of space and time, something which was lost in the 'container universe' of Isaac Newton. However, Torrance claims, more recent physics stemming from Einstein has redis-covered a view of space and time that is strikingly similar to that found in the early centuries of the Christian tradition.

Torrance draws attention to various aspects of the new scientific view of the universe which help to support his position. That includes a dynamic view of the world as a continuously integrated network of fields and forces. It also includes a relational view of space and time, rejecting the Newtonian view of absolute space and time as providing a 'container' universe. Torrance also makes use of a multilevel view of the structure of human knowledge in which things can be described at multiple different levels, and he sees that the universe itself has a stratified structure with different levels of reality.

Steiner, in a parallel way, holds that Christ, through his resurrection, fundamentally changed the nature of the relationship between matter and the spirit. He sees this relationship as having gone awry in what is known as the 'fall', and it is the work of Christ in his resurrection to restore a healthy relationship between the material and the spiritual. That is what makes the resurrection body possible. As Steiner sees it, matter and spirit were separated from each other at the fall; matter became denser, and was cut off from spirit. He sees Christ as having re-established the possibility of a closer relationship between matter and spirit, which in turn made Jesus' own particular resurrection body possible.

Both Steiner and Torrance understand the resurrection to be the culmination of something that was going on before the crucifixion. It was not just some kind of emergency correction of what went wrong at his crucifixion. The Eastern tradition of Christianity similarly sees the spiritual body as co-existing with the body of flesh and blood prior to death, but obscured until death. It is a view developed particularly by Kallistos, a fourteenth-century Patriarch of Constantinople, which can be found in the Philokalia.

Steiner's view is that Jesus' earthly body had been lived in by a remarkable spiritual being, and that had already made an impact on his body of flesh and blood, preparing the way for his resurrection body to emerge. The earthly Jesus already represented a remarkable integration of matter and spirit. For Steiner, the work of transforming the relationship between matter and spirit was already well advanced by the time of the crucifixion, though it reached its culmination in the resurrection.

It is surprising that there has not been more theological discussion of the relationship between the story of Jesus' transfiguration (e.g. Luke 9.28–36) and his resurrection. It seems that the transfigured body seen by Jesus' closest disciples was a step towards the process of creating the resurrection body through which Jesus manifested himself to his disciples. It may be significant that, according to the gospel narrative, it was only after the success of the transfiguration that Jesus decided to move towards his death. It is as though the transfiguration was a kind of dress rehearsal for the resurrection.

It helped Steiner in developing his understanding of the resurrection body that he was working with a more complex conceptual framework for the human being than the dualistic one of body and soul that has been so pervasive in the Christian era. Steiner never works with less than a fourfold conception of a human being, though in places he elaborates that fourfold scheme further. His fourfold scheme is similar, though not quite identical with, St Paul's scheme of spirit, psyche, body and flesh.

Steiner also makes a distinction between the etheric and physical bodies. The etheric body is a body of formative forces. The relationship between the etheric and physical body in Steiner is analogous to the relationship between the spiritual body and a body of flesh and blood in St Paul. St Paul's point is that the resurrection body is a body of some kind, but not a body of flesh and blood. Steiner sees the etheric body as playing a crucial role in the appearances of the risen Jesus, and in his eventual second coming. It was essentially a resurrection of Jesus' etheric body rather than his physical body. This is a close counterpart to St Paul saying that the resurrection body was a spiritual body, not a body of flesh and blood.

Rudolf Steiner and those influenced by him have a strong view of the transformation of matter that began with the transformation of the physical body of Jesus, so that Jesus' body gradually became no longer an ordinary physical body, but one that was shot through with spirit and transformed by it. We can speculate that this transformative process may have begun at Jesus' baptism, when the Spirit came upon Jesus in a new way, and reached a provisional culmination at his transfiguration.

Teilhard de Chardin

The transformation of matter represented in the resurrection stories is seen in the Christian tradition as what St Paul calls a 'first fruits', blazing the trail for something that eventually happens more pervasively. The French Jesuit palaeontologist, Teilhard de Chardin, has developed a more comprehensive view of this spiritualization of matter, in which the sharp division between matter and spirit is gradually overcome in the whole of creation, with spirit being materialized and matter being spiritualized (Teilhard de Chardin, 1955). His vision provides a helpful perspective from which to understand the resurrection body of Jesus.

Teilhard de Chardin was once widely regarded as an inspirational thinker, but he has been under a cloud for a while. I think that stemmed from the fact there has been very little acceptance of his views among scientists, which has made theologians cautious about him. My own view is that the scientific rejection of Teilhard de Chardin has more to do with dogmatic scientism than with current scientific theory or data. However, there has recently been a revival of theological interest in Pierre Teilhard de Chardin, by Celia Deane-Drummond (2017), David Grummett (2005), and Ursula King (2015) and others. Just as Torrance argues that his view of how Jesus transforms space and time is consistent with the new physics, so one can argue that Teilhard de Chardin is consistent with the new physics of the twentieth century (Davies, 1983). Physics now knows that 'matter' is not the hard, solid stuff we used to take it to be.

Teilhard de Chardin's view of the gradual spiritualization of matter potentially offers a way of handling one of the most difficult problems at the interface of science and religion. It is hard to reconcile the Christian fundamental hope for God's creation with the scientific prediction that the universe will gradually disperse, cool, and become unable to support life. That has led John Polkinghorne, who generally dislikes an interventionist view of divine action, to resort to postulating that God will create a new heaven and earth, to rescue his creation (Polkinghorne, 2002). However, Teilhard de Chardin's view of the gradual spiritualization of matter implies that the assumptions on which scientific predictions of the far future are based will cease to hold true (Watts, 2012).

Appearances

The Gospels describe the appearances of the risen Jesus to his disciples as happening particularly in the days immediately following the crucifixion. This period of frequent manifestation of Jesus to his disciples is said to last 40 days, and to come to an end with his ascension into heaven. For Torrance, the Ascension marks a change to a new plane of existence that is unconstrained by space and time. Steiner suggests that there is normally a period of about 40 days after physical death in which the etheric body hovers around, and that Jesus made use of that time to manifest himself to his disciples, and was able, at will, to use his etheric body to manifest himself in material form (Steiner, 1991). In this view, the Ascension marks the end of the association of Jesus with a particular time and place.

Nevertheless, the tradition maintains that there were continuing manifestations or apparitions of Jesus after the 40 day period. The most significant one, described in the New Testament, is Jesus' appearance to St Paul on the road to Damascus. However, over the years there have been many other such appearances. Phillip Wiebe has for many years been collecting reports of apparitions of Jesus (Wiebe, 2014). For example, Hugh Montefiore, later Bishop of Birmingham, described Jesus appearing to him at the age of sixteen and saying 'follow me'. As a Jew, Montefiore knew almost nothing about Jesus at the time, and it was only later that he read the gospels and became aware that Jesus had said those words to his original disciples. Wiebe describes other appearances of Jesus in recent decades for which there is apparently quite strong corroborating objective evidence.

There are many reports of ghosts, apparitions and visions of various kinds. They are mainly of the departed, but sometimes of the living. There is no doubt that such reports are significantly influenced by a variety of cultural and psychological factors, and Rodney Stark (1999) has set out a helpful framework that indicates the various factors that are relevant. However, the question is whether *all* apparitions of the departed can be explained in that way, or whether there are some that cannot. There is a tendency here for people to read the evidence in a way that confirms their presuppositions. Those who believe that all such apparitions can be explained away in natural terms find evidence of that, whereas those who believe in supernatural or paranormal experiences find evidence of that. There is a marked confirmatory bias at work.

Eysenck and Sargent (1982) helpfully set out some of the features of reports of an apparition that would point towards it *not* being just some kind of hallucination. That includes where several people see the apparition independently in the same place and time, or where there is repeated observation of a particular apparition in the same place but by different people at different times. The extensive Census of Hallucinations carried out in the nineteenth century with 17,000 people found a number of strong cases of dying persons appearing at the time of death, including some cases of which there were independent witnesses and where the time of death could not have been known or predicted (Tyrrell, 1973).

There are also interesting reports of a living person appearing around the time of death, even when the person to whom they appear could not have known they were dying, or where apparitions give some information to the person to whom they appear that they could not have known independently. Laurens Van der Post (1976) has reported that his psychologist friend, C. G. Jung, appeared to him while he was on an ocean voyage. Jung stood on a hilltop and waved his stick saying 'I'll be seeing you'. It was only when Van der Post reached port that he realized that the apparition of Jung had occurred at the time of Jung's death. He interpreted it as an example of what Jung called 'synchronicity'.

Disturbing Presences

The presence of the departed is not always benign and there are also many reports of ghosts or other presences hanging around a particular place in a way that feels disturbing. John Pearce-Higgins, once Vice-Provost of Southwark Cathedral, developed a particular ministry with spirits of the departed who, as he put it, had not gone to their proper rest. He suggested that most people who seek exorcism or ministry of the deliverance are actually troubled by spirits of the departed rather than by evil spirits. That implies that what is required is some kind of requiem to help the departed go to their rest, rather than an exorcism of an evil spirit.

Pearce-Higgins tells the story of an unhappy, lonely, elderly vicar who, after his death, was felt by the young family who moved into the vicarage to be hanging around in an uncomfortable and unsettling way (Pearce-Higgins, 1973). Pearce-Higgins was called out to help and, after taking stock of the situation, instructed the former vicar to go to his proper rest. It seems that the spirit of that vicar left the vicarage, but was then felt to be hanging around the vestry. Pearce-Higgins returned, this time with his diocesan bishop, presumably Mervyn Stockwood. After further discernment they concluded that the former vicar was carrying a burden of guilt that was making it difficult for him to go to his rest. The bishop then pronounced absolution to the departed spirit. Pearce-Higgins remarks laconically that after that they had no more trouble.

There have also been many reports of people reporting factual information that they claim to have known from previous lives, things that they could not have known by ordinary means but which can be corroborated. Some of these reports have proved to be correct, and are inexplicable by ordinary sources of knowledge (Stevenson, 2005). They do not necessarily imply reincarnation and could arise from some other kind of contact with a deceased person. However, they are among the most compelling reports of some kind of contact with a deceased person. There are too many strong cases to be easily dismissed.

Angels

There also numerous reports of encounters with angels, often guardian angels, who are reported to have saved people from disaster. Similar issues arise about the believability of such reports as with apparitions and ghosts. Belief in guardian angels is widespread. An Associated Press/ GfK poll (2011) in the US found that 77% of the sample studied believed in angels; and a Mori poll in the UK found that 46% believed in angels (Ipsos MORI, 2007). Both surveys found that women are more likely than men to believe in angels. Belief in angels was more common in people of lower socio-economic status.

Both polls also found more belief in angels among those who believe in God; but also, strikingly, found significant belief in angels among those who did *not* believe in God. The Mori poll found that 19% of those who did *not* believe in God, *did* believe in angels. I suspect that belief in angels is higher among those who think that the spiritual side of life is important, among those who also believe in departed souls, and among those who meditate on a regular basis. In the Mori poll, three quarters of those who said they believed in angels also said their guardian angels had helped them in everyday life. Belief in angels is not just an abstract belief; it is often rooted in experience. There is a large popular literature of experiences with guardian angels, including the bestselling books of Lorna Byrne (e.g. Byrne, 2010).

Reports from those who see angels say that they have some kind of body, but a spiritual body rather than a body of flesh and blood. Aquinas' formulation was that angels did not actually have bodies, or at least not physical bodies, but that they could assume bodies (Jones, 2011). Spiritual bodies may be somewhat akin to angelic bodies. The bodies of angels are usually described as beautiful, but are of no particular age or gender. Guardian angels are said to stay close to the people they are guarding and are said to be beings of light.

There are quite precise descriptions of the properties of angels in late medieval theologians such as Aquinas. As Rupert Sheldrake and Matthew Fox (1996) have pointed out, the properties of angels set out in medieval theological literature are strikingly similar to the properties of photons in twentieth-century physics. It is a remarkable example of theology anticipating scientific theory. Angels have often been said to be made of fire, but they seem to have the properties of light.

So What are Spiritual Bodies?

In the light of these various findings about apparitions and spiritual bodies, it seems that the appearance of Jesus to his disciples may not have been unique; there are reports of somewhat similar appearances of other people after death. Nevertheless, the appearances of Jesus to his followers were remarkably strong and compelling. There is a parallel with the point made in the last chapter that healings were not unique to Jesus, but that Jesus was nevertheless a remarkable healer.

There will be some who will be resistant to the idea that anyone other than Jesus has appeared after his death, but there are too many other reports for it to be possible to claim that it was unique to Jesus. St Paul says that we will *all* be changed, and *all* will have spiritual bodies (1 Corinthians 15.52). There will also be those who are resistant to the idea that Jesus' resurrection body is being reduced to some kind of 'spook', though I believe what I am suggesting here is in line with St Paul's emphatic point that the resurrection body of Jesus is a 'spiritual' body, not a body of flesh and blood (1 Corinthians 15.50).

It is hard to conceptualize the spiritual body of the risen Jesus because we tend to operate with a sharp dichotomy between spirit and flesh. The risen body of Jesus was neither, at least not in a straightforward way. I am inclined to endorse the views of Torrance and Steiner that Jesus objectively changed the framework within which such appearances occurred, whether that is seen as redemption of space and time (as Torrance does), or as healing of the relationship between matter and spirit (as Steiner does).

The nature of a spiritual body is difficult to grasp precisely because it combines elements of matter and spirit, and is not clearly one or the other. The debate that followed the controversial remarks of Bishop David Jenkins on television about the resurrection being primarily a spiritual event, not a 'conjuring trick with bones', seemed not to grasp that basic point. Spiritual bodies are *both* transformed material bodies *and* embodied spirits. They exist in an in-between realm that defies sharp dichotomization into matter and spirit.

Spiritual Seeing and Hearing

Finally, I want to turn to how spiritual bodies are perceived. There has been much interest in the Christian tradition in the 'spiritual senses', or how people sense the divine. Like James W. Jones (Jones, 2019), I am keen to connect this with human embodiment, and I suggest that the scientific theory and research we now have on religious visions and voices is the most promising way to pursue this.

I think we need an interactional theory of spiritual seeing and hearing. On the one hand, I suggest that spiritual bodies really exist, that there really is something to be perceived. However, spiritual bodies are not seen by everyone, but only by those who are attuned to see them. That is implicit in the gospel stories about appearances of the risen Jesus, who appears only to those who believe in him; there are qualities in the perceiver that are also necessary.

I suggest that we need to weave together two strands in an account of such appearances, one concerned with revelation and the other concerned with the psychology of the perceiver. I don't see any incompatibility between these two strands. Both components are important in any satisfactory account of spiritual appearances as, for example, Christopher Knight (2016) has argued. There is also the connection between the two; visions may depend on some kind of resonance or attunement between the two. What I have in mind here is akin to Polkinghorne's suggestion that we can think about intercessory prayer in terms of resonance (Polkinghorne, 2007).

The issues that arise here are somewhat similar to those that arise in connection with discerning the presence of Christ in the Eucharist. That also seems to be perceived only by the believer and would probably not show up in a scientific analysis of the consecrated bread and wine. Some would take that as indicating that there is nothing really there, that it is all in the mind of the believer. However, I submit that it is equally compatible with an interactional account of a real spiritual presence and the human person, such as I am sketching here in terms of attunement. We have already noted what an active process human perception is. It is not like taking a photographic record. If perceiving external objects is an active process, that is even more true of perceiving visions.

The psychologist Lawrence Barsalou (Barsalou et al., 2004) has offered a good scientific proposal about how visions arise. Even where there are no observable postures or movements, there may be incipient physical actions or other patterns of activity in the nervous system (what Barsalou calls 'simulations') that underlie visions. The role of simulations in cognitive processing is ubiquitous and is apparent in perception, memory, language, thought and social cognition (e.g. Teske, 2013). It may be that it is through people performing cognitive simulations that visions arise, in religion and elsewhere.

Barsalou recognizes that many representations are rather fragmentary and have little impact, whereas religious experiences are often quite intense. Though intensity is a striking feature of religious representations, it is probably not unique to religion. Other forms of mental imagery can also sometimes be intense and in that respect become similar to religious visions.

Barsalou assumes that representations are specific to a particular modality. So, seeing a religious vision would arise out of the visual system; seeing a vision of an angel would be accompanied by a pattern of activation in the visual system similar to what would be found if someone looked at an angel in a painting. Equally, hearing a religious voice would arise out of the auditory system, and so on. So, when a religious person hears God or a spiritual being speaking to them, it will be accompanied by the same pattern of activation in the auditory system as would be found if they were listening to a human voice.

Internal simulations may also be involved in the reception of gestures made by the leader of a religious ritual. For example, in Christian liturgy, the priest makes the orant gesture at several key moments, with arms outstretched and raised, bent at the elbow and with open palms. It is a gesture of both greeting and prayer, inviting those who witness it to join in prayer. The gesture is not normally returned explicitly by the congregation. However, it would be interesting to know whether there is neurological or muscular evidence of that happening in a hidden, incipient way; rather as facial expressions are often instinctively imitated. The reception of the orant gesture might involve some covert simulation of it.

Barsalou focuses on religious visions rather than religious voices, but voices also raise a rich set of issues for simulation theory. It seems likely that when people hear or imagine voices that are not heard by others, the areas of the brain involved are not only those of speech perception but those of speech production too. Neural evidence of both speech reception and production is found with hallucinations (Frith, 1992), and it seems likely to be true of other voices that are heard subjectively, including religious voices. Hearing the voice of God is associated with inner speech (Cook, 2019).

Luhrmann (2012) has argued, on the basis of close observation of prayer experience in evangelical churches, that absorption is relevant to people hearing the voice of God in prayer, and that evangelical prayer practices result in vivid auditory and other imagery, and a pattern of attributing imagery to God. It would be very interesting to explore in more detail the role of simulation processes when people see religious visions or hear the voice of God. There are probably dimensions of individual differences that are relevant to the intensity of mental imagery, such as 'absorption' (e.g. Roche and McConkey, 1990), which is largely a measure of vivid and absorbing imagery. In turn it is correlated with openness to experience, and with the expanded boundaries of consciousness measured by scales of transliminality (Thalbourne and Delin, 1999).

In putting forward a simulation theory of religious visions, Barsalou probably assumed that visions are entirely created by the perceiver. However, I suggest that his account works equally well as the psychological side of the kind of interactional approach that I am proposing here. Simulation theory may have often assumed that there is no divine source of religious voices, but I think it is actually neutral on that point. It can equally be taken as a theory of how a genuine experience of divine voices is mediated within the central nervous system.

12

Concluding Reflections

Like most authors, I hope that this book will make a difference. I have two related objectives, one theoretical, one practical. First, I hope it will enhance our understanding of the significance of the body in religion. Second, I hope it will also enrich how religious people actually use their bodies in the practice of their religious lives.

The neglect of the body in religion is one of the symptoms of the dualism between mind and matter (or mind and body) in which Western civilization has been mired since the seventeenth century. The age of the scientific revolution saw a new, detached, objectifying attention to matter, a new sense that matter existed in its own right, in absolute time and space, independent of us, and independent of God. In other words, it gave rise to 'naturalism'.

At the same time, there was a new sense of the subjective world of inner experience. That was reflected, as we saw in Chapter 9, in a new vocabulary for the experiential aspects of emotion. In turn, that led to a new emphasis on the experiential aspects of religion, evident in the revivalisms of the eighteenth century (Wesleyanism in England etc).

What had been an integrated world polarized into an objectifying approach to matter, and a new emphasis on inner subjectivity. It has been difficult to find a way out of this persistent dualism. The new philosophy of mind that developed after the Second World War took a step in the right direction, but it has not proved to be an adequate solution. It continued to be implicitly physicalist in its assumptions, and to see matter as foundational.

We have fallen into some strange ways of talking in which we assume that our bodies are something different from ourselves. We talk about how our genes or our neurons make *us* do things; similarly, we talk about how *we* can control our bodies through willpower. We talk as though our bodies are not *us*. Little wonder that we assume that our bodies are nothing to do with our religious or spiritual lives.

I believe that the new scientific work that has developed in the last 30 years, under the banner of 'embodied cognition', will have far-reaching consequences, and will prove a crucial step towards a much-needed escape from dualism in Western civilization. It is the primary scientific resource on which I have been drawing throughout this book. It is a way of looking at things that sees mind and body as intimately enmeshed together. It puts mind and body back together again, after a long period of our seeing people in fragmented, atomistic terms.

I think embodied cognition gives us an opportunity to understand how imbued with mind and soul our bodies can be, and how intimately connected with our bodies our mental and spiritual life is. I believe it can lead to a new view of the religious life, one in which we can understand afresh the intimate connection between embodied practices and spiritual experience.

I started writing this book largely for academic reasons. I realized that many of my academic interests in religion were concerned with the role of the body in some way or other. I felt that I had been circling around a centre that I had never quite addressed, and I wanted to bring together these multiple strands of interest in the role of the body in religion. However, as I end the book, the questions I am left with are largely practical. I am asking myself what it would look like to actually live out the spiritual and religious life in a more embodied way.

I remarked in the introduction that the forms of religious and spiritual practice that are growing most conspicuously at the moment are those that are body-focused. In Chapter 3, on the evolutionary origins of religion, I argued that trance dancing is the physical practice out of which religion emerged. Of contemporary forms of Christianity, it is Pentecostalism that is most obviously the heir to that primeval form of religion, and Pentecostalism is the form of Christianity that is growing fastest in the present day.

In Chapter 5, I looked at some of the physically demanding spiritual activities in which people engage, such as pilgrimage, that are increasingly popular. They can provide people with a 'flow' experience that liberates them from the multi-tasking that normally characterizes our lives, and can become a spiritual practice in themselves. In Chapter 6, I looked at how meditation can enable people to lead a spiritual life that rebalances the endless discursive thinking in which many are engaged. Meditation can help them focus on their bodies in a way that enables them to live more fully in the world of experience and in the present moment. Mindfulness is currently the form of body-focused meditation that is most popular; it is spreading like wildfire, bringing healing to many people, giving them a route out of the emotional traps in which they have become mired. These are currently some of the most conspicuous forms of religion and spirituality that make full use of the body, but I suspect that they are not the only ones. There are many other ways in which people who are seeking a richer spiritual life could make better use of their bodies.

To be personal for a moment, I think I have always been a thoughtful, reflective, self-aware person, even though I no doubt have blind spots about myself. For me, as for many religious people, my spiritual life exists primarily in my mind. But I wonder what it would look like if it were otherwise, if it were primarily about what I *did*, or if there was a better balance between thinking, feeling and doing. I have never really managed this. My religious and spiritual life has been a mirror of the highly reflective person that I am.

It is natural for all of us to gravitate to the kind of spiritual practices that come most easily to us; it is almost inevitable that we will start by doing that. However, there is always the possibility of embracing modes of spirituality that don't come so naturally to us. That could lead to a helpful rebalancing of our personalities, and lead us on a journey towards wholeness. So, I conclude by making some practical suggestions arising from the previous chapters. I make these suggestions as much to myself as to others.

I invite those who pray to consider what posture to adopt when they do so. Most of those who pray probably think that it doesn't make much difference what posture they adopt. While I agree that you can pray in any position, I think it *does* make a difference. Prayer works best if you go into a special state of mind, and having a particular posture that you normally use for prayer can help you to do so. After a while, just adopting your prayer posture (kneeling or whatever else) can help you to make the transition into prayer consciousness quickly and effectively.

You may also want to try being creative about the posture you adopt when you pray. You may even try praying silently, and improvise some body language that expresses your prayer. Or you can use minimal words, but use them in a way that enables you to really hear and feel a particular word or words in your mind.

If you meditate already, adopting a particular physical posture will probably be an integral part of your meditation practice. If you have not yet explored the possibilities of body-focused meditation you may want to consider that. As we have seen, some forms of meditation are very focused on the body. Many find that, once they get into them, such practices are very healing and restorative.

There are ways of expressing emotions as part of spiritual practice. For example, the shedding of tears has had a particularly important place in religion. Spiritual tears will not necessarily be tears of sorrow, they can also be tears of joy, or tears that mark an experience of spiritual transformation.

You may already be involved in forms of public worship that make explicit use of your body. If you come from the Charismatic or Pentecostal traditions you may already be raising your hands in worship, or moving your whole body. You will notice that the effect of doing that in the company of other people who are doing the same thing seems to be more powerful than doing it on your own.

Alternatively, if you are in the Catholic tradition, you may find it helpful to join in synchronized movements in church, such as everyone genuflecting together when the sacrament is exposed in Benediction. Synchronized movements have a more powerful effect than each person doing their own thing, and transform a group of individuals into sensing that together they are the body of Christ.

You may also want to explore whether there is a useful place in your spiritual life for physically demanding practices such as a pilgrimage walk. It may be something that you do with other religiously committed people, as you journey towards a place of religious significance.

Alternatively, you might consider how you can take physical activities that are normally entirely secular and imbue them with spiritual significance. You can do that by the intentions with which you carry them out, or by the prayer that surrounds them. A workout in the gym, weeding the garden, or doing the washing up, can become, in effect, a spiritual practice. Work can become prayer.

You may want to consider the role of physical discipline or abstinence in your spiritual life. Such practices are best entered into positively, as an exacting form of spiritual training, rather than in a spirit of self-punishment. Food abstinence may be a good initial focus, as most people in the developed world over-eat, and there are medical and environmental benefits from reducing food consumption, as well as spiritual ones.

If you have not yet engaged in prayers for healing of the body you may want to consider that. In some Christian circles healing prayer is normal, but in others it is considered strange. I come from a religious background in which healing prayer was not the norm but, as I have found my way into it, I have been surprised by just how beneficial it can be. It does not always deliver results, of course, but my experience is that it works sufficiently often to be worthwhile, even in strictly practical terms.

In this last chapter, I have abandoned the usual academic caution and have chosen to summarize some of the conclusions of the earlier chapters in the form of hints and tips for a more embodied spiritual life. Different things are helpful for different people and I am not suggesting that you take up every suggestion offered here. However, if you have a spiritual life at all, there may be things here that resonate with you and will help you to make your spiritual practice more a matter of the whole person, including your body.

In conclusion, there are three things that I hope that readers will take away from this book:

- We are whole people, with minds and bodies that are closely integrated. We are not reducible to our bodies, neither do we need to leave our bodies behind. We are embodied souls and ensouled bodies.
- Our bodies are such an integral part of us that we cannot properly understand our religious and spiritual lives without taking full account of the role of our bodies.
- Our spiritual lives flourish better if we make good use of our bodies. We misunderstand things if we imagine that we need to ignore our bodies to soar into a spiritual realm. On the contrary, wise use of our bodies helps us to connect with God.

Appendix

The Body in World Faith Traditions

SARA SAVAGE

Bodies are often considered peripheral to religion whose 'real' business is belief. In fact, sensorimotor experience provides the foundation for cognitive systems, and religious traditions make great use of the body – both as metaphor and as an instrument for carrying out various ritual practices. Many religious thinkers reflect on the body in terms of its significance for achieving spiritual goals, presenting it as a hindrance, a source of sin, something to be covered, disciplined, or denied. But others regard it as a means of achieving higher states, and in some traditions the body is experienced as a vehicle for divinity itself. In this essay we are primarily concerned with the 'lived body', which entails 'having a body' consciously and reflectively in the context of a religious life world, as opposed to merely 'being a body' unconsciously and unreflectively.

Since the Enlightenment, religion has all too often been understood as something 'detachable' from the rest of culture. It is often reified as an entity or free-standing category. While this is a useful approach for some analyses, it is inadequate for the topic at hand. The experience of living in a human body is thoroughly culturally enmeshed. This complexity forces the first question: where then do we start?

This essay will extend the largely Christian focus of Fraser Watts in this volume and will survey the role of the body in the major faith traditions. Arbitrarily, we begin with the three monotheisms – Judaism, Christianity, and Islam – in terms of their impact on the lived body. We then look, more briefly, at the life worlds of Hinduism and Buddhism. In each case, we consider sacred texts that inform religious beliefs about the body, as well as the specific bodily practices involved in prayer, ritual and dance. However, there is a wide range of views in every faith tradition, and it would be wrong to suggest that all adherents to any religion agree in their views about the body, or in their embodied practices. Important areas of divergence both across and within faiths include:

- the degree of dualism (the body conceptualized as clearly distinct from the soul)
- whether the body is a means to a (spiritual, sacred) end or whether the body as it is lived is important in itself
- the degree to which the body is 'gendered' in ritual practice (with implications for gender hierarchy)
- the degree of disjunction between stated beliefs about the body and how those beliefs are enacted, or subverted, by ritual practices.

Psychology and Posture

Straus notes that the upright posture is, from an evolutionary perspective, the defining, essential, and unique organizing feature of the human species, from which all human faculties flow (Straus, 1952, p. 531). Walking on two legs permits the flexible and articulate mobility of arms and hands. This, in turn, enables us to make tools. It encourages a longer vista, and a dominating, objectifying attitude towards the world, which contrasts with the earthbound, food-orientated, immediate perspective of quadrupeds. Action in horizontal, lateral space is largely governed and directed by vision; sight is more important to humans than bite, as indicated by our forward-facing eyes and relatively small jaw.

Humans do not spring from the womb with these abilities in place (Straus, 1952, p. 534). Every young child has to master an upright posture, learning to walk by trial and error. This achievement continues through life, as we re-master the upright posture every morning after the nightly 'collapse' of sleep (Straus, 1952, p. 535). When upright, our bodies are symmetrical and balanced, but movement produces varying degrees of asymmetry and loss of balance. Walking is 'a continually arrested falling' – the whole weight shifts forward, first falling forward from one leg, and catching that fall as the weight shifts to the other leg, repeating this rhythmic pattern (Straus, 1952, p. 542). This alternation between the stability of upright posture and its relinquishment is a fundamental physical reality underlying human bodily experience.

It is unsurprising, therefore, that many of the metaphors we live by refer to this vertical dimension: happy is up, sad is down; good is up, bad is down (Lakoff and Johnson, 1980). As Straus observes, the ten commandments are revealed to Moses on Mount Sinai, but the underworld and inferno are located below (Straus, 1952, p. 536). To be upright is to be righteous, a pre-condition for relationship with the divine. Marks of respect commonly involve a modification of the vertical position of dominance – when we bow, shake hands or kneel, we volun-tarily relinquish the upright posture that we have previously striven to achieve (Straus, 1952, p. 539).

In *A Different Existence*, J. H. van den Berg notes the evenly balanced, symmetrical posture of those in prayer (as opposed to the 'contrapposto' of a relaxed position), arguing that it emphasizes their concentration on a single task:

> Why, within the memory of man, is the attitude of prayer a symmetrical one? Because the world of the praying person ... has a direction, a direction without conditions, without roundabout ways. He who prays, is praying, expelling all maybes of the things around him for a moment; or rather, that is what he is trying to do. (Van den Berg, 1972, p. 57)

Van den Berg contrasts this with the asymmetrical attitude of the adolescent, for whom everything is 'dubious' and without direction. We find this contrast mirrored in ritual practice, which, we will see in this chapter, makes great use of symmetry, with only occasional use of asymmetry.

From these general observations, we now proceed to the experience of the lived body within major religious cultures.

Judaism

Texts

Given the intermingling of Egyptian, Canaanite, Babylonian, Persian, Greek, Roman, Arab and European influences over nearly four millennia, there is no homogenous Jewish view of the human body. Yet certain writings on the body have particular authority. First and foremost is the Torah, which contains the first five books of the Jewish canon (Genesis, Exodus, Leviticus, Numbers and Deuteronomy). It is traditionally attrib-uted to Moses (de Lange, 2003).

Creation

Genesis begins with two accounts of creation. The first is characterized by divine transcendence – the phases of creation follow immediately from God's commands. Humans are created on the sixth day, after the other living creatures:

> Then God said, 'Let us make humankind in our image, according to our likeness' ... So God created humankind in his image, in the image of God he created them, male and female he created them. (Genesis 1.26–27)[1]

This is followed by God's command to be 'fruitful and multiply' and his judgement that the created world was 'very good'.

The second creation account emphasizes God's immanence (Genesis 2.4b–23). The first man, Adam, is formed from dust, and God gives him life by breathing into his nostrils. God later makes the first woman, Eve, from one of Adam's ribs. The two live in the Garden of Eden, and although they are naked they feel no shame. This innocence does not last, as both Adam and Eve eat fruit from a forbidden tree (Genesis 3). They become aware of the difference between good and evil, realize their nakedness, and are punished by God for their disobedience. Women are henceforth subjected to great pain in childbirth and subordinated to their husbands, men are forced to labour for food, and all humans are condemned to die.

Other scriptural authors have taken up this emphasis on the transience of the human body. The Psalmist writes, 'my flesh and my heart may fail, but the strength of God is the strength of my heart and my portion for ever' (Psalm 73.26). In a similar vein, the Prophet Isaiah declares that 'all people are grass, their constancy is like the flower of the field ... The grass withers, the flower fades; but the word of our God will stand for ever' (Isaiah 40.6,8).

Body and soul

Taken together, these passages might suggest that the human body, created perfect, became an encumbrance as a result of the first sin. But they do not contain the now familiar idea that the supposedly 'true' human comprises an immortal soul, housed temporarily in a bodily container. Rather, in the Torah, the human person is presented as a single entity, which is a complex mixture of physical, mental, emotional, intentional and spiritual attributes. Jewish faith requires all these attributes to be used in the covenantal service of Yahweh:

> Hear, O Israel: The Lord is our God, the Lord alone. You shall love the Lord your God with all your heart, and with all your soul, and with all your might. (Deuteronomy 6.4–5)

In the Jewish canon, the word used to denote the soul is often *nephesh*, which is translated as 'psyche' in Greek. There is no separate word for body, suggesting that it was not conceived separately from the soul.[2] It is therefore unsurprising that the afterlife has been construed in bodily terms, though some Jewish writers (including Philo) later emphasized the distinction between body and soul (Boyarin, 1995, p. 5). This later dualism betrays the influence of Greek thought – Plato famously claimed that philosophy is the practice of death, because death frees the soul from the inconvenience of embodiment (Plato, 1914).

Visual representations

The second of the ten commandments forbids the Jews to create idols, 'whether in the form of anything that is in heaven above, or that is on the earth beneath, or that is in the water under the earth' (Exodus 20.4). This has been taken to include that God is not to be represented in any earthly form.

Marriage and sexuality

Yet marriage and family life are highly valued in Judaism. The command to 'multiply and fill the earth' is taken seriously, and it is incumbent upon all males to fulfil this in the context of marriage. Heterosexual relations between a man and his wife are the only sanctioned form of intercourse, and are regulated by several divisions of the *Mishnah*, including *Ketubot* and *Niddah*.

Ketubot discusses the obligations of a married couple to one another. Men have a sexual duty towards their wives (*onah*), although the regularity with which they must fulfil this duty depends on their profession (Neusner, 1988; Ketubot 5.6).[3] One medieval writer advised husbands to 'please her heart and mind and cheer her in order to bring together your thoughts with hers and your intention with hers,' adding that 'you should attract her with charming words (Anderson, 1998, p.7).'[4] In keeping with the scriptural account of God's punishment of Eve, it is recognized that a wife will feel passion for her husband, but will be dependent upon him to take the lead.

Niddah is concerned primarily with menstruation (Neusner, 1988). Menstrual blood was assigned a special power, as it signifies the life or death of a potential living organism. The loss of menstrual blood is associated with death and carries with it the taboo of death; the absence of blood signifies potential life as the possibility of pregnancy remains. The loss of semen through nocturnal emission or masturbation is similarly understood as a waste of potential life. In Genesis, Onan is put to death by God for having allowed his semen to spill to the ground (Genesis 38.9–10).

According to the *Mishnah*, the wife's primary role is within the home. To serve her husband, she '(1) grinds flour (2) bakes bread (3) does laundry (4) prepares meals (5) feeds her child (6) makes the bed (7) works in wool,' and performs other similar tasks (Neusner, 1988). Women also have a special role in the ritual of the Sabbath, in lighting the candles. But whereas male births are celebrated with the circumcision ceremony, and male entry into puberty is celebrated with a bar mitzvah, female births and female puberty have traditionally passed without any special rite (Greenberg, 1990, p. 5). Women were not required to have religious instruction, and have usually been excluded from religious leadership (until recently within reformed traditions).

Clean and unclean

The Jewish laws of cleanliness and uncleanliness are set out in the third book of the Torah, Leviticus, and are discussed extensively in Rabbinic literature. Some laws concern animals; those that are deemed unclean fall outside proscribed groupings. For instance, animals that 'chew the cud' are clean if they have divided hooves, and animals that have divided hooves are clean if they chew the cud. Camels, rock-badgers and pigs do not meet these requirements, and Jews are therefore forbidden to touch or eat them (Leviticus 11.3–8).

Other rules pertain to human cleanliness. Menstruating women are unclean until seven days after the flow of blood has stopped. Men are made unclean by sexual discharges. Diseases like leprosy render sufferers, clothing and housing unclean:

> The priest shall make an examination, and if there is a white swelling in the skin that has turned the hair white, and there is quick raw flesh in the swelling, it is a chronic leprous disease in the skin of his body. The priest shall pronounce him unclean. (Leviticus 13.9–11)

Leviticus includes instructions for restoring oneself to cleanliness. The purification of lepers is a lengthy affair, beginning with the slaughter of a clean bird and the release of another clean bird that has been dipped in the first bird's blood. It continues with bathing, shaving and cleansing with oil, concluding on the eighth day with an offering for atonement

(Leviticus 14.1–32). Houses infected with leprosy must also be cleansed, and may have to be torn down if the infection persists. Uncleanness may be spread by direct or indirect contact – during menstruation and the seven days of uncleanness that follow, any object that a woman touches becomes unclean for the rest of the day, and any person who touches it will likewise become unclean.

Contemporary Rabbinic Judaism still requires purification. On the eighth day after the menstrual flow has stopped, a woman must immerse herself in a *miqueh* (Klein, 1979, p. 514). This is a pool of natural water, usually rainwater. She must wash thoroughly in advance, and must enter the *miqueh* either naked or in a 'loose-fitting garment', adopting a posture that allows the water to touch the whole of her body (Klein, 1979, p. 514). Following this vertical descent, there is the emergence, like a new birth, into a cleansed condition. Brides also come to the *miqueh* prior to their wedding, as do converts of both sexes. There is a strong implicit message that bodies – an intrinsic part of the human person – need purification, but they are to be enjoyed, and to be used in worship of the Creator.

Liturgy

Prayer

Prayer in the Psalms reflects the vertical dimension described by Straus. It is normal for someone in prayer to be upright, 'lifting holy hands'. The fact that the hands are empty and clean signifies the open, receptive relationship with God, while the upright posture indicates the ability of the faithful to stand in his presence. The words 'Hide not your face from me' (Psalms 143.7) emphasize the psalmist's desire for a direct encounter with God, but other passages remind us of his transcendence – he is 'the Rock who is higher than I' (Psalms 61.2).

The '*Amidah*', the most important Jewish prayer, also has this vertical dimension. Indeed, its name means 'standing', because believers stand to recite it (de Lange, 2003, p. 38). Submission to God is indicated by bowing at the beginning and end of the first and eighteenth benedictions. This is a deviation from the vertical, a partial giving up of the human achievement of uprightness.

Orthodox Jews commonly sway while standing for prayer, with a bodily movement called *shuckling*. Although they remain upright, the hollowing out produced by bending at the waist is another way to indicate submission. It also imitates the body's automatic response to pain or grief – one is 'doubled over' by grief, and crumpled by pain. One twelfth-century text provides two further explanations: it may be done 'in order to arouse natural heat', or it may have resulted from the need to share books, each person bowing in turn to read the next lines of a text set down on the ground (Hallevi, 1931 p. 80).

During prayer, some may wear a shawl known as a *tallit*. Head-covering is not limited to prayer, however, and many Jews will wear a hat or skullcap every day. At weekday morning services, small boxes called *tefillin* are strapped to the head and arm, containing certain passages from the Torah (de Lange, 2003).

Sabbath meal

As Straus has argued, the ability to command lateral space with arms and hands depends on our upright, vertical posture – we require only two limbs to stand, freeing the other two for interaction with our surroundings. On the Sabbath, Jews worship the Creator by limiting such interaction. According to the *Mishnah*, they must not carry certain tools, including swords and spears. There is a list of thirty-nine forbidden activities, reflecting common activities at the time this text was compiled. These include sewing, ploughing, baking, writing and carrying (Neusner, 1988).

Yet the Sabbath is also an important time for the satisfaction of bodily needs: there is special bread, the best food is cooked, and good wine is served. There are three meals rather than the normal two. The day begins and ends with a benediction over wine: 'just as the Sabbath is ushered in with *Quiddush*, which begins with the benediction over wine, so it is ushered out with *Havdalah*, also beginning with the benediction over wine' (Klein, 1979, p. 514). The important point is that the enjoyment of bodily pleasures is bound up with gratitude towards God.

Priestly blessing

The words of the priestly blessing are taken from Numbers, the fourth book of the Torah:

The Lord spoke to Moses, saying: Speak to Aaron and his sons, saying, Thus you shall bless the Israelites: You shall say to them, The Lord bless and keep you; the Lord make his face to shine upon you, and be gracious to you; the Lord lift up his countenance upon you, and give you peace. (Numbers 6.22–26)

Traditionally, this blessing could only be pronounced by a Kohanim, a descendent of Aaron. Standing, his head covered with a prayer shawl, the priest would recite the words with his arms stretched out and his fingers spread like a lattice (Bridger and Wolk, 1976, p. 57). This is reminiscent of a passage in the Song of Songs where the lover gazes through the lattices at his beloved, but here neither the congregation nor the priest himself should look at the priest's hands (Song of Songs, 2.9). Many contemporary Reformed and Conservative congregations have abandoned the priestly blessing altogether, but it might be performed by a Rabbi.

Dance

Dance has an important place in Judaism. In the Hebrew Bible, we are told that King David 'danced before the Lord with all his might', wearing only a linen ephod (undergarment) (2 Samuel 6.4). We are also told that Aaron's sister, Miriam, 'took a tambourine in her hand; and all the women went out after her with tambourines and with dancing' (Exodus 15.20). Today, group dances are common at Jewish weddings and other social occasions, and many involve a circle formation. In the *hora*, the dancers hold the hands or touch the shoulders of their neighbours, emphasizing community (Olitzky and Isaacs, 2004, p. 106). Their concentration on footwork directs their attention towards the land.

Straus' account of posture is limited to the vertical and horizontal dimensions, but human movement has a transversal, oppositional, asymmetrical dimension as well. The human gait differs from that of the orangutan: when one steps forward with the right foot, the left shoulder moves forward in opposition, maintaining a dynamic balance termed *contrapposto*. This was represented in Greek sculpture and rediscovered in the Renaissance.

If the vertical dimension, up and down, involved in prayer and penitence signifies the human–divine relationship, the transversal dimension seems to signify naturalness, dynamic relaxation and sensuality. It is neither the upright military stance that we adopt when called to attention, nor the supine position of sleep, but the posture we have when at ease. But how often is this transverse dimension experienced in Jewish bodily rituals? It seems to have been more common *before* the nineteenth century, when reforms were introduced to improve decorum (de Lange, 2003, p. 43). In his diary entry for 14 October 1663, Samuel Pepys described a great scene of asymmetry at a Sephardi synagogue on the day of Simchat Torah, with men dancing and joyously cavorting with the Torah scrolls.

Christianity

Texts

Christian scripture is contained in the Bible. This begins with the Jewish canon, the 'Old Testament'. To this is added the New Testament, comprising four gospels that recount Christ's life and ministry (Matthew, Mark, Luke and John), an account of the first apostles (Acts), an apocalyptic text (Revelation), and a series of letters (many written by, or attributed to, the apostle Paul). The New Testament does not replace the Old Testament, but Christians follow the New Testament where the two are at odds – not least, as we shall see, by rejecting the Jewish laws of purity.

Authority is claimed for several other Christian texts. The Nicene Creed is a statement of belief shared by Christians of most denominations. The Apostles' Creed and the Athanasian Creed are common in the West. The words of certain theologians and church leaders are also held in high regard. Roman Catholics may look to Thomas Aquinas or to papal pronouncements. Protestants are influenced considerably by the writings of Luther, Calvin and the other Protestant reformers.

The Gospels: Purity, resurrection and incarnation

The Jewish food laws are explicitly overturned in the New Testament book of Acts, following a vision of the apostle Peter:

He saw the heaven opened and something like a large sheet coming down, being lowered to the ground by its four corners. In it were all kinds of four-footed creatures and reptiles and birds of the air. Then he heard a voice saying 'Get up, Peter; kill and eat.' But Peter said, 'By no means, Lord; for I have never eaten anything that is profane or unclean.' The voice said to him again, a second time, 'What God has made clean, you must not call profane.' (Acts 10.11–15)

This event is foreshadowed by Christ's own relaxed attitude towards purity laws. The gospels record that he touched a leper (Matthew 8.1–4; Mark 1.40–45; Luke 5.12–16), and that his cloak was touched by a woman who had been bleeding for twelve years (Mark 5.21–43; Matthew 9.18–26; Luke 8.40–56). In both cases, the touch is enough to heal them. Jesus makes no effort to cleanse himself from these defiling encounters, and he disregards statutes about ritual cleansing and the Sabbath. He declares that uncleanliness arises from our own evil actions, not from food or contact with other people and objects. As he puts it, 'there is nothing outside a person that by going in can defile, but the things that come out are what defile' (Mark 7.14).

This clash of frameworks brings him into conflict with the Jewish authorities. He is handed to the Romans for crucifixion and dies on a cross. In one account his side is pierced so that blood and water run out, demonstrating that his body is fully human (John 19.34). On the third day, his tomb is found empty. He appears to Mary Magdalene and later to the disciples. There are some indications that his appearance is changed; Mary does not recognize him immediately, and nor do the disciples when he appears by the Sea of Tiberias (John 20.14). Yet he still bears the marks of crucifixion, for Thomas is invited to touch the nail marks in Jesus' hands and the hole in his side (John 21.4). Crucially, he has overcome the fate of all human bodies – he has defeated death, and ascends into heaven alive in his body (yet still bearing the marks of the cross) (Acts 1.9). His death is understood to demolish the barriers between Jew and Gentile, male and female, slave and free. Hierarchy is turned on its head.

Christ's birth also has an important bodily dimension, but the gospel accounts differ significantly, and Mark does not mention it at all. Matthew and Luke claim that Jesus' virgin mother was impregnated by the Holy Spirit (Matthew 1.18; Luke 1). This might be taken as evidence that Christianity has a negative attitude towards normal sexual intercourse, but the prologue to John's gospel emphasizes the uniquely elevated status of the body in the Christian religion:

In the beginning was the Word, and the Word was with God, and the Word was God ... And the Word became flesh and lived among us, and we have seen his glory, the glory as of a father's only son, full of grace and truth. (John 1.1,14)

With these words, John proclaims that Jesus of Nazareth was no mere prophet, but God incarnate in human flesh.

Paul's Epistles

Yet some of Paul's pronouncements on the body portray it as a means of sin though, as Watts notes in this volume, he is more negative about the 'flesh' than about the 'body'. In his letter to the Romans he observes, 'with my mind I am a slave to the law of God, but with my flesh I am a slave to the law of sin' (Romans 7.25). He commands them not to succumb to bodily emotions and drives, writing, 'do not let sin exercise dominion in your mortal bodies, to make you obey their passions' (Romans 6.12). We will consider Paul's view of sexuality in more detail below. His argument in Romans may be traced back to Christ, who is said to have advised believers, 'If your right eye causes you to sin, tear it out and throw it away; it is better for you to lose one of your members than for your whole body to be thrown into hell' (Matthew 5.29).

Yet Paul's view of the body is not wholly negative. He believes that it can be misused, but he also declares that it is 'a temple of the holy spirit' (1 Corinthians 6.19). Moreover, while the Gospels tell us of the bodily resurrection of Christ, Paul foretells the bodily resurrection of believers. In his first letter to the nascent church in Corinth, he considers the form that this will take:

> What is sown is perishable, what is raised is imperishable. It is sown in dishonour, it is raised in glory. It is sown in weakness, it is raised in power. It is sown a physical body, it is raised a spiritual body. (1 Corinthians 15.42–44)

Paul affirms that Christ has conquered death. Through his own resurrection, he has reversed the curse pronounced upon Adam. At the end of our earthly life our bodies return to dust, but we are not truly dead. Rather, we are 'changed' (1 Corinthians 15.51). We do not know what form our new spiritual body will take, except that it will be imperishable and immortal (1 Corinthians 15.53). So whereas Plato insists that the philosopher's soul is freed from the encumbrance of the body at death, Paul writes that the Christian's body is transformed so that it is no longer an encumbrance.

Creeds and Church Fathers

The Apostles' Creed, which can be traced back the furthest, contains three important passages pertaining to the body. It tells us that Christ was conceived by the Holy Spirit and born of a virgin, that he rose from the dead having been buried for three days, and that others also experience bodily resurrection (Schaff and Schaff, 1983, p. 45). The Nicene Creed includes all of these claims, and also refers explicitly to the incarnation (Schaff and Schaff, 1983, pp. 58–59).

Again, this suggests a positive image of the body – God himself takes bodily form in Christ and overturns death, so that our bodies do not perish but are raised to new life. Most Christian theologians have accepted this Pauline view, though a handful have taken the Platonic stance that death is good because it frees the soul from the body. Even St Augustine, in an early work, writes that supernal light 'deigns not even to show itself to those shut up in this cage of the body' (Miles, 1979, p. 97).[5] His mature position is more orthodox; the separation of soul and body at death is an evil, as the two belong together like a husband and wife (Miles, 1979, p. 97). Hence the need for bodily resurrection, and not mere immortality of the soul.

Visual representations

Christians are strongly divided on the matter of sacred images. In Roman Catholic art, paintings and statues of religious figures are permitted, though visual representations of God are rare. Icons are an important part of Eastern Orthodoxy, but these religious images must be two-dimensional. The Protestant reformers opposed all such art – as Graham Howes explains, 'to make material images of the uncircumscribable, all-creating Creator, whose real images were already around us in the form of fellow creatures and also present at the Eucharist itself, was evident idolatry' (Howes, 2007, p. 9).

Sexuality and marriage

The gospels often subvert traditional expectations of marriage and pro-creation. We have seen that Jesus is said to be born of a virgin. He never marries, and rebuffs the claims of his immediate family upon him, and declares, 'whoever does the will of my father is my mother, brother and sister' (Matthew 12.50). His teachings emphasize liberation from prior commitments and prior bondages, and the welcome of believers into a new family of disciples.

St Paul's attitude to marriage is ambivalent. On the one hand, it saves us from sexual immorality. Paul explicitly condemns extra-marital sex, whether heterosexual or homosexual, and writes that 'it is better to marry than to be aflame with passion' (1 Corinthians 7.9). On the other hand, the Christian must focus on the second coming of Christ, and marriage may prove a distraction. He suggests this compromise:

> I think that, in view of the impending crisis, it is well for you to remain as you are. Are you bound to a wife? Do not seek to be free. Are you free from a wife? Do not seek a wife. But if you marry, you do not sin, and if a virgin marries, she does not sin. (1 Corinthians 7.26–28)

Some of Paul's epistles contain the seeds of gender equality, with the radical idea that a man's body belongs to the wife as much as her body belongs to him, and that both must submit to each other 'as unto to the Lord' (1 Corinthians 7.4). And yet, in the same letter, he adds that 'the husband is the head of his wife'. He also declares that women should not speak in church – 'if there is anything they desire to know, let them ask their husbands at home' (1 Corinthians 14.35). Many denominations still forbid the ordination of women.

Ritual

Certain rites are common to most branches of Christianity, including baptism, communion and funerals. Yet the timing of baptism, the regularity of communion, and the amount of bodily movement involved varies considerably from denomination to denomination. At various prescribed points of a Catholic service, for example, members of the congregation will bow, kneel, genuflect, and make the sign of the cross (by touching their forehead and each shoulder). In many Protestant churches, by contrast, such practices would be strongly discouraged – although the body has a largely positive status in Christian texts and doctrine, this largely has been denied ritual expression.

Baptism

Entrance into the Christian faith is celebrated by baptism, signifying the believer's identification with Christ in his death and resurrection, and the washing away of sin. Infant baptism is still the norm in the Roman Catholic, Anglican and Orthodox churches, with promises made by adult 'Godparents' on the child's behalf. The baby is held in the priest's arms; vertical movement is usually limited to the pouring or sprinkling of water on the baby's forehead. Baptists favour full immersion in adulthood (in a baptismal pool or a natural body of water), reflecting the descent of death and ascent of rebirth. Quakers understand baptism as purely inward, and do not generally baptize with water (Dandelion, 2007, p. 212).

Prayer

The common practice of kneeling to pray involves the relinquishment of the human's normal upright posture. This disarming position is usually reserved for royal or other powerful persons, and emphasizes the superiority of God. Bowing the head reveals the back of the neck, and is therefore a gesture of supreme trust and vulnerability. Placing the hands together precludes the use of a tool or weapon, and the arms are stilled from labour. The symmetrical alignment of the spine when kneeling allows a peace and stillness to be maintained in the body; breathing may become regular and deep. These calming practices facilitate a real effect – the under-arousal of the cortical system (d'Aquili and Newberg, 1999, pp. 97–102).

Behaviour in church

Church services are characterized by synchronized movement. This is a powerful blockade to individualistic behaviours in favour of those of a norm-supported group. Although the points at which the congregation sit, stand and kneel may vary between (and even within) traditions, and some may not kneel at all, they invariably make these movements in unison. Church services borrow a number of structural elements from the synagogue; in fact, unison movement is a feature of all public ritual. In church, all face forward, awaiting directions from the minister or priest, reinforcing the authority of clergy, who in some denominations ascend a pulpit to deliver sermons from 'on high'. Lateral movements are rare; any movement around the church takes the form of an orderly procession. The passing of the peace, in which individuals greet and shake hands with their neighbours, is a comparatively recent addition to services. It is sometimes fiercely boycotted by the more traditionally minded.

When entering a church, people typically modify their gait. They avoid swinging their arms, along with any other asymmetrical posture or movement. There is no written instruction that they must do so; they may be, in part, responding to the strong symmetry of church architecture. Whatever the reason, people know that they must leave their normal way of inhabiting their body outside the church door.

This is also reflected in the choice of clothing. Many people wear their best clothes to attend church, suggesting a high view of the person in

Christianity, a sense of celebration and raised status. In many denominations, priests and their assistants have special garments. In the early church, these were based on Roman patrician clothing, and this remains the inspiration for Roman Catholic and Anglican clerical wear. The Protestant reformers rejected these traditional clothes speaking of social status, and adopted a style of dress more similar to the 'ordinary person' of that period. The simple garb corresponds to a preference for 'plain speaking' as an expression of a character that is direct and straightforward.

Communion

According to the Gospels, the service of Holy Communion (also termed the Eucharist, the Mass and the Lord's Supper) was inaugurated by Christ himself. While eating with his disciples on the night that he was handed over to the Jewish authorities,

> he took a loaf of bread, and when he had given thanks, he broke it and gave it to them, saying, 'This is my body, which is given for you. Do this in remembrance of me.' And he did the same with the cup after supper, saying, 'This cup that is poured out for you is the new covenant in my blood.' (Luke 22.19–20)

Communion services vary in accordance with denominational interpretations of this command. The Roman Catholic Church teaches the doctrine of transubstantiation; during the Mass, the elements of bread and wine *become* the body and blood of Christ *in substance*, even though they retain the appearance of bread and wine. Most Anglicans reject this doctrine, maintaining that the elements are changed through Christ's *spiritual* presence.[6]

In both traditions, the change is held to occur when the elements are consecrated, when the priest may lift the wafer of bread, cover it with his hand, or make the sign of the cross above it, while recalling Christ's words. He then repeats this process with the chalice of wine. At the end of the prayer, the congregation are called forward. The priest consumes some of the bread and wine first, and whatever is left at the end. The communicants, standing or kneeling, receive a piece of consecrated bread in their hands or on their tongue. In Anglican and some Roman Catholic churches, they also receive a sip of consecrated wine.

For many Protestants, communion is nothing more than a memorial, and the bread and wine are only symbolically the body and blood of Christ. In these traditions, the emphasis is usually on preaching. The pulpit is the dominant architectural focus, not the altar. The ceremony may be far less elaborate, and in some churches the vessels containing the consecrated elements are simply passed laterally around the congregation. In contrast, a Catholic may experience the rituals of the Mass as a heightening of God's mystery and presence. The consecrated Body, here, is an end in itself.

Liturgical dance

Dance was largely forbidden by the early church as a form of worship, not least because of its associations in Greek culture with sensuality and mystery rites. Although dance in the church has continued to appear at a grass-roots level at various points throughout the centuries (notably the Middle Ages with various dances and mystery plays), there have been repeated campaigns against dance since the time of the early Church Fathers. Since the Shaker movement in the nineteenth century, Christian dance subsided. The blossoming of modern dance, influenced by German expressionism in the 1930s, seeded the first liturgical dance artists in New York in the 1960s, a movement that spread across a number of US and European churches.

The Pentecostal revival, especially among black Americans, represents another major shift. Movement and dance are a normal part of Pentecostal services (as it is among Christians in Africa) with the choir, congregation and ministers moving along every dimension, vertically, laterally, transversally, in both spontaneously and choreographed ways. Charismatic Christians also make use of physical freedom, lifting their hands in worship. The 'charismatic hop' is a joyful jigging up and down, moving from one leg to another. In most charismatic or 'liturgical' dance, however, the transverse, sensuous dimension is still studiously avoided. Postmodern, 'alternative' styles of worship, that eschew much of the hierarchical traditional ways, seek to overturn this unstated ban, and draw on images, rhythmic music, and movement to a much greater extent, with less observance of strict 'verticality'.

Islam

Texts

The Qur'an is said to be a written record of God's final revelation, received by the Prophet Muhammad through the Angel Gabriel in 610

CE, and is widely accepted as the direct speech of God. It incorporates much of the narrative of Jewish and Christian scripture, including the creation of heaven and earth in six days (The Koran Hud 11.7),[7] the creation of woman from man (The Koran, The Hordes 39.6), and the temptation of Adam and his banishment from paradise (The Koran, The Cow 2.35). Jesus features prominently, but Muslims do not believe that he was the Son of God, nor that he was crucified.

The food laws of the Jewish canon, which were overturned by Jesus and his apostles, are reinstated in the Qur'an with very few changes: 'He has forbidden you carrion, blood, and the flesh of swine; also any flesh that is consecrated other than in the name of God' (The Koran, The Cow 2.175). There is, however, one important addition. Muslims are forbidden to drink alcohol: 'Believers, wine and games of chance, idols and divining arrows, are abominations devised by Satan' (The Koran, The Table 5.90). Other commandments concerning the body relate to sexual behaviour; we will consider these below. In each of these cases, the problem is not with the body itself, but with its misuse.

Islam also teaches full bodily resurrection, and the Qur'an suggests responses for believers to offer to those who cannot accept this doctrine:

> 'What!' they say. 'When we are turned to bones and dust, shall we be restored to life?' Say: 'You shall; whether you turn to stone or iron, or any other substance which you may think unlikely to be given life.' They will ask: 'Who will restore us?' Say: 'He that created you at first'.
> (The Koran, The Night Journey 17.49–51)

Turning to the *ahadith*, some sayings concern modesty. We are told, for example, that 'Allah's Apostle ... forbade Al-Ihtiba [a way of sitting] while wrapping oneself with a single garment, without having a part of it over the private parts (al-Bukhari, 1983, 1.363). Posture is also important. During prayer, one must move in time with the Imam – 'if he prays standing then pray standing, and bow when he bows, and raise your heads when he raises his head; prostrate when he prostrates,' and so forth. These prostrations are not merely aesthetic, for on the Day of Resurrection the angels are said to remove believers from hell, 'recognizing them from the traces of prostrations' (al-Bukhari, 1983, 1.770).

The Prophet himself is reported to have prayed in a very specific manner: Abu Humaid As-Sa'idi said, 'I remember the prayer of Allah's Apostle better than any one of you. I saw him raising both his hands up to the level of the shoulders on saying the Takbir; and on bowing he placed his hands on both knees and bent his back straight, then he stood up straight from bowing till all the vertebrae took their normal positions. In prostrations, he placed both his hands on the ground with the fore-arms away from the ground and away from his body, and his toes were facing the Qibla.' (al-Bukhari, 1983, 1.791)

Other sayings concern ritual washing. We are told in some detail, for example, how the Prophet Muhammad undertook the mandatory cleans-ing after sexual intercourse (Janaba), washing his hands, performing an ablution as if for prayer, running his fingers through the roots of his hair and pouring water over his head and body (al-Bukhari, 1983, 1.248). We also hear that Muhammed left instructions for his dead daughter's body to be washed three times with 'water and Sidr', to have camphor applied, and to be wrapped in his waist-sheet (al-Bukhari, 1983, 2.344). Such respect for the body is not limited to corpses; Muhammad is said to have reprimanded a follower who fasted every day and prayed all night, saying, 'If you keep on doing this, your eyes will become weak and your body will get tired' (al-Bukhari, 1983, 3.198).

Certain sayings point to wider theological issues concerning the body. First, we may be led astray by Satan. According to Muhammad, 'when any human being is born Satan touches him at both sides of the body with his two fingers' (al-Bukhari, 1983, 4.506). Moreover, 'Satan reaches everywhere in the human body as blood reaches in it' (al-Bukhari, 1983, 3.251). Second, as set out in the Qur'an, believers will be resurrected from the dead. Muhammad explains that 'there is nothing of the human body that does not decay except one bone; that is the little bone at the end of the coccyx of which the human body will be recreated on the Day of Resurrection' (al-Bukhari, 1983, 6.457).

Visual Representations

The most important elements of Islamic religious art are geometrical patterns and calligraphy. This speaks of a radical view of God's tran-scendence. Immanence is eschewed, and images of people (as well as animals) are avoided, and many would regard images of God or Muham-mad as highly offensive. There was much controversy in 2005 after a Danish newspaper, *Jyllands-Posten*, published several cartoons depicting the Prophet.

APPENDIX

Marriage and Sexuality

The Qur'an teaches modesty for both men and women alike. In 'Light',
men are commanded to 'turn their eyes away from temptation and to
restrain their carnal desires' (The Koran, Light 24.30). Women are told
to do the same, but also to 'draw their veils over their bosoms and not
to reveal their finery' except to their husbands and certain relations (The
Koran, Light, 24.31). Similarly, in 'The Confederate Tribes', chastity
is one characteristic of those men and women upon whom Allah 'will
bestow forgiveness and a rich reward' (The Koran, The Confederate
Tribes 33.35). Extra-marital sexual intercourse is forbidden, and adultery
is punishable by one hundred lashes (The Koran, Light 24.1). Women are
again encouraged to veil in order to avoid inappropriate male attention,
and to be recognized as Muslim women rather than 'available' non-
Muslims or slaves:

> Prophet, enjoin your wives, your daughters, and the wives of true believers
> to draw their veils close round them. That is more proper, so that they
> may be recognized and not be molested. (The Koran, The Confederate
> Tribes 33.59)

The Qur'an states that all human beings are equal in the sight of
Allah (except in their faith and righteousness). Yet like Genesis and 1
Corinthians, the Qur'an also states that women are subordinate to men.
In 'Women', members of the female sex are told to obey their husbands;
it is declared that 'men have authority over women because God has
made one superior to the other, and because they spend their wealth to
maintain them.' Men are told to beat those who do not obey (The Koran,
Women 4.34) but also to seek 'mutual agreement' with wives who 'fear
ill-treatment or desertion' (The Koran, Women 4.128). A man may take
up to four wives; one verse assumes that men will have multiple wives,
yet suggesting that it is impossible to treat them equally. Another asserts
that monogamy is preferable where equality cannot be ensured.

Ritual

With the 'five pillars', Sunni Islam sets out five essential practices for
all Muslims: profession of faith (*shahadah*), prayer (*salat*), giving alms
(*zakat*), fasting in Ramadan (*sawm*) and pilgrimage to Mecca (*hajj*). The
first two are performed most regularly, with prayers offered five times a

day (men can pray in the mosque, but women are encouraged to pray at home.) The *hajj*, by contrast, might be performed once in a lifetime. Shi'a Muslims do not subscribe to the five pillars, but to the 'ten ancillaries of the faith'. These include prayer, fasting, pilgrimage and giving alms, to which are added further charity (*khums*), the struggle to please God (*jihad*), enjoining what is good and forbidding what is evil (*amr-bil-ma'ruf* and *nahi-anil-munkar*), loving the family of Muhammad and disassociating with their enemies (*tawalla* and *tabarra*).

Prayer

After ritual washing, the worshipper turns to face Mecca (Robinson, 1999, pp. 100–101). He stands upright, with both hands by his ears, and declares 'Allahu Akbar' (God is great). This stance emphasizes that he is attuned and listening to God alone, symmetrical and focused. In each unit of prayer, he recites the first chapter of the Qur'an, followed by further verses from other chapters, bowing and prostrating at certain prescribed points. When bowing, he bends three times with a straight back. When prostrating, he kneels with his forehead, nose, hands and knees all touching the ground. Prostration embodies the concept of surrender to an even greater extent than the kneeling position adopted by Christians; it is a total relinquishing of the normal human capacities in the vertical and horizontal dimensions.

On Fridays, Muslims are encouraged to attend a prayer session at the Mosque. Notably, worshippers must remove their shoes when entering the building. This is a mark of respect, but also suggests vulnerability and freedom from everyday dirt.

The intention of Muslim prayer is one of recollection and concentration on God. There is no attempt to achieve an altered level of consciousness, but rather to embody the core precept of Islam: submission. However, this method of prayer undoubtedly affects the cardiovascular system. The impact of repeated prostration, lowering and lifting the entire weight of the body, not to mention the impact of being shoulder to shoulder with your brethren, is similar to running up and down the stairs – it is refreshing and enlivening for the body and emotions. For those who practise it, the regular rhythm of the five daily prayers 'holds' the believer in a lived experience of being a body submitted to the divine. The attitudes towards the body, the importance of bodily and family life, the body's need of purification and modesty, reveals something of its membership in the Abrahamic tradition, albeit one held in dynamic tension with radical transcendence.

Hajj

As well as being the last of the five pillars, the hajj to Mecca (reversing the dangerous flight *from* Mecca undertaken by the Prophet and his persecuted companions) is commanded in the Qur'an for all those who can manage it:

> Make the pilgrimage and visit the Sacred House for His sake. If you cannot, send such offerings as you can afford and do not shave your heads until the offerings have reached their destination. (The Koran, The Cow 2.196)

Today, the itinerary of this pilgrimage is closely controlled, although it is still an arduous undertaking for most. It takes place in the final month of the year. All wear the same clothing – namely two white strips of cloth. They begin by processing seven times around the sacred house (Ka'bah) and seven times between the hills of Safa and Marwa. Pilgrims to Mecca report a profound sense of unity with other believers; differences in social status are temporarily erased by the white garb. The slow circumambulation *en masse* has a 'centring' effect; the jagged crises of individual life stories can feel smoothed and absorbed by the larger enacted story of circling around the Ka'bah. Pilgrims must spend time in prayer at Mount Arafat, and traditionally throw seven stones at three pillars in Mina, commemorating the temptation of Ibrahim by the devil. Ibrahim's readiness to sacrifice his son is celebrated by the pilgrims with a feast of animal sacrifice (Eid al-Adha) (Robinson, 1999, p. 182). This once-in-a lifetime ritual summarizes in physical experience the over-arching narrative of Islam.

Hinduism

Texts

Hinduism is even more disparate than Judaism, Christianity and Islam, and its roots are even more ancient than the first of the monotheisms (whose oral tradition has roots as far back as 1800 BCE). Hinduism has no centralized religious leadership, and no single holy text. The vast range of sects and practices makes it impossible to identify one Hindu attitude towards the body. Here, we are forced to concentrate on a very limited number of important scriptures.

Vedas and Upanishads

The *Rigveda* comprises hymns to many Hindu deities, and details their characteristics. We are told that Agni's physique is particularly remarkable: 'Fierce is his gait and vast his wondrous body: he champeth like a horse with bit and bridle, And darting forth his tongue, as 'twere a hatchet, burning the woods, smelteth them like a smelter' (Griffith, 1896). That a god can be praised in such corporeal terms suggests that the body is embraced rather than avoided.

The *Artharvaveda* acknowledges that the human body is imperfect, and subject to fever, bowel problems, leprosy, poison and ultimately death. But this veda includes many prayers to ward away these afflictions, and others positively celebrate the body. A prayer for virility ends with the plea, 'the strength of the horse, the mule, the goat and the ram, moreover the strength of the bull bestow upon him, O controller of bodies!' (Hymns of the Atharva-Veda, IV, 4). Another, for admittance to heaven, suggests a bodily afterlife that is free from all defect: 'in that bright world where our pious friends live in joy, having cast aside the ailments of their own bodies, free from lameness, not deformed in limb, there may we behold our parents and our children' (Hymns of the Atharva-Veda, IV, 4).

The *Katha Upanishad* provides a different perspective. The author divides body and soul, presenting the body as the soul's chariot:

> Know thou the soul (atman, self) as riding in a chariot / The body as the chariot. / Know thou the intellect (buddhi) as the chariot-driver / And the mind (manas) as the reins.
> The senses (indriya), they say, are the horses; / The objects of sense, what they range over. / The self combined with senses and mind / Wise men call 'the enjoyer' (bhoktr). (Katha Upanishad, 3.3–4)

Those without understanding are unable to master the senses and go on to reincarnation; those with understanding take control of the senses and are freed from endless rebirth. The stability of the immortal soul is contrasted with the impermanence of earthly objects; the author observes that 'the childish go after outward pleasures; they walk into the net of widespread death.' In a striking parallel with Plato, who uses similar chariot imagery in the *Phaedrus*, the author longs for freedom from the body, since 'when liberated [from the body], he is liberated indeed' (Katha Upanishad, 5.1).

Dharmasutras

The Dharmasutras are part of the *vedanga*, which supplement the Vedas; here we will consider the version attributed to the sage Apastamba. Like the Jewish canon and the Qur'an, this includes many rules about purity and impurity. Those in the first stage of the Hindu life, the students, are forbidden to eat certain categories of animal – including carnivorous birds, carnivorous fish, and animals with five claws or one hoof (Apastamba 1.17.14–39). Alcohol is not permitted, and certain vegetables are also disallowed, including garlic, onion and leek. Meat is only forbidden at certain times in this text, though many Hindus now have a wholly vegetarian diet.

The provenance of food may also make it unsuitable. We are told that 'he shall not eat the food given by a corporate body or announced through a public invitation; the food of anyone who lives by practising a craft or using weapons'; and so forth. Likewise, he must not eat in a house where someone has died in the last ten days, in the presence of a corpse, or 'after a birth before the mother comes out of the birthing room'(Apastamba 1.16.18–20). Food that has come into contact with an impure person is itself impure.

The student must purify himself 'by sipping water collected on the ground,' or by sipping water offered by a pure person. This is necessary after contact with any bodily fluid, as well as 'hair, fire, cattle, a Brahmin, or a woman' (Apastamba 1.16.14). Clothing, like wood for the sacred fire, must be purified by sprinkling with water. Contact with dogs requires more thorough ablutions: 'he should plunge into water with his clothes on; or he becomes pure after he has washed that spot, touched it with fire, washed that spot again, as well as his feet, and sipped water' (Apastamba 1.15.16–17).

Ritual

Temple worship

We have already noted that Hinduism encompasses a wide range of traditions and practices. A particularly detailed set of instructions for worshippers at Siva's temple was compiled by Armunga Navalar of Jaffna, Sri Lanka, in the nineteenth century. Navalar begins by noting that adherence to Siva is worthless unless a believer possesses (Hudson, 1995, 3, p. 311) certain virtues, represented as Siva's 'limbs'. Many of these require us to exercise control over our own bodies – followers must not eat meat, drink liquor, commit adultery, and so forth. But although possession of these virtues is essential, it is not enough; certain physical deeds and ritual practices are also required.

First, the believers must be appropriately attired, wearing ash and the 'eyes of Rudra' beads. Indeed, if someone performs a deed for Siva without wearing these, it 'will not produce the slightest benefit' (Hudson, 1995, 3, p. 311). Second, they must attend the temple each day to 'obtain the sight of Siva'. The temple has within it a 'womb' or 'inner sanctum' which contains the 'Siva linga' (literally, the Siva symbol). This is the holiest part of the temple; it is encircled by four further enclosures, which are themselves encircled by the village. Only Siva brahmans may touch the linga, but they do so 'for the sake of others'. The bodily metaphors here are apparent; the body is a means to understanding the divine.

The process by which one obtains the sight of Siva begins with extensive ritual washing, purification and dressing:

> Those who want to obtain the vision of Siva ought to go to an auspicious temple once they have bathed according to the rules in the Siva bathing place near Siva's abode and, standing on its bank, dry themselves with a dry cloth, place ash on the forehead, tie the hair into a knot, remove the wet loincloth and replace it with a dry one, purify both hands, tie two pieces of clean cloth that are untorn and have been washed and dried around the waist, and complete the rites and prayers. (Hudson, 1995, 12, p. 313)

These preparations show one's respect for the deity, and Navalar compares those who omit them to 'those who sneer at Siva'. (Hudson, 1995, 12, p. 313). The believer should come to the temple with a plate of food or some flowers as an offering for the god. They should venerate the gateway, and enter with 'both hands piled on the head'. Men prostrate themselves with both legs fully stretched out, and touch the ground with the head, the two hands, the two ears, the chin and the two arms. Women prostrate with only the lower part of the leg stretched out, and touch the ground with head, hands and knees (Hudson, 1995, 16, p. 313).

Having performed the appropriate prostration, they walk around the inner sanctum a set number of times in the following manner:

> They ought to arise and join the hands in worship and conduct a circumambulation while thinking steadily of the Lord Siva, holding prayer beads in the hand and uttering the five-syllable mantra (namah sivaya) of folding both hands together at the region of the heart. (Hudson, 1995, 21, p. 314)

As they walk, they must tread carefully, concentrating on the ground in case they kill any living creature. After further venerations they enter the inner sanctum. They reach the icon of the Lord of Obstacles, clench their fists, hit themselves on the forehead three times, and bow three times by pulling down each ear with the opposite hand (Hudson, 1995, 30, p. 315). Finally, they gaze at Siva, 'join the hands at the head and the heart, and while the mind dissolves, body hair stands on end, and joy wells up and overflows, sing hymns of praise to him' (Hudson, 1995, 31, p. 315). The priest then makes the offering, ash is applied, and further goddesses and gods are approached and worshipped. When leaving the inner sanctum, the believer must avoid showing his backside to either Siva or Nandi. Through the myriad of ritual practices and proscriptions glimpsed above, the faith pervades every aspect of life, personal and social.

Verticality among worshippers performing puja, with its control of the body as means to holiness, is in contrast with the rhythmic, asymmetrical and transversal poses of statues of deities adorning thousands of temples. An outsider to the faith may see this contrast as a disjunction, but a larger, unspoken gestalt may be at work, creating an implicit unity for the body as it is lived in Hinduism. The gods are depicted having in abundance what humans have imperfectly, or even problematically. The dynamic poses of the deities provide a rare glimpse into a fine-grained awareness that the upright, bi-pedal human gait also involves asymmetrical moments of falling and relaxation. Only the gods appear to handle this tension gracefully.

Meditation and yoga

The principles of meditation are set out in many Hindu texts, not least the famous *Bhagavad Gita*. There, the believer is advised by the deity to find a secret, solitary environment, and to sit down on a covering of cloth, deerskin and grass. Then:

> Fixing his mind exclusively on one point, with the workings of the mind and senses restrained, he should practice devotion for purity of self. Holding his body, head and neck even and unmoved (remaining) steady, looking at the tip of his own nose, and not looking about in (all) directions, with a tranquil self ... he should restrain his mind, and (concentrate it) on me, and sit down in engaged devotion, regarding me as his final goal. (Bhagavad Gita)

The aim of this process is complete tranquillity, 'final emancipation', and 'assimilation' with the deity; control of the body, and the body itself, is the vehicle to this end. In this text, the form of assimilation is not explicitly stated. In the *Yoga Tattva Upanishad*, by contrast, we are told that the emancipated have a choice between bodily and non-bodily existence:

> Samadhi is that state in which the Jivatman (lower self) and the Paramatman (higher self) are differenceless (or of equal state). If he desires to lay aside his body, he can do so. He will become absorbed in Paramatman ... But if he does not so desire and if his body is dear to him, he lives in all the worlds possessing the Siddhis of Anima, etc. (Yogatattva Upanishad, p. 199)

The author of this Upanishad identifies several stages on the path to emancipation, as well as several meditative postures and practices. Breathing exercises are prescribed for beginners – sitting as described in the *Bhagavad Gita*, they should breathe in slowly through the left nostril, hold their breath as long as possible, and then exhale through the right nostril, closing the unused nostril with their thumb (Yogatattva Upanishad, p. 194). In time, this has benefits for the body – including leanness and 'brilliancy of complexion'. At more advanced stages, levitation is said to be possible (Yogatattva Upanishad, p. 196). But the body may also hinder meditation through laziness and lust.

Buddhism

Texts

The supreme Buddha, Siddhartha Gautama, was born circa 580 BCE to a royal and privileged Hindu family in Nepal (Harvey, 1990, pp. 14–29).[8] He married and had a child. Tradition recalls that, after that, he left the enclosure of his royal residence for the first time, and was confronted by the reality of human suffering. This shocked him into seeking an answer to the problematic nature of embodied human existence – and our inevitable fate of old age, sickness and death. He embarked on a path of extreme asceticism, but this proved unfruitful. Eventually, his 'middle way' of disciplined meditation enabled him to experience Enlightenment, and thus release from the endless cycle of birth, suffering, death and re-birth. Buddhism in not theistic in the strict sense; it is a cycle of teaching to enable disciples to attain enlightenment.

As with the other religions examined here, there is no single Buddhist attitude to the body, and it is important to distinguish between the two major branches of this faith, Theravada and Mahayana. However, discipline is a common theme in Buddhist texts. The rules contained in the *Patimokkha* require monks to be dressed appropriately, 'under proper control', and quiet, and to move about 'with downcast eye' (The Patimokkha, Sekhiya Dhamma, 1–14). The body is to be tamed, and distanced. Regarding posture, a vertical stance is key – monks must proceed without swaying the body, head or arms. The eating of alms is strictly regulated, from the amount to the manner of consumption. Those who keep these rules are considered to be 'pure'.

The Theravadin *Mahavagga*, which records the life of the Gautama Buddha, places the same emphasis on discipline. The Buddha sets out four noble truths (The Mahavagga, First Khandhaka, 6.19–22). First, existence is suffering, from birth to death. Second, the cause of suffering is desire or 'thirst'. Third, suffering is overcome when desire is overcome – one must therefore purge oneself of every passion. Fourth, in order to achieve this one must follow the 'eightfold path', which consists of 'right belief, right aspiration, right speech, right conduct, right means of livelihood, right endeavour, right memory, right meditation.'

Not all of these pertain to the body, but the Buddha also advocates a 'Middle Path' between bodily pleasure and mortification:

> There are two extremes, O Bhikkhus, which he who has given up the world ought to avoid. What are these two extremes? A life given to pleasures, devoted to pleasures and lusts: this is degrading, sensual, vulgar, ignoble, and profitless; and a life given to mortifications: this is painful, ignoble, and profitless. (The Mahavagga, First Khandhaka, 6.17)

The Buddha also teaches that the self is separate from the body, reasoning that the true self cannot be perishable and a cause of pain. He remains in a body, but his body can be transformed – for instance, he can convert into flames and withstand fire (The Mahavagga, First Khandhaka, 15.4–5).

Other Buddhist texts portray the body in a more explicitly negative light. The Theravadin *Ganda Sutta*, for example, compares it to a boil:

> A boil, monks, is another word for this body ... Whatever would ooze out from it would be an uncleanliness oozing out, a stench oozing out, a disgust oozing out ... For that reason, you should become disenchanted with this body. (Ganda Sutta)[9]

Similarly, the Theravadin *Vijaya Sutta* warns against those who consider the body to be beautiful, encouraging them to visualize corpses and the body's discharges.

Ritual

Bowing

Bowing is very common in Buddhist societies. Buddhists may bow once to their superiors, whether parents, teachers, monks or the elderly. They may bow three times towards sacred objects, representing the three 'jewels' or 'refuges' (the Buddha, *dhamma* or teaching, and *sangha* or the monastic community). Harvey describes the procedure:

> A person stands or kneels with palms joined in a gesture known as namaskara. They are held at the chest and forehead or, in Northern Buddhism, at the head, lips and chest: symbolizing respect offered by mind, speech and body. From a kneeling position, a person then places the elbows, hands and head on the ground. In Northern Buddhism, a fuller form known as a 'grand prostration' involves laying full-length on the ground. (Vijaya Sutta)[10]

Representations of the Buddha embody the teaching of the Eightfold Path to Enlightenment. The Buddha is depicted always in repose, with eyes closed. The most common depiction is of the Buddha seated, with his back erect and legs folded in the lotus position, arms relaxed with palm upwards (holding a lotus, or thumb and middle finger touching in meditation). As with the examples of bowing and prostration that we encountered in other religions, the Buddhist practice of bowing to representations of the Buddha involves the voluntary abandonment of the human achievement of vertical posture, indicating humility and wilful submission.

Meditation

Buddhist meditation may be divided into two interlinked categories – calm meditation (Samatha) and insight meditation (Vipissana). Calm meditation often takes the form of 'mindfulness of breathing' (Harvey, 1990, pp. 248–249). In the *Satipatthana Sutta*, which is accepted in both the Theravada and Mahayana traditions, the Buddha himself describes this practice. He notes that the individual finds an empty place, where he 'sits down with his legs crossed, keeps his body erect and his mindfulness alert'. The eyes may be closed (Harvey, 1990, p. 249). Then:

> Always mindful, he breathes in; mindful he breathes out. Breathing in long, he discerns that he is breathing in long; or breathing out long, he discerns that he is breathing out long. (Satipatthana Sutta)[11]

Breathing is the only direct link we have to our brain's limbic system, the more primitive, middle structure of the brain. Magnetic resonance imaging (MRI) studies indicate that the stress response (fight, flight, freeze response), as well as other powerful emotions, all have their seat within the limbic system. Slow, deep breathing calms the limbic system; it reverses the chemical/hormonal cascade triggered by the stress response. The neo-cortex thereby regains its normal ascendency in the symphony that is brain functioning. The felt experience is calm.

The Buddha's position on insight meditation is set out in the same text, and is identified as the sole path to enlightenment:

> This is the direct path for the purification of beings, for the overcoming of sorrow and lamentation, for the disappearance of pain and distress, for the attainment of the right method, and for the realization of Unbinding – in other words, the four frames of reference. (Satipatthana Sutta)

The four frames of reference are closely related to the body – contemplation of the body itself, contemplation of feeling, contemplation of consciousness, and the contemplation of mental objects (including both negative and positive emotions). With each frame of reference, the key is to be 'mindful'. Building on mindfulness of breathing, we must always be aware of what our bodies are doing. We must also recognize what we are feeling, how we are conscious, and which mental objects we are contemplating. The results are swift:

> Let alone half a month. If anyone would develop these four frames of reference in this way for seven days, one of two fruits can be expected for him: either gnosis right here and now, or – if there be any remnant of clinging/sustenance – non-return. [i.e., at death they will not be reborn into the human world]. (Satipatthana Sutta)

To be mindful of our emotions, our bodies, our breathing, our thoughts, is to 'own' them, to be conscious of more of ourselves. In neurological terms, it is about increasing the links between different parts of our neo-cortex and the more primitive parts of our brain, and its direct links to our bodies. Part of the 'problem' of being human is a widely reported sense of inner divide, or some form of self-alienation. In this divided state, we do not know what deep emotions are, or that our perceptions of self and others may be distorted. Enlightenment (understood to be the search for reality, the search for truth) requires disciplined, hard work. To bring all that we are into consciousness is a humanizing process.

Concluding Comments

We are now in a position to reflect on the questions posed at the beginning of this chapter – are the religions discussed here dualist towards the body? Do they present the body as a means to something else or as something important in itself? Do their ritual practices have a gendered, hierarchical dimension, and do these practices enact or subvert their stated beliefs about the body? Inevitably, given the range of views held by the leaders (let alone members) of each religion, our comments can be nothing more than guides.

Notwithstanding the influence of Plato (which became quite pronounced in Christianity), the three monotheisms preclude soul/body dualism insofar as they affirm a bodily afterlife. For the most part, Jewish, Christian and Islamic writers portray the body as an integral part of the person. The body has a special place in Christianity because of the central doctrines of incarnation and resurrection. However, the three monotheisms also emphasize that the body is open to misuse. The Jewish and Islamic purity laws suggest a struggle against defilement. Christians reject such laws, but the New Testament upholds strict controls on bodily activity (especially sexual behaviour). Despite the seeds of equality between human beings present in the monotheisms, all three distinguish between men and women, and have traditionally limited religious leadership to men.

The essential goodness of the body is reflected in bodily acts of worship and fellowship. In Judaism, the importance of the upright posture is reflected in the name of the Amidah. The observance of the Sabbath centres around family meals. The five daily prayers that Muslims must undertake involve bowing and prostration, and the Hajj consists of a series of physical activities. Catholic and Orthodox Christian services involve a significant amount of ritual movement, including bowing, kneeling, making the sign of the cross and genuflecting. While Protestants have somewhat ignored the body in ritual, Charismatic and Pentecostal churches often embrace dance. The body is a means of worship and, in the Catholic mass, Christ's Body is an object of worship in itself.

In Hinduism, the Katha Upanishad does strongly suggest soul/body dualism. Yet Hinduism is not opposed to the body, as evinced by the exuberant bodily depictions of deities and the elaborate bodily rituals. It is the gods who possess perfection and whose bodies are life-giving. In meditation, the body serves as a vehicle for emancipation and assimilation with the deity – it is quite clearly a means to an end. Buddhist meditation also has a more transcendent aim, namely freedom from rebirth, but mindfulness techniques reinforce the connection between mind and body too, by encouraging us to concentrate on bodily actions that we usually take for granted. Like the monotheistic faiths, Hinduism and Buddhism have traditionally emphasized gender differences, with women barred from many leadership roles.

It is perhaps surprising that some religious groups strongly object to ritual movement, including some Protestant Christians; this might imply that the body is a tool for sin – not for worship. When religion neglects the bodily dimension, or when belief (for example, Christianity's view of the importance of the body) is at odds with its normative ritual practice, religion risks becoming contradictory in human experience. Piaget asserts that we know reality first through our bodies. As human life unfolds and becomes more cognitively, propositionally driven, our bodies remain a wordless but final arbiter concerning what is 'real'. As Martha Graham puts it, the body does not lie. This contradiction may well be reflected in current patterns of religious decline (for example in Christianity generally), and religious growth (for example, among Pentecostal and Charismatic churches), along with a host of other influences in late (or post) modernity.

The line of reasoning here relies on written records. It may be a sheer coincidence that early hominid evolution involved becoming upright and bi-pedal millions of years before lateral mastery through hunting, tool making, and cooking meat over fires fuelled the gradual development of large brains among the homo species. Even so, something deeper may be afoot. Pre-monotheistic empires such as Egypt and Mesopotamia seem fixed upon a single message of power expressed through the immensity, symmetry and verticality of their statuary and architecture. The ancient king was fused with deity in order to exert control over chaos. The lived body of ancient worshippers (apart from priests or priestesses) remains unknown. However, bodily rituals such as those summarized here, evidenced in written records and lived contemporary experience, seem to provide us with tools that help us to solve some of the dilemmas of human experience. These tools may have been particularly needed at the height of agrarian, stratified civilizations with their onerous demand for cooperation. The religions covered in this chapter point to a call, and a resource, for people to be fully human, fully conscious, fully evolved, through a near constant verticality. In many rituals, the faithful move upwards towards purity and divinity and downwards in submission and detachment. In the presence of the divine, humans are to limit their lateral and transverse mastery. The symmetry of movement maintains the single focus of the religious quest. The bodily control required in ritual points to a balancing of the needs of the individual (drives, wants and desires) with the needs of the wider community, with its requirement for individual self-control, and the society's maintenance of gender distinctions. Immense social control no doubt accrued to religion through these implicitly expressed means. But these rituals also served, and continue to serve, individuals' needs. Bodily rituals help to unite the different faculties of the worshipper (emotions, thoughts, will, physical drives). Bodily rituals provide tools for cognition (including purity laws and gender distinctions protecting basic categories). Perhaps most importantly, our bodies provide a framework, and a vehicle, for a lived experience of our relatedness to the Divine.

Notes

1 All biblical quotations are from the New Revised Standard Version (2007), Anglicized Edition (Cambridge University Press).

2 Compare Deuteronomy 6.4–5 with Leviticus 21.11, Jeremiah 12.12 and Psalm 63.1. The word *basar* is often translated as 'flesh' but it has a far wider range of meanings: it may denote a corpse, a person in his or her entirety, or the soul.

3 See also Judith Reesa Baskin (2002), *Midrashic Women: Formations of the Feminine in Rabbinic Literature*, Brandeis Series on Jewish Women (University Press of New England), p. 93.

4 Taken from Nachmanides (attrib.), *Iggeret Hakodesh*, Chapter 6.

5 See also Margaret R. Miles (1979), *Augustine on the Body* (Scholars Press), p. 97.

6 For example, The 'Articles of Religion', number 28, in the *Book of Common Prayer* (1662).

7 References from the Koran are taken from the version translated by N. J. Dawood (1990) (Penguin).

8 For an account of the life of the Buddha, see Peter Harvey (1990), *An Introduction to Buddhism: Teachings, History and Practices* (Cambridge University Press).

9 *Ganda Sutta: A Boil* (AN 9.15), trans. Thanissaro Bhikkhu, *Access to Insight* (BCBS edn), 4 July 2010, www.accesstoinsight.org/tipitaka/an/an09/an09.015.than.html, accessed 10.9.2020.

10 *Vijaya Sutta: Vijaya* (SN 5.4), trans. Bhikkhu Bodhi, *Access to Insight* (BCBS edn), 13 June 2010, www.accesstoinsight.org/tipitaka/sn/sn05/sn05.004.bodh.html, accessed 10.9.2020.

11 *The Way of Mindfulness: The Satipatthana Sutta and its Commentary*, Soma Thera, *Access to Insight* (BCBS edn), 30 November 2013, http://www.accesstoinsight.org/lib/authors/soma/wayof.html, accessed 10.9.2020.

References and Further Reading

Albertson, E. R., Neff, K. D. and Dill-Shackleford, K. E. (2014), 'Self-Compassion and Body Dissatisfaction in Women: A Randomized Controlled Trial of a Brief Meditation Intervention', *Mindfulness*, 6:3, pp. 444–54.

al-Bukhari, Muhammed Ibn Ismail. (1983), *Sahih Al Bukhari* (trans. Muhammad Muhsin Khan) (Kazi Publications).

Anderson, H. (1998), *The Family Handbook* (Westminster John Knox Press).

Anderson, M. L. (2003), 'Embodied Cognition: A Field Guide', *Artificial Intelligence*, 149:1, pp. 91–130.

Arbib, M. and Hesse, M. (1986), *The Construction of Reality* (Cambridge University Press).

Asch, S. E. (1958), 'The Metaphor: A Psychological Enquiry', in: R. Tagiuri and L. Petrullo (eds), *Person Perception and Interpersonal Behaviour* (Stanford University Press), pp. 86–94.

Asma, S. T. (2018), *Why We Need Religion* (Oxford University Press).

Assagioli, R. (1993), *Psychosynthesis: A Manual of Principles and Techniques* (Penguin).

Associated Press/GfK (2011), The AP-GfK Poll: A Telephone Survey of the American General Population (ages 18+) (December), accessed 22 September 2020 at: http://surveys.associatedpress.com/data/GfK/AP-GfK%20Poll%20December%202011%20Topline_Santa.pdf

Augustine (1994), 'Soliloquies', in: P. Schaff (ed.), *Nicene and Post-Nicene Fathers: First Series*, 7 (Hendrickson).

Averill, J. R. (1982), *Anger and Aggression: An Essay on Emotion* (Springer-Verlag).

Baddeley, A. D. (2004), *Your Memory: A User's Guide* (Carlton).

Baddeley, A. D. (2007), *Working Memory, Thought and Action* (Oxford University Press).

Baker, A. (1964), *Holy Wisdom* (Anthony Clarke Books).

Barfield, O. (1953), *History in English Words* (Faber and Faber).

Barfield, O. (1957), *Saving the Appearances: A Study in Idolatry* (Faber).

Barfield, O. (1984), *Poetic Diction: A Study in Meaning* (Wesleyan University Press).

Barfield, O. (2012), *Romanticism Comes of Age* (Barfield Press).

Barfield, O. (2014), *What Coleridge Thought* (Barfield Press).

Barnard, P. J. (2019), 'Sticks, Stones, and the Origins of Sapience,' in: K. A. Overmann and F. L. Coolidge (eds), *Squeezing Minds from Stones: Cognitive Archaeology and the Evolution of the Human Mind* (Oxford University Press), pp. 102–27.

Barrett, J. L. (2004), *Why Would Anyone Believe in God* (AltaMira).

Barrett, J. L. (2012), *Born Believers: The Science of Children's Religious Belief* (Atria Books).

Barrett, L. F. (2006), 'Are Emotions Natural Kinds?' *Perspectives on Psychological Science* 1:1, pp. 28–58.

Barrington-Ward, S. (2011), *The Jesus Prayer: A Way to Contemplation* (Pauline Books).

Barsalou, L., Barbey, A. K., Simmons, W. K. and Santos, A. (2004), 'Embodiment in Religious Knowledge', *Journal of Cognition and Culture*, 5:1–2, pp. 14–57.

Barsalou, L., Pecher, W. D., Zeelenberg, R., Simmons, W. K. and Hamann, S. B. (2005), 'Multi-Modal Simulation in Conceptual Processing,' in: W. Ahn, R. Goldstone, B. Love, A. Markman and P. Wolff (eds), *Categorization Inside and Outside the Lab: Festschrift in Honor of Douglas L. Medin* (American Psychological Association), pp. 249–70.

Bartholomew, C. G. and Hughes, F. (2004), *Explorations in a Christian Theology of Pilgrimage* (Ashgate).

Baskin, J. R. (2002), *Midrashic Women: Formations of the Feminine in Rabbinic Literature* (University Press of New England).

Baumeister, R. (1991), *Escaping the Self: Alcoholism, Spirituality, Masochism and Other Flights from the Burden of Selfhood* (Basic Books).

Baumeister, R. and Tierney, J. (2012), *Will Power: Why Self-Control is the Secret to Success* (Penguin).

Beharrell, W. (2019), 'Transformation and the Waking Body: A Return to Truth via our Bodies', *Zygon: Journal of Religion and Science*, 54:4, pp. 984–1003.

Bellah, R. N. (2011), *Religion in Human Evolution: From the Paleolithic to the Axial Age* (Belknap Press).

Benor, D. J. (1993), *Healing Research: Holistic Energy Medicine and Spiritual Healing* (Helix).

Benson, H. (2001), *The Relaxation Response* (Harper).

Benson, H., Dusek, J. A., Sherwood, J. B., Lam, P., Bethea, C. F., Carpenter, W., Levitsky, S., Hill, P. C., Clem, D. W. Jr., Jain, M. K., Drumel, D., Kopecky, S. L., Mueller, P. S., Marek, D., Rollins, S. and Hibberd, P. L. (2006), 'Study of the Therapeutic Effects of Intercessory Prayer in Cardiac Bypass Patients: A Multi-center Randomized Trial of Uncertainty and Certainty of Receiving Intercessory Prayer', *American Heart Journal*, 151:4, pp. 934–42.

'Bhagavadgita, with the Sanatsugatiya and the Anugita', in: Kashinath Trimbak Telang (trans.), *Sacred Books of the East, vol 8* (1882), (Clarendon Press).

The Bible (New Revised Standard Version) (2007), (Cambridge University Press).

Blake, W. (1968), *The Letters of William Blake* (Hart-Davis).

Bloxham, G. and Gentry, W. D. (2010), *Anger Management for Dummies* (John Wiley).

Bock, E. (1955), *The Three Years: The Life of Christ Between Baptism and Ascension* (Christian Community Press).

Boivin, M.J. and Webb, B. (2011), 'Modelling the Biomedical Role of Spirituality through Breast Cancer Research', in: F. Watts (ed.), *Spiritual Healing: Scientific and Religious Perspectives* (Cambridge University Press), pp. 128–39.

Book of Common Prayer (1662), (2004 edn) (Cambridge University Press).

Bortoft, H. (1996), *The Wholeness of Nature: Goethe's Way Toward a Science of Conscious Participation in Nature* (Floris Books).

Bourne, C. and Watts, F. (2011), 'Conceptualizations of Spiritual Healing: Christian and Secular', in: F. Watts (ed.), *Spiritual Healing: Scientific and Religious Perspectives* (Cambridge University Press), pp. 77–89.

Bouyer, L. (1955), *Christian Asceticism and Modern Man*, trans. W. Mitchell (Blackfriars).

Boyarin, D. (1995), *Carnal Israel: Reading Sex in Talmudic Culture* (University of California Press).

Boyer, P. (2001), *Religion Explained: The Human Instincts that Fashion Gods, Spirits and Ancestors* (William Heinemann).

Bragazzi, N. L. and Puente, Giovanni del (2013), 'Chronic Kidney Disease, Spirituality and Religiosity: A Systematic Overview with the List of Eligible Studies', *Health Psychology Research* 1:2, pp. 135–40.

Bretherton, R., Collicutt, J. and Brickman, J. (2016), *Being Mindful, Being Christian* (Monarch Books).

Bretherton, R. and Dunbar, R. I. M. (2020), 'Dunbar's Number goes to Church: The Social Brain Hypothesis as a Third Strand in Church Growth Studies', *Archive for the Psychology of Religion*, 42:1, pp. 46–62.

Bridger, D. and Wolk, S. (1976), *The New Jewish Encyclopaedia* (Behrman House).

Bromiley, H. and Bromiley, K. (2001), *In Search of a Miracle: God's Path to Healing* (Writers Club Press).

Brown, C. G. (2012), *Testing Prayer: Science and Healing* (Harvard University Press).

Brown, P. (2008), *The Body and Society: Men, Women and Sexual Renunciations in Early Christianity* (Columbia University Press).

Brown, W., Murphy, N. and Newton Malony, H. (eds) (1998), *Whatever Happened to the Soul? Scientific and Theological Portraits of Human Nature* (Fortress Press).

Brown, W. and Strawn, B. D. (2012), *The Physical Nature of Christian Life: Neuroscience, Psychology, and the Church* (Cambridge University Press).

Brown, W. and Reimer, K. S. (2013), 'Embodied Cognition, Character Formation, and Virtue', *Zygon: Journal of Religion and Science*, 48:3, pp. 832–45.

Bultmann, R. (1958), *Jesus Christ and Mythology* (Scribner).

Burch, V. and Penman, D. (2013), *Mindfulness for Health: A Practical Guide to Relieving Pain, Reducing Stress and Restoring Wellbeing* (Piatkus).

Burkan, T. (2016), *Extreme Spirituality: The Secret Key to Empowerment* (CreateSpace Independent Publishing Platform).

Burrus, V. (2007), *The Sex Lives of Saints: An Erotics of Ancient Hagiography* (University of Pennsylvania Press).

Byrne, L. (2010), *Angels in My Hair: A Memoir* (Arrow).

Capps, D. (2008), *Jesus the Village Psychiatrist* (Westminster John Knox Press).

Cartwright, N. (1983), *How the Laws of Physics Lie* (Oxford University Press).

Catechism of the Catholic Church (1999), (Geoffrey Chapman).

Cave, D. and Norris, R. B. (2012), *Religion and the Body: Modern Science and the Construction of Religious Meaning* (Brill).

Charles, S. J., Mulukom, V. van., Farias, M., Brown, J. E., Delmonte, R., Maraldi, E., Turner, L., Watts, F., Watts, J. and Dunbar, R. I. M. (in press), 'Religious Rituals Increase Social Bonding and Pain Threshold' in: *Evolution and Human Behavior*.

Chasteen, A. L., Burdzy, D. C. and Pratt, J. (2010), 'Thinking of God Moves Attention', *Neuropsychologia*, 48:2, pp. 627–30.

Church of England (2000), *A Time to Heal: A Report for the House of Bishops on the Healing Ministry* (Church House Publishing).

Clark, A. and Chalmers, D. (1998), 'The Extended Mind,' *Analysis*, 51:1, pp. 7–19.

Clark, A. (2008), *Supersizing the Mind: Embodiment, Action and Cognitive Extension* (Oxford University Press).

Clarke, I. (2008), *Madness, Mystery and the Survival of God* (John Hunt Publishing).

Clarke, I. (2010), *Psychosis and Spirituality: Consolidating the New Paradigm*, 2nd edn (Wiley).

Clayton, P. and Davies, P. (2006), *The Re-Emergence of Emergence: The Emergentist Hypothesis from Science to Religion* (Oxford University Press).

Clayton, P. (2011), 'The Theology of Spiritual Healing', in: F. Watts (ed.), *Spiritual Healing: Scientific and Religious Perspectives* (Cambridge University Press), pp. 44–63.

Coakley, S. and Shelemay, K. K. (2007), *Pain and its Transformations: The Interface of Biology and Culture* (Harvard University Press).

Coakley, S. (2010), *Religion and the Body* (Cambridge University Press).

Coakley, S. (ed.) (2012), *Faith, Rationality and the Passions* (Wiley-Blackwell).

Coakley, S. (2015), *The New Asceticism: Sexuality, Gender and the Quest for God* (Bloomsbury Continuum).

Coakley, S. (2020), *Spiritual Healing: Science, Meaning, and Discernment* (Eerdmans).

Coleman, S. and Elsner, J. (1995), *Pilgrimage: Past and Present in the World Religions* (Harvard University Press).

Coles, A. and Collicutt, J. (2019), *Neurology and Religion* (Cambridge University Press).

Colliander, T. (1985), *Way of the Ascetics: The Ancient Tradition of Discipline and Inner Growth* (St Vladimir's Seminary Press).

Cook, C. C. H. (2019), *Hearing Voices, Demonic and Divine: Scientific and Theological Perspectives* (Routledge).

Cook, C. C. H. (2020), 'Mental Health and the Gospel: Boyle Lecture 2020', *Zygon: Journal of Religion and Science*, 55:4, pp. 1107–23.

Corrigan, J. (ed.) (2004), *Religion and Emotion: Approaches and Interpretations* (Oxford University Press).

Corrigan, J. (ed.) (2016), *The Oxford Handbook of Religion and Emotion* (Oxford University Press).

Corwin, A. I. (2012), 'Changing God, Changing Bodies: The Impact of New Prayer Practices on Elderly Catholic Nuns' Embodied Experience', *Ethos: Journal of the Society for Psychological Anthropology* 40:4, pp. 390–410.

Corwin, A. I. (2020), 'Care in Interaction: Aging, Personhood, and Meaningful Decline', *Medical Anthropology*, accessed 12 September 2020 at: https://doi.org/10.1080/01459740.2019.1705297

Corwin, A. I. and Erikson-Davies, C. (2020), 'Experiencing Presence: An Interactive Model of Perception', *HAU: Journal of Ethnographic Theory*, 10:1, pp. 166–82.

Csikszentmihalyi, M. (1975), *Beyond Boredom and Anxiety: Experiencing Flow in Work and Play* (Jossey-Bass).

Csikszentmihalyi, M. (1990), *Flow: The Psychology of Optimal Experience* (Harper and Row).

Csordas, T. (1994), *The Sacred Self: Cultural Phenomenology of Charismatic Healing* (University of California Press).

Csordas, T. (2002), *Body/Meaning/Healing* (Palgrave Macmillan).

Dailey, E. W. (2018), *The Fit Shall Inherit the Earth: A Theology of Sport and Fitness* (Pickwick Publications).

Damasio, A. (2000), *The Feeling of What Happens: Body and Emotion in the Making of Consciousness* (Mariner).

Dandelion, P. (2007), *An Introduction to Quakerism* (Cambridge University Press).

D'Aquili, E. and Newberg, A. B. (1999), *The Mystical Mind: The Biology of Religious Experience* (Fortress Press).

Darwin, C. (2009), *The Expression of the Emotions in Man and Animals* (Penguin).

Davies, D. J. (2011), *Emotion, Identity and Religion: Hope, Reciprocity and Otherness* (Oxford University Press).

Davies, J. G. (1984), *Liturgical Dance: An Historical, Theological and Practical Handbook* (SCM).

Davies, O. (2014), 'Neuroscience, Self and Jesus Christ', in: L. Boeve, Y. de Maeseneer and E. Van Stichel (eds), *Questioning the Human: Toward a Theological Anthropology for the Twenty-First Century* (Fordham University Press).

Davies, P. (1983), *God and the New Physics* (Penguin).

Davies, S. (1995), *Jesus the Healer: Possession, Trance and the Origins of Christianity* (SCM).

Davy, C. (1958), *Towards a Third Culture* (Faber and Faber).

Deane-Drummond, C. (2017), *Pierre Teilhard de Chardin on People and Planet* (Routledge).

De Cruz, H. (2020), 'Awe and Wonder in Scientific Practice: Implications for the Relationship Between Science and Religion', in: D. Evers, M. Fuller, A. Runehov, K-W Saether and B. Michollet (eds), *Issues in Science and Theology. Nature – and Beyond: Transcendence and Immanence in Science and Theology* (Springer), pp. 155–68.

Deikman, A. J. (1990), 'De-Automatization and the Mystic Experience', in: C. Tart (ed.), *Altered States of Consciousness* (Harper), pp. 34–57.

Dein, S. (2019), 'God Cured My Cancer: Assessing the Efficacy of Religious Healing', *Journal for the Study of Religious Experience*, 5:1, pp. 37–48.

Dein, S. (2020), 'Transcendence, Religion and Social Bonding', *Archive for the Psychology of Religion*, 42:1 pp. 77–88.

De Lange, N. R. M. (2003), *Judaism* (Oxford University Press).

De Sousa, R. (1987), *The Rationality of Emotion* (MIT).

De Waal, F. (2013), *The Bonobo and the Atheist: in Search of Humanism Among the Primates* (W. W. Norton).

Dharmasutras: The Law Codes of Apastamba, Gautama, Baudhayana, and Vasistha (1999), (trans. Patrick Olivelle) (Oxford University Press).

Dixon, T. (2003), *From Passions to Emotions: The Creation of a Secular Psychological Category* (Cambridge University Press).

Dixon, T. (2015), *Weeping Britannia: Portrait of a Nation in Tears* (Oxford University Press).

Douglas-Klotz, N. (2001), *The Hidden Gospel: Decoding the Spiritual Message of the Aramaic Jesus* (Quest Books).

Dow, J. (1986), 'Universal Aspects of Symbolic Healing: A Theoretical Synthesis', *American Anthropologist*, 88:1, pp. 56–69.

Dubisch, J. and Winkelman, M. (eds) (2005), *Pilgrimage and Healing* (University of Arizona Press).

Duffey, F. D. (1950), *Psychiatry and Asceticism* (B. Herder).

Dunbar, R. (2014), *Human Evolution: A Pelican Introduction* (Pelican).

Dunbar, R. (2020), 'Religion, the Social Brain and the Mystical Stance', *Archive for the Psychology of Religion* 42:1, pp. 46–62.

Dunbar, R. (in press), *How Religion Evolved* (Pelican).

Durt, C., Fuchs, T. and Tewes, C. (2017), *Embodiment, Enaction and Culture: Investigating the Constitution of the Shared World* (MIT).

Dutton, K. R. (1995), *The Perfectible Body: The Western Ideal of Physical Development* (Cassell).

Easton, D. and Hardy, J. W. (2004), *Radical Ecstasy: SM Journeys to Transcendence* (Greenery Press).

Edwards, J. (1959), *A Treatise Concerning Religious Affections* (ed. J. Smith) (Yale University Press).

Eilberg-Schwartz, H. (1992), *People of the Body: Jews and Judaism from an Embodied Perspective* (State University of New York Press).

Ekman, P. (2003), *Emotions Revealed: Recognizing Faces and Feelings to Improve Communication and Emotional Life* (Holt).

Elias, N. (1984), *The Civilizing Process* (Blackwell).

Elochukwu, U. (1996), *A Listening Church: Autonomy and Communion in African Churches* (Orbis).

Erikson, E. H. (1977), *Toys and Reasons: Stages in the Ritualization of Experience* (Norton).

Exline, J. J., Park, C. L., Smyth, J. M. and Carey, M. P. (2011), 'Anger toward God: Social-Cognitive Predictors, Prevalence, and Links with Adjustment to Bereavement and Cancer', *Journal of Personality and Social Psychology*, 100:1, pp. 129–48.

Eysenck, H. J. and Sargent, C. (1982), *Explaining the Unexplained: Mysteries of the Paranormal* (Weidenfeld and Nicolson).

Farb, N., Daubenmier, J., Price, C, J., Gard, T., Kerr, C., Dunn, B.D., Klein, A. C., Paulus, M. P. and Mehling, W. E. (2015), 'Interoception, Contemplative Practice, and Health', *Frontiers in Psychology*, accessed 12 September 2020 at: https://doi.org/10.3389/fpsyg.2015.00763

Farias, M. and Wikholm, C. (2015), *The Buddha Pill: Can Meditation Change You?* (Watkins).

Farias, M., Coleman, T.J., Bartlett, J. E., Oviedo, L., Soares, P., Santos, T. and Bas, María del C. (2019), 'Atheists on the Santiago Way: Examining Motivations to Go on Pilgrimage', *Sociology of Religion*, 80:1, pp. 28–44.

Farley, E. (1990), *Good and Evil: Interpreting a Human Condition* (Fortress).

Farré-i-Barril, N. (2012), 'Sleep Deprivation: Asceticism, Religious Experience and Neurological Quandaries', in: D. Cave and R. S. Norris (eds), *Religion and the Body: Modern Science and the Construction of Religious Meaning* (Brill), pp. 217–34.

Festinger, L. (1957), *A Theory of Cognitive Dissonance* (Stanford University Press).

Firth-Godbehere, R. (2019), 'A Brief History of English Disgust', *History and Philosophy of Psychology*, 20:1, pp. 3–12.

Flegg, C. G. (1992), *Gathered Under Apostles: A Study of the Catholic Apostolic Church* (Clarendon).

Forest, J. (2008), *Praying with Icons* (Orbis).

Francis, A. L. and Beemer, R. C. (2019), 'How does Yoga Reduce Stress? Embodied Cognition and Emotion Highlight the Influence of the Musculoskeletal System', *Complementary Therapies in Medicine*, 43:2, pp. 170–5.

Frith, C. D. (1992), *The Cognitive Neuropsychology of Schizophrenia* (Erlbaum).

Fuchs, T. (2017), *Ecology of the Mind: The Phenomenology and Biology of the Embodied Mind* (Oxford University Press).

Fuentes, A. (2020), *Why We Believe: Evolution and the Human Way of Being* (Yale University Press).

Fuller, R. C. (2008), *Spirituality in the Flesh: Bodily Sources of Religious Experience* (Oxford University Press).

Fuller, R. C. and Montgomery, D. E. (2015), 'Body Posture and Religious Attitudes', *Archive for the Psychology of Religion*, 37:3, pp. 227–39.

Gallagher, S. (2006), *How the Body Shapes the Mind* (Clarendon).

Gallese, V. (2006), 'Embodied Simulation: From Mirror Neuron Systems to Inter-personal Relations,' in: G. Bock and J. Goode (Novartis Foundation Symposia) (eds), *Empathy and Fairness* (Wiley), pp. 3–19.

Gallwey, W. T. (2015), *The Inner Game of Tennis: The Ultimate Guide to the Mental Side of Peak Performance* (Pan).

Ganda Sutta: A Boil (AN 9.15), (trans. Thanissaro Bhikkhu), Access to Insight (BCBS Edition), 4 July 2010, accessed 10 September 2020 at: http://www.access toinsight.org/tipitaka/an/an09/an09.015.than.html

Gebser, J. (1986), *The Ever-Present Origin* (Ohio University Press).

Gerbag, P. L. (2008), 'Yoga and Neuro-Psychoanalysis', in: F. S. Anderson (ed.), *Bodies in Treatment: The Unspoken Dimension* (The Analytic Press), pp. 127–50.

Gibson, J. J. (1977), *The Ecological Approach to Visual Perception* (Houghton Mifflin).

Gibson, J. J. (2019), 'Mindfulness, Interoception and the Body: A Contemporary Perspective', *Frontiers in Psychology*, accessed 16 September 2020 at: https://doi.org/10.3389/fpsyg.2019.02012

Gibson, W. and Begiato, J. (2017), *Sex and the Church in the Long Eighteenth Century: Religion, Enlightenment and the Sexual Revolution* (Bloomsbury).

Gilbert, P. (2010), *The Compassionate Mind: A New Approach to Life's Challenges* (Constable).

Gilbert, P. and Gilbert. H. (2011), 'Spiritual Healing in the Context of the Human Need for Safeness, Connectedness and Warmth: A Biopsychosocial Approach', in: F. Watts (ed.), *Spiritual Healing: Scientific and Religious Perspectives* (Cambridge University Press), pp. 112–27.

Gjelsvik B., Lovric D. and Williams, J. M. G. (2018), 'Embodied Cognition and Emotional Disorders: Embodiment and Abstraction in Understanding Depression', *Journal of Experimental Psychopathology*, 9:3, pp. 1–41.

Goldberg, E. (2005), 'Cognitive Science and Hathayoga', *Zygon: Journal of Religion and Science*, 40:3 pp. 613–30.

Goleman, D. (1995), *Emotional Intelligence: Why it can Matter More than IQ* (Bantam Books).

Goodall, J. and Berman, P. (2000), *Reason for Hope: A Spiritual Journey* (Grand Central Publishing).

Gooder, P. (2016), *Body: Biblical Spirituality for the Whole Person* (SPCK).

Gosling, D. A. (2013), 'Embodiment and Rebirth in the Buddhist and Hindu Traditions', *Zygon: Journal of Religion and Science*, 48: 4, pp. 908–15.

Grainger, R. (2004), 'Forgiveness and Liturgy', in: F. Watts and L. Gulliford (eds), *Forgiveness in Context: Theology and Psychology in Creative Dialogue* (T. and T. Clark), pp. 69–82.

Graiver, I. (2018), *Asceticism of the Mind: Forms of Attention and Self-Transformation in Late Antique Monasticism* (Pontifical Institute of Mediaeval Studies).

Greenberg, B. (1990), 'Female Sexuality and Bodily Functions in the Jewish Tradition', in: Jeanne Becher (ed.), *Women, Religion, and Sexuality: Studies on the Impact of Religious Teachings on Women* (WCC), pp. 1–44.

Grenz, S. J. (2001), *The Social God and the Relational Self: A Trinitarian Theology of the Imago Dei* (John Knox Press).

Griffith, R. T. H. (1896), *The Hymns of the Rigveda* (E. J. Lazarus).

Grummett, D. (2005), *Teilhard de Chardin: Theology, Humanity and Cosmos* (Peeters).

Guindon, A. (1976), *The Sexual Language: An Essay in Moral Theology* (University of Ottawa Press).

Guindon, A. (1986), *The Sexual Creators: An Ethical Proposal for Concerned Christians* (University Press of America).

Haidt, J. (2012), *The Righteous Mind: Why Good People are Divided by Politics and Religion* (Pantheon).

Hallevi, J. (1931), *Kitab Al Khazari* (trans. Hartwig Hirschfeld) (M. L. Cailingold).

Hammond, C. (2015), *The Sound of Liturgy: How Words Work in Worship* (SPCK).

Hardman, O. (1924), *The Ideals of Asceticism: An Essay in the Comparative Study of Religion* (Macmillan).

Harper, K. (2013), *From Shame to Sin: The Christian Transformation of Sexual Morality in Late Antiquity* (Harvard University Press).

Harré, R. (ed.) (1986), *The Social Construction of the Emotions* (Blackwell).

Harré, R. (1998), *The Singular Self: An Introduction to the Psychology of Personhood* (Sage Publications).

Harvey, L. (2014), *A Brief Theology of Sport* (SCM).

Harvey, P. (1990), *An Introduction to Buddhism: Teachings, History and Practices* (Cambridge University Press).

Hay, D. (1982), *Exploring Inner Space: Scientists and Religious Experience* (Penguin).

Heidenreich, A. (1969), *The Risen Christ and the Etheric Christ: An Esoteric Study* (Rudolf Steiner Press).

Henriksen, J-O. and Sandnes, K. O. (2016), *Jesus as Healer: A Gospel for the Body* (Eerdmans).

Hillman, J. (1998), 'Peaks and Vales', in: James Hillman (ed.), *Puer Papers* (Spring Publications), pp. 54–74.

Hood, R. W. Jr. and Williamson, W. P. (2008), *Them That Believe: The Power and Meaning of the Christian Serpent-Handling Tradition* (University of California Press).

Hood, R. W. Jr., Hill P. C. and Spilka, B. (2018), *The Psychology of Religion: An Empirical Approach* (Guilford Press).

Househam, A. M., Peterson, C. T., Mills P. J. and Chopra, D. (2017), 'The Effects of Stress and Meditation on the Immune System, Human Microbiota, and Epigenetics', *Advances in Mind-Body Medicine* 31:4, pp. 10–25.

Howes, G. (2007), *The Art of the Sacred: An Introduction to the Aesthetics of Art and Belief* (I.B. Tauris).

Hubel, D. H. (1988), *Eye, Brain and Vision* (Scientific American Library).

Hudson, D. D. (1995), 'How to Worship at Siva's Temple', in: Donald S. Lopez (ed.), *Religions of India in Practice* (Princeton University Press).

Hudson, J. (2019), *How to Survive: Lessons for Everyday Life from the Extreme World* (Macmillan).

'Hymns of the Atharva-Veda, Together with Extracts from the Ritual Books and the Commentaries', in: Maurice Bloomfield (trans.) (1897), *Sacred Books of the East, vol 42* (Clarendon Press).

Ipsos MORI, Schott, B. (2007), 'Survey on Beliefs', accessed on 23 September 2020 at: https://www.ipsos.com/ipsos-mori/en-uk/survey-beliefs

James, W. (1884), 'What is an Emotion?' *Mind*, 9, pp. 188–205.

James, W. (2012), *The Varieties of Religious Experience: A Study in Human Nature* (Oxford University Press).

Jansen, W. and Notermans, C. (eds) (2012), *Gender, Nation and Religion in European Pilgrimage: Old Routes, New Journeys* (Ashgate).

Jeeves, M. (ed.) (2015), *The Emergence of Personhood: A Quantum Leap?* (Eerdmans).

Jewell, A. (ed.) (2004), *Ageing, Spirituality and Well-Being* (Jessica Kingsley).

Johnson, M. and Walker, J. (eds) (2016), *Spiritual Dimensions of Ageing* (Cambridge University Press).

Jones, D. A. (2011), *Angels: A Very Short Introduction* (Oxford University Press).

Jones, J. W. (2005), 'Brain, Mind, and Spirit – A Clinician's Perspective, or Why I am not Afraid of Dualism,' in: K. Bulkeley (ed.), *Soul, Psyche, Brain: New Directions in the Study of Religion and Brain-Mind Science* (Palgrave Macmillan), pp. 36–60.

Jones, J. W. (2015), *Can Science Explain Religion? The Cognitive Science Debate* (Oxford University Press).

Jones, J. W. (2019), *Living Religion: Embodiment, Theology, and the Possibility of a Spiritual Sense* (Oxford University Press).

Jones, J. W. (2020), 'Embodying theological understanding', in: R. Re Manning (ed.), *Mutual Enrichment Between Psychology and Theology* (Routledge), pp. 61–72.

Jordan, M. D. (2001), *The Ethics of Sex* (Blackwell).

Jordan, M. D. (2015), *Convulsing Bodies: Religion and Resistance in Foucault* (Stanford University Press).

Kabat-Zinn, J. (2013), *Full Catastrophe Living: How to Cope with Stress, Pain and Illness Using Mindfulness Meditation* (Piatkus).

Katz, R. (1982), *Boiling Energy: Community Healing among the Kalahari Kung* (Harvard University Press).

Katz, S. T. (1978), *Mysticism and Philosophical Analysis* (Sheldon Press).

Kazen, T. (2011), *Emotions in Biblical Law: A Cognitive Science Approach* (Sheffield Phoenix Press).

Kelley, D. M. (1972), *Why Conservative Churches are Growing: A Study in Sociology of Religion* (Harper and Row).

Kelsey, D. H. (2009), *Eccentric Existence: A Theological Anthropology, vol. 1* (John Knox Press).

Kelsey, M. T. (1973), *Healing and Christianity: In Ancient Thought and Modern Times* (SCM).

Keltner, D. and Haidt, J. (2003), 'Approaching Awe, A Moral, Spiritual, and Aesthetic Emotion', *Cognition and Emotion*, 17:2, pp. 297–314.

Keys, A., Henschel, A. and Brožek, J. (1950), *The Biology of Human Starvation*, 2 vols. (University of Minnesota Press).

King, U. (2015), *Spirit of Fire: The Life and Vision of Teilhard de Chardin* (Orbis).

Kinsey. B. (2011), 'The Psychodynamics of Spiritual Healing and the Power of Mother Kissing It Better', in: F. Watts (ed.), *Spiritual Healing: Scientific and Religious Perspectives* (Cambridge University Press), pp. 90–111.

Kirkpatrick, L. A. (2004), *Attachment, Evolution, and the Psychology of Religion* (Guilford Press).

Klein, I. (1979), *A Guide to Jewish Religious Practice* (Jewish Theological Seminary of America).

Knight, C. (2016), 'The Psychology of Religion and the Concept of Revelation', *Theology and Science*, 14:4, pp. 482–94.

Koenig, H., King, D. E. and Carson, V. B. (2012), *Handbook of Religion and Health* (Oxford University Press).

Kohler, W. (1927), *The Mentality of Apes* (Harcourt, Brace).

König, K. (2006), *The Human Soul* (Floris).

Konvalinka, I., Xygalatas, D., Bulbulia, J., Schjødt, U., Jegindø, E-M., Wallot, S., van Orden, G. and Roepstorff, A. (2011), 'Synchronized Arousal between Performers and Related Spectators in a Fire-Walking Ritual', *Proceedings of the National Academy of Sciences U.S.A.*, 108:20, pp. 8514–9.

The Koran (1990), (trans. N. J. Dawood) (Penguin).

Kroll, J. and Bachrach, B. (2006), *The Mystic Mind: The Psychology of Medieval Mystics and Ascetics* (Routledge).

Kugelmann, R. (2011), *Psychology and Catholicism: Contested Boundaries* (Cambridge University Press).

Lakoff, G. and Johnson, M. (1980), *Metaphors We Live By* (University of Chicago Press).

Lakoff, G. (2003), 'How the Body Shapes Thought: Thinking with an All-Too-Human Brain', in: A. J. Sanford and P. Johnson-Laird (eds), *The Nature and Limits of Human Understanding* (T&T Clark), pp. 49–74.

Lampe, G. W. H. (1977), *God as Spirit* (Clarendon).

Lash, N. (1995), 'Observation, Revelation and the Posterity of Noah', in: R. J. Russell, W. R. Stoeger and G. V. Coyne (eds), *Physics, Philosophy, and Theology: A Common Quest for Understanding* (Vatican Observatory), pp. 203–18.

Lee, M. T., Poloma, M. M. and Post, S. G. (2013), *The Heart of Religion: Spiritual Empowerment, Benevolence, and the Experience of God's Love* (Oxford University Press).

LeShan, L. (1980), *Clairvoyant Reality: Towards a General Theory of the Paranormal* (Turnstone).

Levey, A.B., Aldaz, J.A., Watts, F.N. and Coyle, K. (1991), 'Articulatory Suppression and the Treatment of Insomnia', *Behaviour Research and Therapy*, 29:1, pp. 85–9.

Lewis, M. (2014), *The Rise of Consciousness and the Development of Emotional Life* (Guilford Press).

Linacre Institute (2006), *After Asceticism: Sex, Prayer and Deviant Priests* (Linacre Institute).

Lockley, M. (2010), *How Humanity Came into Being: The Evolution of Consciousness* (Floris).

Luhrmann, T. (2012), *When God Talks Back: Understanding the American Evangelical Relationship with God* (Vintage).

MacKendrick, K. (1999), *Counterpleasures* (State University of New York).

Macmurray, J. (1961), *Persons in Relation* (Faber).

Malan, J. (1932), 'The Possible Origin of Religion as a Conditioned Reflex', *The American Mercury* 25, pp. 314–17.

Marchant, J. (2016), *Cure: A Journey into the Science of Mind over Body* (Canongate).

Marsh, M. (2010), *Out-Of-Body and Near-Death Experiences: Brain-State Phenomena or Glimpses of Immortality?* (Oxford University Press).

Marshall, L. (2000), *Nyae Nyae !Kung: Beliefs and Rites* (Harvard University Press).

Marshall, L. (2001), *The Body Speaks: Performance and Physical Expression* (Bloomsbury).

Martin, P. (1997), *The Sickening Mind: Brain, Behaviour, Immunity and Disease* (Flamingo).

Maslow, A. (1954), *Motivation and Personality* (Harper).

McClenon, J. C. (2002), *Wondrous Healing: Shamanism, Human Evolution and the Origin of Religion* (Northern Illinois University Press).

McFadden, S. H. (2013), 'Old Persons, Old Age, Aging and Religion', in: R. F. Paloutzian and C. L. Park (eds), *Handbook of the Psychology of Religion and Spirituality*, 2nd edn (Guilford Press), pp. 198–212.

McFadyen, A. I. (1990), *The Call to Personhood. A Christian Theory of the Individual in Social Relationships* (Cambridge University Press).

McGilchrist, I. (2009), *The Master and His Emissary: The Divided Brain and the Making of the Western World* (Yale University Press).

McGuire, M. B. (2008), *Lived Religion: Faith and Practice in Everyday Life* (Oxford University Press).

Meggitt, J. (2011), 'The Historical Jesus and Healing: Jesus' Miracles in Psychosocial Context', in: F. Watts (ed.), *Spiritual Healing: Scientific and Religious Perspectives* (Cambridge University Press), pp.17–43.

Meier, B. P., Hauser, D. J., Robinson, M. D., Friesen, C. K. and Schjeldahl, K. (2007), 'What's "Up" with God? Vertical Space as a Representation of the Divine', *Journal of Personality and Social Psychology,* 93:5, pp. 699–710.

Melzack, R. and Wall, P. D. (1996), *The Challenge of Pain* (Penguin).

Merton, T. (1949), *The Waters of Siloe* (Harcourt, Brace).

Midgley, M. (1991), *Wisdom, Information and Wonder: What is Knowledge For?* (Routledge).

Midgley, M. (2010), *The Solitary Self: Darwin and the Selfish Gene* (Cambridge University Press).

Miles, M. R. (1979), *Augustine on the Body* (Scholars Press).

Mithen, S. J. (1996), *The Prehistory of the Mind: The Cognitive Origins of Art, Religion and Science* (Thames and Hudson).

Moerman, D. (2002), *Meaning, Medicine and the 'Placebo Effect'* (Cambridge University Press).

Morris, P. A. (1982), 'The Effects of Pilgrimage on Anxiety, Depression and Religious Attitude', *Psychological Medicine*, 12:2, pp. 291–4.

Morris, T., Greer, S., Pettingale, K. W. and Watson, M. (1981), 'Patterns of Expression of Anger and their Psychological Correlates in Women with Breast Cancer', *Journal of Psychosomatic Research*, 25:2, pp. 111–17.

Moss, C. R. (2019), *Divine Bodies: Resurrecting Perfection in the New Testament and Early Christianity* (Yale University Press).

Murdoch, I. (2013), *The Sovereignty of Good* (Routledge).

Murphy, G. R. (1979), 'A Ceremonial Ritual: The Mass', in: E. G. d'Aquili., C. D. Laughlin, and J. McManus (eds), *The Spectrum of Ritual: A Biogenetic Structural Analysis* (Columbia University Press), pp. 318–41.

Murphy, M. (1992), *The Future of the Body: Explorations into the Further Evolution of Human Nature* (J. P. Tarcher/Perigee).

Neusner, J. (1988), *The Mishnah: A New Translation* (Yale University Press).

Nevrin, K. (2008), 'Empowerment and Using the Body in Modern Postural Yoga', in: M. Singleton and J. Byrne (eds), *Yoga in the Modern World: Contemporary Perspectives* (Routledge), pp. 119–39.

Newen, A., Bruin, L. de and Gallagher, S. (eds) (2018), *Oxford Handbook of 4E Cognition* (Oxford University Press).

Norenzayan, A. (2013), *Big Gods: How Religion Transformed Cooperation and Conflict* (Princeton University Press).

Norenzayan, A., Shariff, A., Gervais, W., Willard, A., McNamara, R., Slingerland, E. and Henrich, J. (2016), 'The Cultural Evolution of Prosocial Religions', *Behavioral and Brain Sciences*, 39, pp. 1–65.

Numbers, R. L. and Amundsen, D. W. (1986), *Caring and Curing: Health and Medicine in the Western Religious Traditions* (Macmillan).

Oden, A. G. (2017), *Right Here Right Now: The Practice of Christian Mindfulness* (Abingdon Press).

Olitzky, K. M. and Isaacs, R. H. (2004), *The Complete How To Handbook for Jewish Living* (KTAV Publishing House).

Owen-Jones, P. (2010), *Letters from an Extreme Pilgrim: Reflections on Life, Love and the Soul* (Rider).

Pagitt, D. and Prill, K. N. (2005), *Body Prayer: The Posture of Intimacy with God* (WaterBrook Press).

Paloutzian, R. F. and Park, C. L. (eds) (2013), *Handbook of the Psychology of Religion and Spirituality* (Guilford Press).

Park, C. L. (2010), 'Making Sense of the Meaning Literature: An Integrative Review of Meaning Making and its Effects on Adjustment to Stressful Life Events', *Psychological Bulletin*, 136:2, pp. 257–301.

Park, L. E., Streamer, L., Huang, L. and Galinsky, A. D. (2013), 'Stand Tall, but

Don't Put Your Feet Up: Universal and Culturally-Specific Effects of Expansive Postures on Power', *Journal of Experimental Social Psychology* 49:6, pp. 965–71.

Pattison, S. (2008), *Shame: Theory, Therapy, Theology* (Cambridge University Press).

Patton, K. C. and Hawley, J. H. (2005), *Holy Tears: Weeping in the Religious Imagination* (Princeton University Press).

Pearce-Higgins, J. D. and Stanley Whitby, G. (eds) (1973), *Life, Death and Psychical Research: Studies on Behalf of the Churches' Fellowship for Psychical and Spiritual Studies* (Rider).

Pilch, J. (2000), *Healing in the New Testament: Insights from Medical and Mediterranean Anthropology* (Fortress).

Plamper, J. (2015), *The History of Emotions: An Introduction* (Oxford University Press).

Plato (1914), 'Phaedo', in: *Euthyphro/Apology/Crito/Phaedo/Phaedrus* (William Heinemann).

Polanyi, M. (1997), *Personal Knowing: Towards a Post-Critical Philosophy* (Routledge).

Polkinghorne, J. (1998), *Belief in God in an Age of Science* (Yale University Press).

Polkinghorne, J. (2002), *The God of Hope and the End of the World* (Yale University Press).

Polkinghorne, J. (2007), *Science and Providence: God's Interaction with the World* (SPCK).

Porterfield, A. (2005), *Healing in the History of Christianity* (Oxford University Press).

Powell, S. M. (2016), *The Impassioned Life: Reason and Emotion in the Christian Tradition* (Fortress Press).

Power, M. and Dalgleish, T. (1997), *Cognition and Emotion: From Order to Disorder* (Psychology Press).

Prokofieff, S. O. (2010), *The Mystery of the Resurrection in the Light of Anthroposophy* (Temple Lodge Publishing).

Proudfoot, W. (1985), *Religious Experience* (University of California Press).

Purzycki, B. G., Haque, O. and Sosis, R. (2014), 'Extending Evolutionary Accounts of Religion beyond the Mind: Religion as Adaptive Systems', in: F. Watts and L. Turner (eds), *Evolution, Religion, and Cognitive Science: Critical and Constructive Essays* (Oxford University Press), pp. 74–91.

Rachman, S J. (1978), *Fear and Courage* (W. H. Freeman).

Ransom, M. R. and Alicke, M.D. (2013), 'On Bended Knee: Embodiment and Religious Judgments', *Current Research in Social Psychology* 21:9, accessed 16 September 2020 at: https://crisp.org.uiowa.edu/sites/crisp.org.uiowa.edu/files/2020-04/21.9.pdf

Richardson, A. (1950), *A Theological Word Book of the Bible* (SCM).

Ricœur, P. (1977), *Freud and Philosophy: An Essay on Interpretation* (Yale University Press).

Riis, O. and Woodhead, L. (2010), *A Sociology of Religious Emotions* (Oxford University Press).

Rittelmeyer, F. (1969), *Meditation: Letters on the Guidance of the Inner Life based on the Gospel of St. John* (trans. M. L. Mitchell) (Christian Community Press).

Robinson, J. (2014), *Divine Healing: The Formative Years, 1830–1890: Theological Roots in the Transatlantic World* (Pickwick Publications).

Robinson, N. (1999), *Islam: A Concise Introduction* (Curzon).

Roche, S. M. and McConkey, K. M. (1990), 'Absorption: Nature, Assessment, and Correlates', *Journal of Personality and Social Psychology* 59:1, pp. 91–101.

Ruse, M. (1988), *Homosexuality: A Philosophical Inquiry* (Wiley-Blackwell).

Ryle, G. (2000), *The Concept of Mind* (University of Chicago Press).

Ryrie, A. and Schwanda, T. (eds) (2016), *Puritanism and Emotion in the Early Modern World* (Palgrave Macmillan).

Sansom, C. (1956), *The Witnesses and Other Poems* (Methuen).

Savage, S. (2001), 'Prayer and the Body', in: F. Watts (ed.), *Perspectives on Prayer* (SPCK), pp. 97–109.

Savage, S. (2013), 'Head and Heart in Preventing Religious Radicalization', in: F. Watts and G. Dumbreck (eds), *Head and Heart: Perspectives from Religion and Psychology* (Templeton Press), pp. 157–94.

Schachtel, E. G. (1959), *Metamorphosis: On the Development of Affect, Perception, Attention, and Memory* (Basic Books).

Schaefer, D. O. (2015), *Religious Affects: Animality, Evolution and Power* (Duke University Press).

Schaff, P. and Schaff, D. S. (1983), *The Creeds of Christendom: with a History and Critical Notes* (6th edn) (Baker Books).

Schilder, P. (1950), *The Image and Appearance of the Human Body: Studies in the Constructive Energies of the Psyche* (International Universities Press).

Schleiermacher, F. (1988), *On Religion: Speeches to its Cultured Despisers* (trans. R. Crouter) (Cambridge University Press).

Schlitz, M. (2011), 'Spirituality and Health: Assessing the Evidence', in: F. Watts (ed.), *Spiritual Healing: Scientific and Religious Perspectives* (Cambridge University Press), pp. 140–52.

Schloss, J. and Murray, M. (2010), *The Believing Primate: Scientific, Philosophical, and Theological Reflections on the Origin of Religion* (Oxford University Press).

Schüler, S. (2012), 'Synchronized Ritual Behavior: Religion, Cognition and the Dynamics of Embodiment', in: D. Cave and R. S. Norris (eds), *Religion and the Body: Modern Science and the Construction of Religious Meaning* (Brill), pp. 81–101.

Shapiro, L. (2019), *Embodied Cognition* (Routledge).

Sharma, K. (2015), *Interdependence: Biology and Beyond* (Fordham University Press).

Shaw, J. (2011), *Octavia: Daughter of God: The Story of a Female Messiah and her Followers* (Jonathan Cape).

Sheldrake, R. (1988), *The Presence of the Past: Morphic Resonance and the Habits of Nature* (Times Books).

Sheldrake, R. and Fox, M. (1996), *The Physics of Angels: Exploring the Realm Where Science and Spirit Meet* (HarperCollins).

Sheldrake, R. (2011), *The Sense of Being Stared At: And Other Aspects of the Extended Mind* (Arrow).

Sheldrake R. (2017), *Science and Spiritual Practices* (Coronet).

Sheldrake, R. (2019), *Ways to Go Beyond and Why They Work: Seven Spiritual Practices in a Scientific Age* (Coronet).

Shepherd, P. (2010), *New Self, New World: Recovering Our Senses in the Twenty-First Century* (North Atlantic Books).

Slade, H. E. W. (1977), *Contemplative Intimacy* (Darton, Longman and Todd).

Smith, G. S. (2010), *Sports Theology: Finding God's Winning Spirit* (Dog Era Publishing).

Soliman, T. M., Johnson, K. A. and Song, H. (2015), 'It's Not "All in Your Head": Understanding Religion from an Embodied Cognition Perspective', *Perspectives on Psychological Science*, 10:6, pp. 852–64.

Solomon, R. C. (2002), *Spirituality for the Skeptic: The Thoughtful Love of Life* (Oxford University Press).

Stark, R. (1999), 'A Theory of Revelations', *Journal for the Scientific Study of Religion*, 38:2, pp. 287–308.

Stead, T. (2016), *Mindfulness and Christian Spirituality: Making Space for God* (SPCK).

Stearns, C. Z. and Stearns, P. N. (1986), *Anger: The Struggle for Emotional Control in America's History* (University of Chicago Press).

Steinberg, M. (2012), *A New Biology of Religion: Spiritual Practice and the Life of the Body* (Praeger).

Steiner, R. (1971), *The Wisdom of Man, of the Soul and of the Spirit: Anthroposophy, Psychosophy, Pneumatosophy* (Anthroposophic Press).

Steiner, R. (1991), *From Jesus to Christ: Eleven Lectures Given in Karlsruhe Between 4 and 14 October, 1911* (Rudolf Steiner Press).

Steiner, R. (2004), *Knowledge of the Higher Worlds: How is it Achieved?* (trans. D. S. Osmond) (Rudolf Steiner Press).

Stevenson, I. (2005), 'Reincarnation', in: J. Henry (ed.), *Parapsychology: Research on Exceptional Experiences* (Routledge), pp. 224–32.

Stewart, J., Gapenne, O. and Di Paolo, E. A. (eds) (2010), *Enaction: Toward a New Paradigm for Cognitive Science* (MIT).

Straus, E. W. (1952), 'The Upright Posture', *Psychiatric Quarterly*, 26:1, pp. 529–61.

Straus, E. W. (1966), 'The Upright Posture', in: E. W. Straus (ed.), *Phenomenological Psychology: The Selected Papers of Erwin W. Straus* (Basic Books), pp. 137–65.

Strawn, B. D. and Brown, W. S. (2020), *Enhancing Christian Life: How Extended Cognition Augments Christian Community* (IVP Academic).

Swatos, W. H. and Tomasi, L. (eds) (2002), *From Medieval Pilgrimage to Religious Tourism: The Social and Cultural Economics of Piety* (Praeger).

Swinburne, R. (1970), *The Concept of Miracle* (Macmillan).

Taylor, G. J., Bagby, M. R. and Parker, J. D. A. (1999), *Disorders of Affect Regulation: Alexithymia in Medical and Psychiatric Illness* (Cambridge University Press).

Taylor, G. R. (1973), *The Angel Makers: A Study in the Psychological Origins of Historical Change, 1750–1850* (Secker and Warburg).

Tearfund (2018), 'Half of Adults in the UK Say That They Pray', accessed 23 September 2020 at: https://www.tearfund.org/en/media/press_releases/half_of_adults_in_the_uk_say_that_they_pray

Teasdale, J. D. and Barnard, P. J. (1993), *Affect, Cognition and Change: Re-Modelling Depressive Thought* (Erlbaum).

Teilhard de Chardin, P. (1955), *The Phenomenon of Man* (Collins).

Teske, John A. (2013), 'From Embodied to Extended Cognition', *Zygon: Journal of Religion and Science*, 48:3, pp. 759–87.

Thalbourne, M.A. and Delin, P.S. (1999), 'Transliminality: Its Relation to Dream-Life, Religiosity and Mystical Experience', *International Journal for the Psychology of Religion*, 9:1, pp 45–61.

Theissen, G. (1983), *The Miracle Stories of the Early Christian Tradition* (T&T Clark).

Theissen, G. (1984), *Biblical Faith: An Evolutionary Approach* (SCM).

Theissen, G. (2014), 'Sarx, Soma and the Transformative Pneuma: Personal Identity Endangered and Regained in Pauline Anthropology', in: M. Welker (ed.), *The Depth of the Human Person: A Multidisciplinary Approach* (Eerdmans), pp. 166–85.

Thirteen Principle Upanishads (1931), trans. Robert E. Hume (Oxford University Press).

Thompson, E. (2005), 'Empathy and Human Experience', in: James D. Proctor (ed.), *Science, Religion, and the Human Experience* (Oxford University Press), pp. 261–85.

Thompson, E. (2007), *Mind in Life: Biology, Phenomenology, and the Sciences of Mind* (Harvard University Press).

Tillich, P. (1957), *Dynamics of Faith* (Harper and Row).

Tomkins, S. S. (1963), *Affect Imagery Consciousness: Vol 2, The Negative Affects* (Tavistock).

Tomlin, G. (2006), *Christian Character in a Consumer Society* (Continuum).

Torrance, T. F. (1976), *Space, Time and Resurrection* (Handsel Press).

Tracy, J. L., Robins, R. W. and Tangney, J. P. (eds) (2007), *The Self-Conscious Emotions: Theory and Research* (Guilford Press).

Tremlin, T. (2010), *Minds and Gods: The Cognitive Foundations of Religion* (Oxford University Press).

Trimble, M. (2012), *Why Humans Like to Cry: Tragedy, Evolution, and the Brain* (Oxford University Press).

Trotter, W. (1953), *Instincts of the Herd in Peace and War* (Oxford University Press).

Tsai, J. L., Koopmann-Holm, B., Miyazaki, M. and Ochs, C. (2013), 'The Religious Shaping of Feeling: Implications of Affect Valuation Theory', in: R. F. Paloutzian and C. L. Park (eds), *Handbook of Religion and Spirituality* (Guilford Press), pp. 274–91.

Tsakiris, M. and Critchley, H. (2016), 'Interoception Beyond Homeostasis: Affect, Cognition and Mental Health', *Phil. Trans. R. Soc. Lond. B. Biol. Sci*, 371:1708:20160002.

Tsakiris, M. and Preester, H. de (2018), *The Interoceptive Mind: From Homeostasis to Awareness* (Oxford University Press).

Turner, L. (2013), 'Individuality in Theological Anthropology and Theories of Embodied Cognition', *Zygon: Journal of Religion and Science*, 48:3, pp. 808–31.

Turner, L. (in press a), 'Ritual Bonding: Brain Opioids and the Origins of Religion', *Religion, Brain and Behavior*.

Turner, L. (in press b), 'Isolating the Individual: Theology, the Evolution of Religion, and the Problem of Abstract Individualism', *Zygon: Journal of Religion and Science*.

Turner, V. (1979), *Process, Performance and Pilgrimage: A Study in Comparative Symbology* (Concept Publishing Company).

Tyler, P. (2018), *Christian Mindfulness: Theology and Practice* (SCM).

Tyrrell, G. N. M. (1973), *Apparitions* (Society for Psychical Research).

Valantasis, R. (2008), *The Making of the Self: Ancient and Modern Asceticism* (James Clarke).

Van Cappellen, P. and Saroglou, V. (2012), 'Awe Activates Religious and Spiritual Feelings and Behavioral Intentions', *Psychology of Religion and Spirituality*, 4:3, pp. 223–36.

Van Cappellen, P. and Edwards, M. E. (2021), 'The Embodiment of Worship: Relations Among Postural, Psychological, and Physiological Aspects of Religious Practice', *Journal for the Cognitive Science of Religion*, 6(1–2), pp. 56–79.

Van den Berg, J. H. (1972), *A Different Existence: Principles of Phenomenological Psychopathology* (Duquesne University Press).

Van der Post, L. (1976), *Jung and the Story of our Time* (Hogarth Press).

Van Huyssteen, J. Wentzel. (2013), 'Should Theology take Evolutionary Ethics Seriously? A Conversation with Hannah Arendt and Maxine Sheets-Johnstone', *NGTT* (*Dutch Reformed Theological Journal*), 54, Supplement 5, pp. 275–84.

Varela, F. J., Rosch E. and Thompson, E. (2017), *The Embodied Mind: Cognitive Science and Human Experience* (MIT).

Vennard, J. E. (1998), *Praying with Body and Soul: A Way to Intimacy with God* (Augsburg).

Verney, S. (1976), *Into the New Age* (Fontana).

Vijaya Sutta: Vijaya (SN 5.4), (trans. Bhikkhu Bodhi), Access to Insight (BCBS Edition), 13 June 2010, accessed 10 September 2020 at: *http://www.accesstoinsight. org/tipitaka/sn/sn05/sn05.004.bodh.html*

'Vinaya Texts', in: W. Rhys Davids and Hermann Oldenberg (trans.) (1881), *The Sacred Books of the East, vol 13* (Clarendon Press).

Vingerhoets, A. (2013), *Why Only Humans Weep: Unravelling the Mysteries of Tears* (Oxford University Press).

Wachholtz, A. B. and Pargament, K. (2008), 'Migraines and Meditation: Does Spirituality Matter?' *Journal of Behavioral Medicine*, 31:4, pp. 351–66.

Waldram, J. B. (2000), 'The Efficacy of Traditional Medicine: Current Theoretical and Methodological Issues', *Medical Anthropology Quarterly*, 14:4, pp. 603–25.

Walker, J. L. (1971), *Body and Soul: Gestalt Therapy and Religious Experience* (Abingdon Press).

Washburn, M. (2003), *Embodied Spirituality in a Sacred World* (State University of New York Press).

Watts, F. and Bennett, D.H. (1983), *Theory and Practice of Psychiatric Rehabilitation* (Wiley).

Watts, F. and Williams, M. (1988), *The Psychology of Religious Knowing* (Cambridge University Press).

Watts, F. (1998), 'Science and Religion as Complementary Perspectives', in: N. H. Gregersen and J. W. van Huyssteen (eds), *Rethinking Theology and Science: Six Models for the Current Dialogue* (Fortress Press), pp. 157–9.

Watts, F. (2000a), 'Psychological Research Questions about Yoga', *Mental Health, Religion and Culture*, 3:1, pp. 71–83.

Watts, F. (2000b), 'The Multi-Faceted Nature of Human Personhood: Psychological and Theological Perspectives,' in: H. Gregersen, W. B. Dress and U. Gorman (eds), *The Person: Perspectives from Science and Theology* (T&T Clark), pp. 41–63.

Watts, F. (2001), 'Shame, Sin and Guilt', in: A. McFadyen and M. Sarot (eds), *Forgiveness and Truth* (T&T Clark), pp. 53–69.

Watts F. (2002a), *Theology and Psychology* (Ashgate).

Watts, F. (2002b), 'Transsexualism and the Church', *Theology and Sexuality*, 9:1, pp. 63–85.

Watts, F. and Gulliford, L. (eds) (2004), *Forgiveness in Context. Theology and Psychology in Creative Dialogue* (T&T Clark).

Watts, F. (2007), 'Emotion Regulation and Religion', in: J. J. Gross (ed.), *Handbook of Emotion Regulation* (Guilford Press), pp. 504–20.

Watts, F. (2011a), *Spiritual Healing: Scientific and Religious Perspectives* (Cambridge University Press).

Watts, F. (2011b), 'Morphic Fields and Extended Mind: An Examination of the Theoretical Concepts of Rupert Sheldrake', *Journal of Consciousness Studies*, 18:11, pp. 203–24.

Watts, F. (2012), 'Theology and Scientific Cosmology', in: F. Watts and C. C. Knight (eds), *God and the Scientist: Exploring the Work of John Polkinghorne* (Ashgate), pp. 139–52.

Watts, F. (2013a), 'Embodied Cognition and Religion', *Zygon: Journal of Religion and Science*, 48:3, pp. 745–58.

Watts, F. (2013b), 'Dual System Theories of Religious Cognition', in: F. Watts and G. Dumbreck (eds), *Head and Heart: Perspectives from Religion and Psychology* (Templeton Press), pp. 125–56.

Watts, F. (2014), 'Religion and the Emergence of Differentiated Cognition', in: F. Watts and L. Turner (eds), *Evolution, Religion and Cognitive Science: Critical and Constructive Essays* (Oxford University Press), pp. 109–31.

Watts, F. and Turner, L. (eds) (2014), *Cognitive Approaches to the Evolution of Religion: Critical Perspectives* (Oxford University Press).

Watts, F. (2015), 'Coventry Cathedral's Theology of Society', *Theology*, 118:6, pp. 429–37.

Watts, F. (2016), 'Self-Conscious Emotions, Religion and Theology', in: D. Evers, M. Fuller, A. Runehov and K-W. Saether (eds), *Issues in Science and Theology: Do Emotions Shape the World?* (Springer), pp. 201–10.

Watts, F. (2017a), 'The Origins and Functions of Religion: Social and Cognitive Aspects', in: S. Khalili and F. Watts (eds), *Science and/or Religion; A 21st Century Debate* (Cambridge Scholars Press), pp. 88–103.

Watts, F. (2017b), *Psychology, Religion and Spirituality: Concepts and Applications* (Cambridge University Press).

Watts, F. and Bretherton, R. (2017), '"Religion" is Complex and Diverse', *Religion, Brain and Behavior*, 7:4, pp. 378–82.

Watts, F. and Reiss, M. (2017), 'Holistic Biology: What it is and Why it Matters', *Zygon: Journal of Religion and Science*, 52:2, pp. 419–41.

Watts, F. (2018), 'Theology and Science of Mental Health and Wellbeing', *Zygon: Journal of Religion and Science*, 53:2, pp. 336–55.

Watts, F. (2019a), 'The Concept of Emotion: An Historical Perspective', *History and Philosophy of Psychology*, 20, pp. 13–18.

Watts, F. (2019b), 'Psychology and Theology of Place', in: V. Counted and F.

Watts (eds), *Religion and Place: Psychological Perspectives* (Palgrave Macmillan), pp. 81–96.

Watts, F. (2019c), 'Introduction: Rethinking Biology', in: M. J. Reiss, F. Watts, and H. Wiseman (eds), *Rethinking Biology: Public Understandings* (World Scientific), pp. 3–15.

Watts, F. (2020), 'The Evolution of Religious Cognition', *Archive for the Psychology of Religion* 42:1, pp. 89–100.

Wegner, D. M. (1994), *White Bears and Other Unwanted Thoughts: Suppression, Obsession, and the Psychology of Mental Control* (Guilford Press).

Weiss, D. H. (2013), 'Embodied Cognition in Classical Rabbinic Literature', *Zygon: Journal of Religion and Science*, 48:3, pp. 788–807.

Welker, M. (ed.) (2014), *The Depth of the Human Person: A Multidisciplinary Approach* (Eerdmans).

West, M. A. (ed.) (2016), *The Psychology of Meditation: Research and Practice* (Oxford University Press).

White, V. (1996), *Paying Attention to People: An Essay on Individualism and Christian Belief* (SPCK).

White, V. (2006), *Life Beyond Death: Threads of Hope in Faith, Life and Theology* (Darton, Longman and Todd).

Wiebe, P. H. (2014), *Visions and Appearances of Jesus* (Leafwood).

Wiech, K., Farias, M., Kahane, G., Shackel, N., Tiede, W. and Tracey, I. (2008), 'An fMRI Study Measuring Analgesia Enhanced by Religion as a Belief System', *Pain*, 139:2, pp. 467–76.

Wilber, K. (2007), *Up from Eden: A Transpersonal View of Human Evolution* (Quest).

Williams, J. Mark G, Teasdale, J., Segal, Z. and Kabat-Zinn, J. (2007), *The Mindful Way Through Depression: Freeing Yourself from Chronic Unhappiness* (Guilford Press).

Williams, J. Mark G. and Penman, D. (2011), *Mindfulness: A Practical Guide to Finding Peace in a Frantic World* (Piatkus).

Williams, J. Mark G. and Kabat-Zinn, J. (2013), *Mindfulness: Diverse Perspectives on its Meaning, Origins and Applications* (Routledge).

Williams, J. Mark G., Fennell, M., Barnhofer, T., Crane, R. and Silverton, S. (2015), *Mindfulness-Based Cognitive Therapy with People at Risk of Suicide* (Guilford Press).

Williams, R. (1982), *Eucharistic Sacrifice: The Roots of a Metaphor* (Grove).

Williams, R. (1999), *On Christian Theology* (Blackwell).

Williams, R. (2014), 'Is there a Christian Sexual Ethic?' in: R. Williams (ed.), *Open to Judgement: Sermons and Addresses* (Darton, Longman and Todd), pp. 161–7.

Williams, R. (2018), *Being Human: Bodies, Minds and Persons* (SPCK).

Williams, R. (2019), 'Epiphany Philosophers Afterword', *Zygon: Journal of Religion and Science*, 54:4, pp. 1036–44.

Williams, R. J. and Watts, F. (2014), 'Attributions in a Spiritual Healing Context: An Archival Analysis of a 1920s Healing Movement', *Journal for the Scientific Study of Religion*, 53:1, pp. 90–108.

Williams, R. J., Watts, F. and Lockhart, A. (in press), 'Health Help-Seeking Behaviour in Spiritual Healing: Records from the Panacea Society's Healing Department, 1924–1997', *Journal of Religion and Health*.

Wilson, B. C. (2011), 'Mirroring Processes, Religious Perception, and Ecological Adaptation: Toward an Empathic Theory of Religion', *Journal for the Study of Religion, Nature and Culture*, 5:3, pp. 307–26.

Wimbush V. L. and Valantasis, R. (2002), *Asceticism* (Oxford University Press).

Winkelman, M. and Baker, J. R. (2008), *Supernatural as Natural: A Biocultural Approach to Religion* (Routledge).

Winnicott, D. W. (1971), *Playing and Reality* (Basic Books).

Wirzba, N. (2011), *Food and Faith: A Theology of Eating* (Cambridge University Press).

Wiseman, H. (2019), 'Am I my Brain? Neurocentrism and the Law', in: M. J. Reiss, F. Watts and H. Wiseman (eds), *Rethinking Biology: Public Understandings* (World Scientific), pp. 141–64.

Wright, N. T. (2017), *The Resurrection of the Son of God* (SPCK).

Xygalatas, D. (2012), *The Burning Saints: Cognition and Culture in the Fire-Walking Rituals of the Anastenaria* (Equinox).

'Yogatattva Upanishad', in: K. Narayanasvami Aiyar (trans.) (1914), *Thirty Minor Upanishads* (Madras), pp. 193–201.

Zeidan, F., Vago, D. (2016), 'Mindfulness Meditation-Based Pain Relief: A Mechanistic Account', *Annals New York Academy of Science*, 1373:1 pp. 114–27.

Zizioulas, J. D. (1985), *Being as Communion: Studies in Personhood and the Church* (St Vladimir's Seminary Press).

Index of Names and Subjects

Adam and Eve/good and evil 38
addiction, asceticism and 50
Africa, dancing in 87
afterlife *see* resurrection of the
  dead
age
  body dissatisfaction and 78–9
  cognitive deterioration 79
Alicke, M. D. 82
The Angel Makers (Taylor) 15
angels, beliefs and reports of
  152–3
anger and aggression
  management of 123
  as religious emotion 122–3
Anglican Church
  baptism 175–6
  Blessed Sacrament and 86
  communion 100
  Eucharist and 106
  A Time to Heal 128
animals
  emotions and 110–11
  primates 28, 29, 84
  snake-handling 7, 59–60
apparitions *see* spiritual bodies
Aquinas, St Thomas 96, 153, 171
The Ascetic Mind (Kroll and
  Bacharach) 41
ascetic practices
  addiction to 50
  adjusting to 52–3

benefits and effectiveness 35,
  41–3
the Buddha and 188
chosen or imposed 51–2
critiques of 39–40
dualist assumptions of 68
extreme 7, 49–50
historical accounts of 42–3
identifying with Jesus 46–7, 48
intensifying experience 41, 45–7
psychological perspective of
  40–2
religious context of 51–4
sado-masochism and 50–1
self-regulation 41, 44–5, 48
sense of vocation 50–1
sport and 64
surrendering to God 46
see also spiritual practices
Asceticism of the Mind (Gravier)
  41
Asch, Solomon 90
Assagioli, Roberto 68
Augustine of Hippo
  *Commentary on the Epistle to
  the Galatians* 14
  on sexuality 14
awe and wonder 115–17

Bacharach, B. 42, 43
  The Ascetic Mind (with Kroll) 41
Baker, Augustine 41

Balthrop, Mabel 127
baptism 13, 175–6
Baptist Church, disgust and 121
Barfield, Owen 121
  awe and wonder 117
  etymology of supernatural 38
  individuality 24, 98
  language and emotions 113
  on metaphors 89
  Saving the Appearances 97
Barnard, Philip
  human cognitive architecture 92
  implicational/propositional
    cognition 93
  Interacting Cognitive Subsystems
    37
Barrett, Justin 38
Barrett, Lisa Feldman 111–12
Barsalou, Lawrence
  simulations 112
  on visions 155
Baumeister, Roy
  ascetic self-regulation 44
  escape from self 50, 65
  strength and self-control 7
Beatrice of Nazareth 43
Being Human (Williams) 5
Being Mindful, Being Christian
  (Bretherton et al) 73
Bellah, Robert N. 27, 36–7
Benson, H. 131
Beyond Boredom and Anxiety
  (Csikszentmihalyi) 59
biopsychokinesis 130
Blake, William 39
blessing 8
blood-letting 7
Bock, Emil 146
the body
  anatomy and physiology 17–18
  bodily functions 13

dissatisfaction with 77–8,
  77–80
emotions and 110–12
extending beyond 100–2
failings of 8, 78–80
flesh and spirited body 6, 16–18,
  52, 145
ideals and image of 8, 78
mindfulness 71–3
privatization of function 118
psychosynthesis 68
resurrection of 143–50, 145–54
role in religious life 1–3
state of 4
using in religion 159–61
vertical/horizontal axis of 83
we are embodied 157–8
see also brain and nervous
  system; mind-body dualism
body language 8
  acting inner states 85–6
  posture and gestures 81–94
Bourne, Charles 128
brain and nervous system
  emotions and 116–17
  human brain size 31–2
  illness and age 79
  left- and right-brain 73, 93, 139
  mirror neurons 23
  social brain theory 31
  transcendent experiences 32–3
  see also endorphin release
Brazil
  healing in 132
  trance dancing 29
Bretherton, R.
  Being Mindful, Being Christian
    (et al) 73
Britain
  tears and 118
  see also Anglican Church

Brown, Candy Gunther
  effervescence of healing 138
  healing in community 132
  Pentacostal healing 141–2
Brown, Peter 14
Brown, Thomas 110
Brown, Warren
  Enhancing Christian Life 5
  learned morality 98
  non-reductive physicalism 21
  *The Physical Nature of Christian
    Life* (with Strawn) 5
Buddhism
  bowing 83, 190
  in Chinese monastery 55
  compassion 115
  the Eightfold Path 189, 190
  embodied cognition 4
  meditation 190–1
  mind-body dualism and 192
  mindfulness 70
  texts of 188–9
  Therevada and Mahayana 189
  Varela et al and 3–4
  weeping and 118–19
al-Bukhari, Muhammad bin Ismail
    179–80
Bultmann, Rudolf 90
Burkan, T. 56, 57–8
Burrus, V. 50
Byrne, Lorna 153

Calvin, John 171
Catholic Church
  ageing nuns and 78–9
  baptism 175–6
  Blessed Sacrament and 86
  charismatic healing 137
  criteria for miracles 133
  Eucharist and 106
  healing and 127, 132

  submission and 50
  tears and 118
cave art 33
Census of Hallucinations 151
Charismatic Christianity 160, 178
Chasteen, A. L. 90
child abuse 41
China, Buddhists in 55
Christian Scientists (Church of
    Jesus Scientist) 76, 127, 132
Christianity
  afterlife beliefs 143–52
  ambivalence about the body 11,
    12–16, 25–6
  cleanliness/uncleanliness 170–1
  Creeds and Church Fathers 18,
    144, 148, 173–4
  dance and synchronized
    movement 87–8
  embodied cognition 4
  external mind and 102
  flesh and body 16–18
  Gospels of 171–2
  healing in community 132
  the Jesus prayer 69
  mantra-based meditation 69
  mind-body dualism and 192
  mindfulness and 73–5
  pilgrimages 61–3
  rituals 175–8
  sexuality and marriage 15–16,
    174–5
  social context of emotions 114
  soul and psyche 18–19
  texts of 171–4
  visual representations 174
  see also baptism; communion/
    Eucharist; Jesus Christ;
    resurrection of the dead
Church of England *see* Anglican
  Church

Cistercians
  religious focus 42
  sleep deprivation 43
  sleep deprivation and prayer 47
  zero tolerance 44
Clayton, Philip 126
cleanliness/uncleanliness
  Christianity 170–1
  Hinduism 186
  Judaism 167–8
clothing 176–7, 186
The Cloud of Unknowing 71
Coakley, Sarah 5
  asceticism or repression 40
  Freud and asceticism 46, 52
  The New Asceticism 49
  reshaping desire 51
cognition
  '4 Es' approach 95
  child development 38
  embedded 95, 98–100
  enactive 95–8
  extended 95, 100–2
  implicational/propositional 93
  literature 8
  see also embodied cognition
Cognition and Emotion journal
  109
cognitive dissonance 47
Cognitive Science of Religion
  (CSR)
  early religion and 35
  natural and supernatural 37–8
Coleridge, Samuel Taylor 20
Commentary on the Epistle to
  the Galatians (Augustine of
  Hippo) 14
communion/Eucharist 177–8
  Christ's presence in 104, 155
  community and 100, 105–6
  enactive approach to 96

enactment of 104–7
gestures of giving 84
mystery and 105–6
Protestant and Catholic beliefs
  177–8
community/society
  the embedded mind 98–100
  Eucharist and 106–7
  the external world 101–2
  of healing 138
  herd instinct 101
  hunter-gatherer societies 35
  positives of religion 129–30
  regulation of sex 15
  social contexts 114–15
consciousness
  disembodied 94
  evolution of 36–7
coordinated movement
  Christian liturgy 178
  external mind and 102
  inter-subjectivity 87
  Jewish dance 170–1
  religious rituals and 87–8
  see also trance dancing
Coptic monastery 55
coronavirus pandemic 1, 139, 144
Corporeal Theology (Tanton) 5
Corwin, A. I. 106
costly signalling theory 58
Coventry Cathedral 99
Csikszentmihalyi, M.
  Beyond Boredom and Anxiety 59
Csordas, T. 137

Damasio, Antonio 23
dance see coordinated movement;
  trance dancing
Darwin, Charles
  The Expression of the Emotions
  110

David, King 170
Davies, Douglas 115
Davies, Oliver 24
  *Neuroscience, Self and Jesus
  Christ* 22
Davies, Stevan 126
De Cruz, H. 116
de Waal, Frans 28
Deane-Drummond, Celia 149
death
  appearances of the departed
  151–2
  funerals 119
  near-death experiences 32
  prehistoric burial practices 33
  separating mind from 21
  see also resurrection of the dead
Deikman, Arthur 71
demons, ascetic control of 41
demythologization 90
depression 112
Desert Fathers 55
desire, ascetic practices and 51
despair and hope 115
A Different Existence (Van den
  Berg) 164
Dixon, Thomas 109, 110, 118
  From Passions to Emotions 108
Donald, Merlin 36–7
Donne, John 98
Douglas-Klotz, Neil 90
Dow, J. 125
Dowland, John 118
Duffey, F. D. 41
Dunbar, Robin 6
  150 person limit 31
  brain size and social networks
  31–2
  religion in human evolution 27
  trance dancing 29
Durkheim, Emile 138

Eastern Orthodox Church
  baptism 175–6
  icons 174
  spiritual and flesh body 148
Ecology of the Mind (Fuchs) 96
Eddy, Mary Baker 127
Edwards, Jonathan
  'Religious Affections' 109
Edwards, M. 83
Egypt, Desert Fathers and 55
Eilberg-Schwartz, Howard 13
Ekman, Paul 110–11
Elias, Norbert 118
embodied cognition 157–8
  '4 Es' approach 95
  conceptualizing persons 23–5
  defining 'embodiment' 4
  dual-aspect monism 22–3
  embodied religion 193–4
  facets of humans 12
  human intelligence and 92–4
  integrated processes of 59
  posture and gesture 81–4
  rising interest in 3–4
  understanding practices 9
*The Embodied Mind: Cognitive
  Science and Human
  Experience* (Varela, Rosch and
  Thompson) 3–4, 96
emergentism 21–2
emotions
  anger and aggression 122–3
  apophatic 116
  awe and wonder 115–17
  biological and contextual
  111–12
  characteristic of religion 115
  compared to thoughts 18–19
  disgust 121
  embodiment and 4, 110–12
  emotional disorders 112

healing energy 138
passions 109
reason and 109–10
religious context of 9, 108
self-evaluative 119–20
shame and guilt 119–21
social context of 114–15, 117–18
subjective 113
tears and grief 117–19
empathy
embodied cognition and 93
mirror neurons 23
enactive cognition 95–8
endorphin release
dance 29, 88
fire-walking 59
immune response and 140
self-harming and 43, 50
social bonding and 30
sport and 64–5
Enhancing Christian Life (Strawn and Brown) 5
Erikson, E. H. 85
Estabany, Oskar 130
The Ever-Present Origin (Gebser) 36
Exline, Julie 122
The Expression of the Emotions in Man and Animals (Darwin) 110
Extreme Pilgrim (television) 55–6
Eysenck, H. J. 130–1, 151

Faber, Frederick William
'My God, How Wonderful Thou art' 86
faith, enactive mind and 96
Farias, M. 62
Farley, Edward 19
Farré-i-Barril, N. 53
fasting 160
ascetic practices 7, 41

benefits to religion 51–3
chosen or imposed 51–2
effects of 42–3, 52–3
Jesus and 46–7
feelings *see* emotions
Festinger, Leon 47
fire-walking 7, 56–9
flagellation, self- 7, 42, 50
see also self-harming practices
flow experiences 158
extreme sport 7
fire-walking 59
pilgrimage 63
sport and 65
forgiveness, guilt and 115
Foucault, Michel 39
Fox, Matthew 153
St Francis of Assisi 68
Freeman, Lawrence 69
Frege, Gottlob 20
Freud, Sigmund
neurotic *versus* realistic guilt 120
understanding asceticism 39, 46, 52
From Passions to Emotions (Dixon) 108
Fuchs, Thomas 100
Ecology of the Mind 96
Fuentes, A. 103
Full Catastrophe Living (Kabat-Zinn) 70–1
Fuller, R. C. 82
The Future of the Body (Murphy) 66

Gabriel, Angel 178
Gallagher, Shaun 78
Gebser, Jean
The Ever-Present Origin 36
gender
dysphoria 77

repressive and permissive periods
15
in ritual practice 163
virginity as ideal state 14
genuflexion 8
Gestalt therapy 86
gestures and posture 4, 8
  behaviour in church 176–7
  Buddhism and 190–1
  communication in gestures 84
  coordination 85, 87–8
  different religions and 87–8,
    192–3
  effects of 83
  embodied cognition and 81–4
  gazing 87
  Hindu worship 186–7
  improvisation 85–7
  Islamic prayer 182
  kneeling 82
  metaphors and 163–4
  for prayer 159
  psychology and 163–4
  religious leaders and 155–6
  uplifted hands 83
  variety of 13
ghosts see spiritual bodies
Gibson, James 97
giving, gestures of 84
Gjelsvik, B. 112
God
  anger at 122
  awe and wonder 115
  belief in 152
  healing and 128, 133–4, 135–6
  hearing the voice of 156
  relation in Trinity 98
  surrendering to 46
  as 'up' 90
Goethe, Johann Wolfgang von
  117

Goodall, Jane
  Reason for Hope 28
Gooder, Paula 145
Grad, Bernard 130
Graham, Billy 99
Graham, Martha 193
Grainger, Roger 105–6
Graiver, Inbar
  Asceticism of the Mind 41
Greece, fire-walking in 56
grief and weeping 117–19
Grummett, David 149
guilt 115
Guindon, André 16
Guthlac, ascetic life of 42–3

Haidt, Jonathan 116, 121
Hammond, Carolyn 82
Hardman, Oscar 49
  The Ideals of Asceticism 40
Harvey, P. 190
healing 9
  biological factors 139–41
  bond of 138
  charismatic 137
  Christian aspiration of 124
  for coping and adjustment 141–2
  'cure' and 'heal' 125
  defining 'miracle' 133
  effectiveness of 129–33
  'flight into health' 137
  hands and 84
  heat sensitivity 140
  Jesus and 124–6
  mind and matter 130–1, 131
  naming power source 135
  placebo factors 125
  for prevention 141
  psycho-social aspects of 136–8
  psychoneuroimmunology
    139–40

psychosomatic problems 125–6
for reduction/elimination 141
religious and non-religious 128
in religious communities 132
revival of 127–8
routine 30
scientific study of 131–3, 136–42
theology of 133–4
trance dancing 29–30
transcendent explanations
    135–6
Heidenreich, Alfred 146
hermits 55
Hillman, James 18
Hinduism
    Dharmasutras 185
    lotus position 83
    meditation and yoga 69–70,
    187–8
    mind-body dualism and 192
    pain as an illusion 76
    temple worship 185–7
    texts of 183–5
    Vedas and Upanishads 184
    wandering holy men 55
Hitler, Adolf 99
Holy Land pilgrimage 61
Holy Spirit, snake-handling and
    59–60
Holy Trinity 98
hope 115
human beings 193
    annual migrations 61
    consciousness and 36–7
    early personhood 24
    evolution of religion 27–38
    integrated view of 9
    interconnectedness of all 12
    many aspects of 18–19
    mind-set in Upper Paleolithic
    35–6

natural and supernatural 37–8
prehistoric burial practices 33
settlement of 35–6
singing Neanderthals 31
see also individuality;
    personhood
Huyssteen, Wentzel van 93

I Am Who I Am (Turner) 5, 23
The Ideals of Asceticism
    (Hardman) 40
identity, pilgrimages and 63
idolatry of an independent world
    97
illness and disease
    body dissatisfaction and 78–80
    diabetes 79
    kidney disease 79–80
    see also healing
imagination 93
India, Hinduism and 55
individuality
    abstract individualism 23
    development of 12
    embodied cognition and 26
    historic sense of 24
    interdependence and 25
    isolation and 98
    see also personhood
intelligence, human embodiment
    and 92–4
Irving, Edward 127
Islam
    five pillars of/ritual 181–3
    hajj 183
    marriage and sexuality 181
    mind-body dualism and 192
    pilgrimage to Mecca 61
    prayer 83, 87, 182
    texts of 178–80
    visual representations 180

James, William
  definition of religion 113
  The Physical Basis of Emotion
    110, 111
  *The Varieties of Religious
    Experience* 32
Jansen, W. 63
Jehovah's Witnesses 99
Jenkins, Bishop David 154
Jesus Christ
  anger and 122, 123
  asceticism of 46–7, 48
  body and blood of 177
  bread and body 86
  cleanliness 171
  embodied existence of 12–13
  enacting Last Supper 100
  gazing at 87
  healing and 124–6, 142
  language and culture of 89–90, 99
  matter and spirit 147–9
  mindfulness and 73–4
  presence in Eucharist 104
  space and time and 146–7
  Stations of the Cross 47
  weeping and 117
  see also Christianity; resurrection
    of Jesus
Jones, James W.
  early enchanted world 37
  emotions and religion 111
  Living Religion 5
  objects to easy solutions 21
  visions and voices 154
Jordan, Mark 50, 51
Josephus, Titus Flavius 124
Judaism
  body and soul 165–6
  body-orientation of 13
  Christian texts and 171
  cleanliness/uncleanliness 172

creation account 164–5
dancing and 87, 170–1
embodied cognition and 5
healers and 124
Hebrew language and 89
liturgy and prayer of 168–9
marriage and sexuality 166–7
mind-body dualism and 192
priestly blessing 169–70
role of disgust 121
Sabbath meal 169
texts of 164
uplifted hands 83
visual representations 166
Jung, C. G. 102, 151

Kabat-Zinn, John
  Full Catastrophe Living 70–1
Kalahari trance dancing 29–30
Kallistos, Patriarch of
  Constantinople 148
Kelsey, Morton 126
Keltner, D. 116
Kempe, Margery 118
Keys, Ancel 43
Kierkegaard, Søren 109
King, Ursula 149
kneeling 82, 83
Knight, Christopher 154–5
Koenig, Harold 129–30
Kohler, W. 28
Kroll, J. 42, 43
  The Ascetic Mind (with
    Bacharach) 41
Kung San trance dancing 29, 32

Lactantius 123
Lampe, Geoffrey 126
language
  Aramaic language 89, 90
  demythologization 90

double-aspect 89–90
  embodiment and 88–90
  Hebrew 89, 90
  Jesus and 89–90
  metaphorical 4, 88–9
  social nature of 98–9
  words for meditation 90–2
L'Arche communities 98
Lash, Nicholas 96
Lee, Matthew 138
LeShan, L. 138
Letters from an Extreme Pilgrim
  (Owen-Jones) 55
The Little Brothers of Jesus 48
liturgy
  cognition 8
  enacting 97–8
Living Religion (Jones) 5
Lockley, M. 36
Lourdes 127
love 115
Luhrmann, T. 156
Luther, Martin 61, 171

McClenon, James 30, 34
McGilchrist, Iain
  The Master and His Emissary
  93, 116–17
McLenon, James 56, 57, 58
Macmurray, John
  Persons in Relation 24
Main, John 69
Malan, J. 28
Marsh, Michael 32
Mary Magdalene 172
Mary of Nazareth
  doesn't recognize Jesus 145
  weeping of 117, 118
Maslow, Abraham 103
The Master and His Emissary
  (McGilchrist) 93

meaning, narratives of 103
meditation 7–8, 158
  compassion-focused 77–8
  focus on body 1, 68, 69–70
  Hindu practices 187–8
  mantra-based 69
  mindfulness 70–2
  posture for 159
  silent prayer 45–6
  snake-handling and 60
  sport training and 65
  words for 90–2
  yoga 69–70
Melzack, R. 75
Merton, Thomas 43
Midgley, Mary 2
mind-body dualism 6, 26
  asceticism and 49–50, 68
  degree of 163
  dual-aspect monism 22–3
  emergentism 21–2
  immortality and 21
  integration 8–9
  major religions considered
    192–3
  making distinctions between
    19–21
  neglect of body and 157
  non-reductive physicalism 20–2
  philosophy moves beyond 2
  physicalism and 11–12
Mind in Life (Thompson) 96
mindfulness 1, 7–8, 70–3, 158
  Christianity and 73–5
  pain and 74–5
Mindfulness: A Practical Guide
  (Williams and Penman) 70
Miriam, dancing 170
Mithen, Steve 31
monastic life
  ascetic practices 42

Chinese Buddhists 55
Coptic 55
Montefiore, Hugh, Bishop of
    Birmingham 150
Montgomery, D. E. 82
moods
    embodied activity and 112
    fasting/sleep deprivation 52
morality
    disgust and 121
    as learned 98
    panic 11, 13–15
morphic fields 100, 102
Morris, P. A. 63
Moss, Candida 146
Mozambique 132
Muhammad the Prophet
    Danish cartoons of 180
    Qur'an and 178–80
Murdoch, Iris 24–5, 98
Murphy, Michael
    The Future of the Body 66
Murphy, Nancy 21
'My God, How Wonderful Thou
    art' (Faber) 86

National Institute for Clinical
    Excellence (NICE) 70
naturalism 157
nature, supernatural and 37–8
Navalar, Armunga 185–7
Neuroscience, Self and Jesus
    Christ (Davies) 22
new age movement 56
The New Asceticism (Coakely) 49
Newen, A., Oxford Handbook of
    4E Cognition (et al) 4
Newton, Isaac 147
Nietzsche, Friedrich 39
Notermans, C. 63

The Only Way is Essex (television)
    16
Opus Dei, ascetic practices of 7,
    43, 50, 56
oratory, community building and
    99
Owen-Jones, Peter
    Letters from an Extreme Pilgrim
    55–6
Oxford Handbook of 4E
    Cognition (Newmen et al) 4

pagan sites, pilgrimages to 62–3
pain
    gate theory of 75
    mindfulness and 74–5
Panacea Society 127, 136
Pargament, K. 76
Pascal, Blaise 109
St Patrick's Breastplate 141
Pattison, Stephen 120
St Paul
    afterlife and 9
    Christians as a body 102
    Jesus appears to 150
    on sex 174–5
    spirit/psyche, body/flesh 16–17,
    148–9
    spiritual fitness 64
    spiritualization of body 145,
    153–4
    writings of 173
Pearce-Higgins, John 151–2
penitence, kneeling and 82
Penman, Danny
    Mindfulness: A Practical Guide
    (with Williams) 70
Pentacostal Churches 158
    dancing and 87, 178
    healing and 127, 132, 140, 141–2
    use of body 1, 160

Pepys, Samuel 171
personhood 12, 23–5, 26
  see also individuality
Persons in Relation (Macmurray)
  24
St Peter 117, 171
Phaedrus (Plato) 184
Philo of Alexandria 166
Philokalia 148
philosophy, mind and body 20–1
The Physical Basis of Emotion
  (James) 110, 111
The Physical Nature of Christian
  Life (Strawn and Brown) 5
physicalism
  mind-body dualism and 11–12
  non-reductive 21–3
Piaget, Jean 38
Pilch, J. 125
pilgrimages 7, 158
  as extreme spirituality 61–3
  the hajj to Mecca 183
  myriad reasons for 62–3
  physical and mental benefits 63
Plato
  death frees soul 166
  reason and emotion 109
  the Upanishads and 184
Polanyi, Michael 97–8
Polkinghorne, John
  God rescues creation 150
  intercessory prayer 135
  resonance and healing 138, 155
posture see gestures and posture
Powell, Samuel 108
prayer
  cognitive deterioration and 79
  externally-focused 86
  healing 131–3
  icons and 87
  Islam and 182

the Jesus prayer 69
Jewish bowing and 168–9
as meditation 45–6, 91–2
postures for 85–6, 159
synchronized movements 87–8
use of body in 8
see also ritual
Prayer of Humble Access 105
Protestantism, tears and 118
Proudfoot, Wayne 111
Psalms, Book of 99
psyche, soul and 18–19
see also mind-body dualism
psychology
  alexithymia 74
  asceticism and 40–2
  controlling 'demons' 41
  embodied cognition 3–4
  healing and 125–6
  mind and healing 130–1
  object relations theory 24
  poor body awareness and 74
  posture and 163–4
  psycho-social healing 136–8
  psychotherapy and emotions
    110
  of sacramentalism 95
  see also cognition; embedded
    cognition
psychoneuroimmunology (PNI)
  139–40
psychosynthesis 68
punishment, supernatural 31

Quaker baptism 176
Quietism 109
Qur'an 178–80

Ransom, M. R. 82
reason, emotion and 109–10
Reason for Hope (Goodall) 28

rebalancing 159
religion
  ageing process and 78–9
  associated with health 129–30
  'big Gods' 28
  characteristic emotions of
    115–23
  Cognitive Science of 35
  different postures of 83
  Dunbar number 31
  embodied cognition and 3–4, 28,
    92–4
  evolution of 27–38
  historical perspective 193–4
  kidney disease and 79–80
  making sense of pain 75–6
  meaning-making and 103
  neglect of the body 1
  posture and gesture 81–4
  practice of 6
  role of body in faiths 162–3
  sense of supernatural 37–8
  using the body 159–61
  see also God; prayer; rituals
resurrection of Jesus 12–13, 17,
  143, 145
  appears to others 148, 150–1,
    153–4, 172
  his body and 143
  unrecognized Jesus 145
resurrection of the dead 9
  apparitions and visions 150–6
  belief and expectations of 143–4
  changes through Jesus 146–9
  more than soul 145
  place of 145–6
  the 'resurrection body' 145–54
  spiritualization of matter
    149–50
Riis, O. 114
Rittelmeyer, Friedrich 91

rituals 8
  baptism 13, 175–6
  behaviour in church 176–7
  Christ's body and blood 13
  dance and coordination 87–8
  embodied cognition and 81
  emotion and 115
  'excess' 85
  Hinduism 185–8
  movements in 193
  posture and gesture 81–4
  prehistoric burials 33
  social bonding 30–2
Road to Santiago (Starkey) 61–2
Robinson, James 127
Rosch, Eleanor
  The Embodied Mind (with
    Varela and Thompson) 3–4
Ruse, M. 121
Ryle, Gilbert 17, 20

sacraments
  '4 Es' cognition and 95
  community-building 100
  meaning-making 103
  see also baptism; communion/
    Eucharist; rituals
sado-masochism in asceticism 40,
  50–1
Sansom, Clive
  John 99
Santiago de Compostela
  pilgrimage 61–2
Sargent, C. 130–1, 151
Satan as 'down' 90
Savage, Sara 4
  improvising posture 85
  postures 82
  role of body in faiths 162–3
  'The Body in World Faith
    Traditions' 162–94

Saving the Appearances: A Study in Idolatry (Barfield) 97
Schachtel, E. G. 72
Schachter, Stanley 111
schizophrenia, transcendent experiences and 33–5
Schleiermacher, Friedrich 109
science
  enactive mind and 96–7
  healing and 125, 131–3, 136–42
  physicalism 11
secularization 15–16, 66
self-control
  ascetic practices and 7, 44–5
self-harming practices 42, 43
  addiction to 50
  asceticism and 41
  mortifying the flesh 15
senses and perception
  accuracy of perceptions 74
  allocentric/autocentric 72
  embodiment and 4
  enactive mind 97
  pain 74–5
  proprioception 74
  vision 97
serpent-handling *see* snake-handling
sex and sexuality
  ascetic practices and 52
  BDSM 50–1
  Christianity and 174–5
  disgust and 121
  effect of fasting 43
  ethics and sacramentalism 104
  gender dysphoria 77
  homosexuality 77, 121
  Islam and 181
  Judaism and 166–7
  kinds of fecundity 16

moral panic about 13–15
  pilgrimages and 63
  repressive and permissive periods 15
  self-control and 45
  virginity as ideal state 14
Shaftesbury, 3rd Earl of 121
Shakers, dance and 178
shamans 6, 30, 34
shame and guilt 119–21
Sheldrake, Rupert
  on angels 153
  benefits of pilgrimage 63
  morphic fields 100, 102
  pilgrimages 61
  Ways to Go Beyond 64
Shepherd, Philip 5
Siddhartha Gautman (the Buddha) 188, 189
signs and symbols, sacramentalism and 104–5
Siva, Lord 185–7
sleep deprivation 42
  ascetic practices and 7, 41
  benefits to religion 51–3
  chosen or imposed 51–2
  effects of 43, 53
  prayer and 43, 47
sleep, mind-body and 22
snake-handling 7, 59–60
social bonding
  Dunbar number 31
  fire-walking 58–9
social brain theory 31
society *see* community/society
sociology of religion 114
Solomon, Robert 116
sorrow and tears 159–60
soul, psyche and 18–19
  see also mind-body dualism
Southwell, Richard

Marie Magdalene's Funeral Tears
118
Space, Time and Resurrection
(Torrence) 146–8
spiritual bodies
angels 152–3
nature of 153–4
the resurrected dead 143–50
sensing the departed 150–2
visions and voices 154–6
spiritual fitness 7
spiritual practices
extreme 55–67, 158
fire-walking 56–9
healing and 9
non-religious spiritual
experiences 66–7
pilgrimage and 61–3
primarily physical 68
snake-handling 59–60
sport and 64–6
using body to enrich 9
see also ascetic practices
sport 7, 25, 64–6
Stark, Rodney 151
Starkey, Walter
Road to Santiago 61–2
Stations of the Cross pilgrimage
61
Steiner, Rudolf 154
afterlife and 144
etheric and physical
bodies 148–9
mission of anger 123
positiveness 117
resurrection spirit body 146,
147–9
on senses 72
stigmata 46
Stockwood, Bishop Mervyn 152
Stonehenge pilgrimages 62

Straus, Edwin W. 83, 163–4
Strawn, Brad
Enhancing Christian Life (with
Brown) 5
*The Physical Nature of Christian
Life* (with Brown) 5
submission, kneeling and 82
Supernatural as Natural
(Winkelman) 27
Swinburne, Richard 133
synchronized movement 160

Tanton, Tobias
Corporeal Theology 5
Taylor, Gordon Rattray
The Angel Makers 15
Tearfund 129
Teilhard de Chardin, Pierre
149–50
Templeton (John) Foundation 5
St Teresa of Avila 18
Thatcher, Margaret 98
Thompson, Evan 23
The Embodied Mind (with
Varela and Rosch) 3–4
Mind in Life 96
thought compared to emotions
18–19
Tillich, Paul 104
A Time to Heal (Church of
England) 128
Tomkins, Silvan 120
Torrance, Thomas 150, 154
Space, Time and Resurrection
146–8
trance dancing
biological explanations 32
cave paintings and 33
in community 99
endorphin release 29
human evolution and 6, 31, 36

hunter-gatherer societies 28, 30
  merging with others 24
trance states, fire-walking and 57,
  58
transcendent experiences
  altered brain states and 33–5
  biological explanations 32–3
  prehistoric burial practices 33
Trotter, Wilfred 101
Turner, Léon 27
  I Am Who I Am 5, 23
Turner, Victor 63

Unitarianism 121
United States, snake-handling in
  59–60

Van den Berg, J. H.
  A Different Existence 164
Van der Post, Laurens 151
Van Huyssteen, Wentzel 93
VanCappellen, P. 83
Varela, Francisco J.
  The Embodied Mind (et al) 3–4,
  96
The Varieties of Religious
  Experience (James) 32
Vennard, J. E. 85
Verney, Bishop Stephen 25
violence, anger and 123

Wachholtz, A. B. 76
walking, bodily experience of 163
Wall, P. 75
Ways to Go Beyond (Sheldrake)
  64

Welby, Justin, Archbishop of
  Canterbury 144
Welker, Michael 17
Wiebe, Phillip 150
Wiech, K. 76
Wilber, Ken 36
will power see ascetic practices;
  self-control
Williams, Bill 99
Williams, Mark 72, 73
  Mindfulness: A Practical Guide
  (with Penman) 70
Williams, Rowan
  Being Human 5
  interoception 74
  pre-modern spiritual experience
  33
  sexual ethics and sacramentalism
  104
Winkelman Michael
  Supernatural as Natural 27
Winnicott, Donald 101
Woodhead, L. 114
World Community for Christian
  Meditation 69
worthiness, Eucharist and 105–6
Wright, Tom 145

Xygalatas, Dimitris 56, 58

yoga 69–70, 187–8

Zaccheus 73
zero tolerance policies 44